# Get started in Greek

## Aristarhos Matsukas

Advisory editor
Anna Stevenson

Also available in ebook

# Contents

# Acknowledgements

Several people have contributed directly or indirectly to the writingof this book. Special thanks go to: Sue Hart, Rebecca Green and Ginny Catmur, my editors at Hodder & Stoughton; my colleagues Sonia Krantonelli, Daniel Gorney and Christine Easthope at the British Hellenic College for comments, corrections and encouragement; one of my most unique students Karl Kirchner for questioning and discussing everything with me; my daughter Arianna for giving me inspiration and my wife Joanna for putting this inspiration in perspective. (1st edition, 2001)

I would like to thank my students who over the years have showed me what is important for them to learn and not what is important for me to teach! Through them I have also realized that teaching is part of learning and learning part of teaching. It just needs ... open minds! (3rd edition, 2010)

Many thanks go to Anna Stevenson, my editor for this last edition. She has lent her expertise to many tricky issues, especially regarding how to simplify complicated aspects of the Greek language. My students at Berlin Community College continue to inspire me and challenge me daily. They have made me be constantly alert and not take anything for granted. Their direct or indirect contribution towards what teacher and/or author I am today is much appreciated. (4th edition, 2014)

# About the author

I have worked as a professional author and language teacher for over 25 years. I have written language books with special focus on Greek as a foreign language, including a bilingual English–Greek, Greek–English pocket dictionary. I have lived about half of my life away from Athens, my birthplace, first in the US for 14 years, where I had studied Teaching English as a Foreign Language (TEFL) and Applied Linguistics, and now in Berlin for the last 14 years.

My accumulated teaching experience of Modern Greek comes from teaching adults and college students in New York City, then Athens, and more recently Berlin. My professional experience also includes university teaching in the USA, working as a head of department in a community college in Athens, as a language school director in Ioannina (Greece) and as the translator of three cookery books.

When not at my desk, I can usually be found in the kitchen, in a bookshop, or at a language book fair. I love travelling (having visited more than 20 countries), watching TV and learning languages.

Aristarhos Matsukas

# How this book works

Learning a foreign language is always exciting, but learning on your own can be daunting. There are no fellow students or tutors to support you. *Get started in Greek* will make the task of learning Greek alone a lot less daunting and much more enjoyable than it might be. Each unit in the book is centred on a single topic and includes two conversations. You can listen to the conversations, practise your pronunciation and speaking, practise reading and writing in Greek, all on a single subject which will reinforce and encourage your comprehension of the language.

Here are the main features of each teaching unit:

**Culture points** give you a short introduction to various aspects of life in Greece and enable you to see some new Greek words in a context that is easy to understand.

**Vocabulary builder** presents new words grouped by theme related to the unit topic. There is also a list of new words and expressions which present additional vocabulary introduced in the unit that you will need to understand the conversations in the unit.

**Conversations** follow a story with characters you will meet throughout the course. Don't be afraid to learn the dialogues by heart like a poem, nursery rhyme or play script. Copy the conversations onto individual pieces of paper such as index cards, sticky notes, etc. (a good writing exercise in itself) and display them on any flat surface (walls, fridge doors, kitchen cupboards, an office noticeboard, in fact anywhere you can see them while doing other things) in the same way as they appear in the book. You can mix the pieces up and put the conversations together again. Translate each conversation into English and display the pieces with just one side of the conversation and try to complete it by saying out loud the other side – the possibilities are endless.

Listen to the conversations several times until you feel confident you understand them well. Don't feel disheartened when, initially, a conversation seems to be just a string of unrecognizable sounds. After listening several times you will begin to hear when one word ends and another begins. After a few more times you will be able to understand everything that is said. And finally, you will feel confident enough to repeat whole sentences.

**Language discovery** previews upcoming information in the unit. You will be asked to note similarities and do other activities that will help you put the language together for yourself. (See below for more information about the learning approach known as the **Discovery method**.)

**Language discovery** is a section that, basically, explains how the Greek in the material you have just studied is put together. You will find varying types of facts and information related to the unit's language points. These may be related grammar, spelling, additional expressions or cultural information.

**Practice** exercises are included at the end of the section to help you test yourself.

**Test yourself** contains exercises that you may turn into your own flash cards, which in turn can be used to create your own language quiz. Just write the correct answers on the back of the card in pencil (so it's not very visible). Collect the cards and keep them close by you so you can spend five, ten or 15 minutes going over the cards every day while waiting for the bus, on the train or at coffee breaks. You can do it any time, anywhere and there's no need to have a textbook with you. Successful learning depends on repetition and revision and the cards are a great help in doing this.

After Units 3, 6 and 10, you will find a **Review test** for checking your understanding of the material, and at the back of the book there is an **Answer key**. Check the **Answer key** when you have completed the exercises to check your progress. You will also find an **English–Greek glossary** and a **Grammar summary** in which all the grammatical and linguistic material discussed in the course is gathered and some additional points explained.

The course is accompanied by audio for the conversations, some exercises and parts of the Practice exercises at the end of each unit.

## SYMBOLS

To make your learning easier and more efficient, a system of icons indicates the actions you should take:

 Culture note

 Play the audio track

 Listen and pronounce

Figure something out for yourself

Exercises coming up!

 Speaking practice

New vocabulary

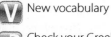 Check your Greek ability (no cheating!)

# Learn to learn

## The Discovery method

There are lots of approaches to language learning, some practical and some quite unconventional. Perhaps you know a few, or even have techniques of your own. In this book we have incorporated the **Discovery method** of learning, a sort of DIY approach to language learning. What this means is that you will be encouraged throughout the course to engage your mind and figure out the language for yourself, through identifying patterns, understanding grammar concepts, noticing words that are similar to English, and more. This method promotes **language awareness**, a critical skill in acquiring a new language. As a result of your own efforts, you will be able to better retain what you have learned, use it with confidence and, even better, apply those same skills to continuing to learn the language (or, indeed, another one) on your own after you've finished this book.

Everyone can succeed in learning a language – the key is to know **how to learn it**. Learning is more than just reading or memorizing grammar and vocabulary. It's about being an **active** learner, learning in real contexts and, most importantly, using what you've learned in different situations. Simply put, if you **figure something out for yourself**, you're more likely to understand it. And when you use what you've learned, you're more likely to remember it.

And because many of the essential but (let's admit it!) dull details, such as grammar rules, are taught through the **Discovery method**, you'll have more fun while learning. Soon, the language will start to make sense and you'll be relying on your own intuition to construct original sentences **independently**, not just listening and repeating.

Enjoy yourself!

## Tips for success

### 1 MAKE A HABIT OUT OF LEARNING

**Study a little every day** – between 20 and 30 minutes is ideal, and create a **study habit** as you would to learn a sport or musical instrument. Give yourself **short-term goals** and time limits, for example, work out how long you'll spend on a unit and work within the time limit. You will need to concentrate, so try to **create an environment conducive to learning** which is calm, quiet and free from distractions.

As you study, do not worry about your mistakes or the things you can't remember or understand.

Languages settle differently in our brains but gradually become clearer as the mind starts to make new connections. Just give yourself enough time and you will succeed.

## 2 EXPAND YOUR CONTACT WITH THE LANGUAGE

Expand your exposure to Greek as part of your study habit. You will find many opportunities. You can listen to radio or television programmes in Greek or about Greece, or read articles and blogs by Greeks or other students of the language. Do you have a personal passion or hobby? Does a news story interest you? Try to access Greek information about them. These are entertaining ways to expand your contact, and to become used to a range of writing and speaking styles.

## 3 VOCABULARY

- ▶ Organize your study of vocabulary. Group new words under **generic categories**, e.g. *food*, *furniture*; **situations** in which they occur, e.g. under *restaurant* you can write *waiter*, *table*, *menu*, *bill*; and functions, e.g. greetings, parting, thanks, apologizing.
- ▶ Say the words out loud as you read them.
- ▶ Write new words over and over. List them on your smartphone or tablet, and remember: you can usually switch the keyboard to include accents and special characters.
- ▶ Listen to the audio several times and say the words out loud as you hear or read them.
- ▶ Cover up the English translations and try to remember the meanings.
- ▶ Associate the words with similar-sounding words in English.
- ▶ Create flash cards, drawings and mind maps.
- ▶ Write Greek words for objects around your house and stick them to objects.
- ▶ Pay attention to patterns in words.
- ▶ Experiment with words. Use the words that you learn in new contexts and find out if they are correct.

## 4 GRAMMAR

▶ Check the **Grammar summary** for terms you don't understand.

▶ Experiment with grammar rules. Sit back and reflect on the rules. Compare the rules for Greek to those of other languages you know. Predict rules, or go looking for them, and be ready to spot exceptions. You'll remember them better and get a feel for the language.

▶ Write your own glossary. Add information as you go along. Look for examples and keep a 'pattern bank' that organizes examples by the structures you've learned.

▶ Use vocabulary to practise new structures. When you learn a new verb form, write the conjugation of different verbs that follow the same form.

## 5 PRONUNCIATION

▶ Study individual sounds, then full words. Make a list of problem words and practise them. Always be aware of intonation; mimic the rising and falling sounds you hear.

▶ Repeat the conversations, line by line. Listen to yourself and try to mimic what you hear. Record yourself if you can.

▶ Keep a section of your notebook for pronunciation rules and practise those that trouble you.

## 6 LISTENING AND READING

The conversations in this book include questions to guide you in your understanding, but you can go further by following some of these tips.

▶ **Imagine the situation.** Try to imagine the scenes, and make educated guesses about the topic and vocabulary – a conversation in a café is likely to be about drinks or food.

▶ **Get the gist.** When watching a foreign film you can usually get the gist of the story from a few scenes. Understanding a foreign conversation or article is similar. Concentrate on the main parts to get the gist and don't worry about individual words.

▶ **Guess the meaning of words.** Use your own experience or knowledge of the topic to guess the sorts of words in a reading or dialogue, and use context – the sense of nearby words, sentences or paragraphs – to guess the meaning of specific words in the passage.

## 7 SPEAKING

Practice makes perfect. Successful language learners learn how to overcome their inhibitions and keep going. Here's how to do it:

▶ Speak out as you go through the course. Answer questions out loud. Rehearse dialogues out loud, then try to replace sentences with ones that are true for you. Remember to mimic the speakers' pronunciation.

▶ Translate the world around you. Look at objects and try to name them in Greek. Look at people and try to describe them in detail. After you have conducted a sales transaction in your own language, do it in Greek. That is, buy the gift or order the food in Greek!

▶ Don't be shy. Seek out native speakers and practise! When you cannot understand what they say, simply ask them to slow down and repeat. Or, ask for clarification.

## 8 LEARN FROM YOUR ERRORS

▶ Don't let errors interfere with getting your message across. Mistakes are part of any normal learning process. Some people get so worried that they won't say anything unless they are sure it is correct, but this leads to a vicious circle as the less they say, the less practice they get and the more mistakes they make.

▶ Realize that many errors are not serious. Some types of errors do not affect meaning, as in using the wrong ending, wrong gender or wrong adjective ending.

## 9 LEARN TO COPE WITH UNCERTAINTY

▶ **Don't give up if you don't understand.** When at some point in the course you feel lost, don't panic! Just keep going and try to guess what is being said or, if you cannot, isolate the expression or words you haven't understood and have them explained to you, then go back to the material and try again.

▶ **Keep talking.** The best way to improve your fluency in a foreign language is to speak it. Talk at every opportunity, and keep the conversations flowing. When you get stuck, don't stop; paraphrase or replace a troublesome word with one you do know, even if you have to simplify what you want to say. As a last resort use a word from your own language. You might even pronounce it with a Greek accent.

▶ **Don't over-use your dictionary.** Don't be tempted to immediately look up every new word. Underline new ones, then read the text several times, concentrating on getting the gist. If after the third time there are still words which prevent you from getting the general meaning of the text, look them up in the dictionary.

# Pronunciation guide

## THE GREEK ALPHABET

The Greek alphabet has 24 capital letters and 25 small letters. This is because the letter **Σ** [sígma] becomes a small **σ** in any position of a word except at the end, where it is **ς**.

 **00.01** You are now going to hear the Greek alphabet. First listen a couple of times without looking at the text. Then look at the text as you listen, and repeat each letter after the speaker.

| | | | | |
|---|---|---|---|---|
| **A α** | [álfa] | | **N ν** | [ni] |
| **B β** | [víta] | | **Ξ ξ** | [ksi] |
| **Γ γ** | [gáma] | | **O o** | [ómikron] |
| **Δ δ** | [THélta] | | **Π π** | [pi] |
| **E ε** | [épsilon] | | **P ρ** | [ro] |
| **Z ζ** | [zíta] | | **Σ σ/ς** | [sígma] |
| **H η** | [íta] | | **T τ** | [taf] |
| **Θ θ** | [thíta] | | **Y υ** | [ípsilon] |
| **I ι** | [yióta] | | **Φ φ** | [fi] |
| **K κ** | [kápa] | | **X χ** | [hi] |
| **Λ λ** | [lámTHa] | | **Ψ ψ** | [psi] |
| **M μ** | [mi] | | **Ω ω** | [oméga] |

Greek, unlike English, is a phonetic language. This means that you can read or pronounce any word once you know the alphabet, something similar to German, Italian or Spanish.

Distinguish the different sound of [TH] and [th]. The first is used to produce the sound of **Δ δ** as in *this*, *though* or *thus*. The second is used to produce the sound of **Θ θ** as in *thin*, *thought* or *thug*.

Be careful with two letters that have almost the same name: **E ε** [épsilon] and **Y υ** [ípsilon].

## VOWELS AND CONSONANTS

There are seven vowels and 17 consonants in Greek.

| Vowels | Consonants |
|---|---|
| **α, ε, η, ι, ο, υ, ω** | **β, γ, δ, ζ, θ, κ, λ, μ, ν, ξ, π, ρ, σ/ς, τ, φ, χ, ψ** |

| Two-letter vowels | Two-letter consonants |
|---|---|
| **αι, ει, οι, ου** | **γγ, γκ, γχ, μπ, ντ, τσ, τζ** |

| Vowel combinations | Two same-letter consonants |
|---|---|
| **αυ, ευ** | **ββ, κκ, λλ, μμ, ππ, ρρ, σσ, ττ** |

The sounds of vowels and consonants in each sub-group above are explained in the following section.

## LETTERS AND SOUNDS

In general, remember that all letters have one sound, except for **Γ γ** [gáma] and **Σ σ/ς** [sígma]. The vowel or consonant sounds are always pronounced in the same way in Greek, in contrast with English where one letter usually has more than one sound, e.g. a as in *mat, mate, mayor*, etc.

## VOWEL SOUNDS

**00.02** You are now going to hear the vowel sounds of the Greek alphabet. First listen a couple of times without looking at the text. Then look at the text as you listen and repeat each letter after the speaker.

| | | |
|---|---|---|
| **Α α** | [álfa] | *a* as in *raft* |
| **Ε ε** | [épsilon] | *e* as in *met* |
| **Η η** | [íta] | *i* as in *sit* |
| **Ι ι** | [yióta] | *i* as in *sit* |
| **Ο ο** | [ómikron] | *o* as in *lot* |
| **Υ υ** | [ípsilon] | *i* as in *sit* |
| **Ω ω** | [oméga] | *o* as in *lot* |

Greek vowels can be short or long. The transliteration system used in this course does not show this since in Greek, unlike English, you will rarely find word pairs such as *fit-feet* or *sit-seat*. Consequently, the Greek word **σπίτι** house is transliterated as [spíti] although the first [i] is longer than the second.

Remember that **Η η, Ι ι** and **Υ υ** have the same sound (**i** as in *sit*).
Also, **Ο ο** and **Ω ω** have the same sound (**o** as in *lot*).

## CONSONANT SOUNDS

**00.03** You are now going to hear the cononant sounds of the Greek alphabet. First listen a couple of times without looking at the text. Then look at the text as you listen, and repeat each letter after the speaker.

| | | |
|---|---|---|
| **Β β** | [víta] | **v** as in **v**et |
| **Γ γ** | [gáma] | 1 **y** as in **y**ield |
| | | 2 **g** as in su**g**ar |
| **Δ δ** | [THélta] | **TH** as in **th**is |
| **Ζ ζ** | [zíta] | **z** as in **z**ip |
| **Θ θ** | [thíta] | **th** as in **th**in |
| **Κ κ** | [kápa] | **k** as in **k**it |
| **Λ λ** | [lámTHa] | **l** as in **l**et |
| **Μ μ** | [mi] | **m** as in **m**et |
| **Ν ν** | [ni] | **n** as in **n**et |
| **Ξ ξ** | [ksi] | 1 **ks** as in ban**ks** |
| | | 2 **x** as in si**x** |
| **Π π** | [pi] | **p** as in **p**et |
| **Ρ ρ** | [ro] | **r** as in **r**est |
| **Σ σ/ς** | [sígma] | 1 **s** as in **s**et |
| | | 2 **z** as in **z**ip |
| **Τ τ** | [taf] | **t** as in **t**ea |
| **Φ φ** | [fi] | **f** as in **f**it |
| **Χ χ** | [hi] | **h** as in **h**it |
| **Ψ ψ** | [psi] | **ps** as in la**ps** |

Remember that these are approximate sounds and only real words in context spoken by native speakers can present precise sounds.

## TWO-LETTER VOWELS

**00.04** You are now going to hear the two-letter vowels of the Greek alphabet. First listen a couple of times without looking at the text. Then look at the text as you listen, and repeat each letter after the speaker.

| | | |
|---|---|---|
| **αι** | [álfa-yióta] | **e** as in m**e**t |
| **ει** | [épsilon-yióta] | **i** as in s**i**t |
| **οι** | [ómikron-yióta] | **i** as in s**i**t |
| **ου** | [ómikron-ípsilon] | **oo** as in c**oo**l |

You are probably wondering about the sound [i] in Greek. Yes, it has five different spellings producing the same sound! Not an easy task for a spell-checker, is it?

## TWO-LETTER CONSONANTS

 **00.05** You are now going to hear the two-letter consonants of the Greek alphabet. First listen a couple of times without looking at the text. Then look at the text as you listen, and repeat each letter after the speaker.

The following two-letter consonants have only one sound:

| | | |
|---|---|---|
| **γγ** | [gáma-gáma] | **ng** as in E*ng*l*a*nd (Not as in e*ng*ine) |
| **γχ** | [gáma-hi] | **nh** as in i*nh*erent |
| **τσ** | [taf-sígma] | **ts** as in se*ts* |
| **τζ** | [taf-zíta] | **dz** as in a*dz*e |

The remaining two-letter consonants have two different sounds each:

| | | |
|---|---|---|
| **γκ** | [gáma-kápa] | 1 **g** as in **g**o<br>2 **ng** as in E*ng*land |
| **μπ** | [mi-pi] | 1 **b** as in **b**oy<br>2 **mb** as in ti*mb*er |
| **ντ** | [ni-taf] | 1 **d** as in **d**ay<br>2 **nd** as in e*nd* |

The **g, b** and **d** sounds occur at the beginning of Greek words, whereas the **ng, mb** and **nd** sounds occur within a Greek word.

## VOWEL COMBINATIONS

 **00.06** You are now going to hear the vowel combinations of the Greek alphabet. First listen a couple of times without looking at the text. Then look at the text as you listen, and repeat each letter after the speaker.

| | | |
|---|---|---|
| **αυ** | [alfa-ipsilon] | 1 **af** as in **af**ter<br>2 **av** as in **av**enue |
| **ευ** | [epsilon-ipsilon] | 1 **ef** as in l**ef**t<br>2 **ev** as in **ev**er |

The difference between the two depends on what letter follows.

## TWO SAME-LETTER CONSONANTS

All two same-letter consonants have the same sound as the corresponding one-letter consonant, e.g. **β** [víta] or **ββ** [víta-víta] have the same sound **v** *as in* **v**et.

The transliteration system used in this book employs all the different sounds presented above. Once again, these sounds are a close approximation and cannot replace real native speakers.

## THE STRESS MARK IN GREEK

A written accent is used in all words of more than one syllable to show where the stress falls, both in the Greek script and in the transliteration. Try to observe this as carefully as possible. Changing the stress can alter the meaning entirely, so pay close attention. When a whole word or phrase is written in capital letters, no stress marks are used.

## FINAL REMARKS

It is not absolutely vital to acquire a perfect accent. The aim is to be understood; here are a number of techniques for working on your pronunciation:

1 Listen carefully to the recordings, native speakers or your teacher. Whenever possible repeat aloud.

2 Record yourself and compare your pronunciation with that of a native speaker.

3 Ask native speakers to listen to your pronunciation and tell you how to improve it.

4 Ask native speakers how a specific sound is formed. Watch them and practise at home in front of a mirror.

5 Make a list of words that give you pronunciation trouble and practise them.

**00.07**

Now practise your pronunciation by saying some names of geographical regions in Greece. Pause after each one and look it up on the map in Unit 2 to see where it is. One of the regions on the map is not on the recording; see if you can find which one is missing.

a [atikí] – [nisiá saronikoó] **ΑΤΤΙΚΗ – ΝΗΣΙΑ ΣΑΡΩΝΙΚΟΥ**

b [kikláTHes] **ΚΥΚΛΑΔΕΣ**

**c** [THoTHekánisos] – **ΔΩΔΕΚΑΝΗΣΟΣ**

**d** [vorioanatoliká nisiá eyéoo] – **ΒΟΡΕΙΟΑΝΑΤΟΛΙΚΑ ΝΗΣΙΑ ΑΙΓΑΙΟΥ**

**e** [thráki] – [samothráki] – **ΘΡΑΚΗ – ΣΑΜΟΘΡΑΚΗ**

**f** [makeTHonía] – **ΜΑΚΕΔΟΝΙΑ**

**g** [thesalía] – **ΘΕΣΣΑΛΙΑ**

**h** [ípiros] – **ΗΠΕΙΡΟΣ**

**i** [évia] – [sporáTHes] – **ΕΥΒΟΙΑ – ΣΠΟΡΑΔΕΣ**

**j** [kendrikí eláTHa] – **ΚΕΝΤΡΙΚΗ ΕΛΛΑΔΑ**

**k** [nisiá ioníoo] – **ΝΗΣΙΑ ΙΟΝΙΟΥ**

**l** [pelopónisos] – **ΠΕΛΟΠΟΝΝΗΣΟΣ**

**m** [kríti] – **ΚΡΗΤΗ**

Did you pick up the word for *Greece* [eláTHa] **Ελλάδα** and the word for *islands* [nisiá] **νησιά**? They will come in handy later on.

[kalí epitihía]! **Καλή επιτυχία!** means *good luck!* Now move on to the first unit.

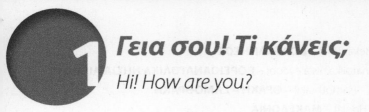

# Γεια σου! Τι κάνεις;

## Hi! How are you?

**In this unit you will learn how to:**

▶ *say hello and goodbye.*
▶ *exchange greetings.*
▶ *ask and say how people are.*
▶ *introduce yourself and your family.*
▶ *address people when you meet them.*

**CEFR: (A1)** *Can establish basic social contact by using and understanding greetings and farewells; Can introduce himself/herself and others; Can use and understand phrases and expressions relating to basic personal information.*

## Χαιρετισμοί, συστάσεις και ευχές
### *Greetings, introductions and wishes*

Native speakers always enjoy hearing foreigners using their language. No matter the number of mistakes you might make or the peculiar pronunciation you might have during these early stages, it is useful to learn some words when you want to greet others or simply say your name. So let's first have a go with some important phrases used as greetings: [kaliméra] **καλημέρα** *good morning*, [kalispéra] **καλησπέρα** *good evening*, [kaliníchta] **καληνύχτα** *goodnight*, [yia soo] **γεια σου** *hi/see you*, [yia sas] **γεια σας** *hello/goodbye*. Apart from [kalispéra] all other phrases can be used both as greetings and as farewells.

Two important phrases to introduce yourself are: [me léne…] **Με λένε ...** *My name's ...* and [íme o/i…] **Είμαι ο/η ...** *I'm ...* You can simply follow either phrase with your name and thus impress native speakers! Just be careful with the second phrase, where you should say either [íme o …] if you are male or [íme i …] if you are female.

What do you say when introducing people to each other in Greek? [na sas sistíso …] **Να σας συστήσω ...** *Let me introduce you to ...* is the most common expression, followed by the names of the people being introduced. [yiásas] **Γεια σας** and [héro polí] **Χαίρω πολύ** are more formal replies. [héro polí] means *Very pleased to meet you* (lit. *I am very pleased*). From the same word root you might hear [hárika] **Χάρηκα** *Nice to have met* *you* (lit. *I was pleased*) when you say goodbye to someone you have met for the first time and [hérete] **χαίρετε** *hello/goodbye* used in formal situations. The phrase [apó eTHó o/i…] **από εδώ o/η …**, or more commonly [apoʹTHó o/i …] **από'δω o/η …** in its contracted form, means *this is/these are* or *here is/here are* (lit. *from here*) and is also used to introduce people.

Finally, two more words are important for you to learn by heart as soon as possible: [efharistó] **ευχαριστώ** *thanks* and [parakaló] **παρακαλώ** *you're welcome*. These words are heard more often in English than in Greek, but you should still learn them and use them as often as possible!

**1** What are the Greek words for *hello* and *goodbye*?

**2** What phrase(s) can you use when you want to introduce yourself?

**3** What phrase(s) do you need to introduce a friend to a Greek person?

 Vocabulary builder

**ΧΑΙΡΕΤΙΣΜΟΙ, ΣΥΣΤΑΣΕΙΣ, ΕΥΧΕΣ** *GREETINGS, INTRODUCTIONS, WISHES*

 **01.01 Listen to the audio as you look at the words and complete the English translations. Then listen again and try to imitate the speakers.**

**Greetings**

| [kaliméra] | καλημέρα | *good morning* |
| [hérete] | χαίρετε | *hello/goodbye* (fml) |
| [yiásoo] | γεια σου | *hi/see you* (infml/sing) |
| [yiásas] | γεια σας | *hello/_____* (fml/pl) |
| [kalispéra] | καλησπέρα | *good evening* |
| [kaliníhta] | καληνύχτα | _____ |

**Introductions**

| [na sas sistíso…] | Να σας συστήσω … | *Let me introduce you to …* (fml/pl) |
| [na soo sistíso…] | Να σου συστήσω … | *Let me introduce you to …* (infml/sing) |
| [apoʹTHó…] | από 'δω … | *This is …* |
| [héro polí] | χαίρω πολύ | *How do you do?/Pleased to meet you.* (lit. *I'm very pleased*) |
| [hárika] | χάρηκα | *Nice to have met you.* (lit. *I was pleased*) |

**Wishes**

| | |
|---|---|
| [kalós orísate]! Καλώς ορίσατε! | *Welcome!* (fml/pl) |
| [kalós órises]! Καλώς όρισες! | _____ (infml/sing) |
| [kalós se/sas vríka]! Καλώς σε/σας βρήκα! | *Nice to see you again!* |
| [efharistó] ευχαριστώ | _____(I) |
| [efharistoóme] ευχαριστούμε | *thank you* (we) |
| [parakaló] παρακαλώ | *you're welcome* (lit. *please*) |

> **LANGUAGE TIP**
> [se] is used in informal situations, [sas] in formal situations.

# Conversation 1 Στο αεροδρόμιο
*At the airport*

 **NEW WORDS AND EXPRESSIONS 1**

 **01.02 Listen to the words and expressions that are used in the conversation and note their meaning. Then listen again and repeat after the speaker.**

| | | |
|---|---|---|
| [sto aeroTHrómio] | στο αεροδρόμιο | *at the airport* |
| [kaliméra] | καλημέρα | *good morning* |
| [yiásoo] | γεια σου | *hi/hello* |
| [ti kánis]? | τι κάνεις; | *How are you?* |
| [íme] [kalá] | είμαι καλά | *I'm fine.* |
| [esí]? | Εσύ; | *You?* |
| [eTHó] | εδώ | *here* |

| | | |
|---|---|---|
| [polí kalá] | πολύ καλά | *just fine* (lit. *very well*) |
| [yiatí]? | γιατί; | *Why?* |
| [íse]? | είσαι; | *Are you?* |
| [periméno] | περιμένω | *I wait/I am waiting* |
| [THío] [fíloos] | δύο φίλους | *two friends* |
| [apó] [to] [lonTHíno] | από το Λονδίνο | *from London* (lit. *from the London*) |

 **01.03** [ángelos] **Άγγελος** *Angelos is at Athens airport when he bumps into his friend* [ána] **Άννα** *Anna.*

**1 Listen to the conversation without looking at the text. What phrase does Angelos use to ask Anna how she is?**

| **Anna** | [kaliméra ángele]! | *Good morning, Angelos!* |
|---|---|---|
| **Angelos** | [yiásoo ána] [ti kánis]? | *Hello, Anna. How are you?* |
| **Anna** | [íme kalá] [esí]? | *I'm fine* (lit. *well*). *You?* |
| **Angelos** | [kalá], [polí kalá]. | *Fine, just fine.* (lit. *Well, very well.*) |
| **Anna** | [yiatí íse eTHó]? | *Why are you here?* |
| **Angelos** | [periméno] [THío fíloos] [apó to lonTHíno]. | *I'm waiting for two friends from London.* |

| **Άννα** | Καλημέρα, Άγγελε! |
|---|---|
| **Άγγελος** | Γεια σου, Άννα. Τι κάνεις; |
| **Άννα** | Είμαι καλά. Εσύ; |
| **Άγγελος** | Καλά, πολύ καλά. |
| **Άννα** | Γιατί είσαι εδώ; |
| **Άγγελος** | Περιμένω δύο φίλους από το Λονδίνο. |

**2 Now read the conversation and answer the questions.**
  **a** How is Angelos?
  **b** How is Anna?
  **c** Why is Angelos at the airport?

 **3 Listen again and pay attention to the words which run together. Practise speaking the part of Angelos and concentrate on getting your pronunciation correct.**

# Language discovery 1

1 **Read the conversation again and find two forms of the verb** *to be* **and one form of the verb** *to wait*. **Did anything catch your attention? Did you only find one word in Greek for each verb?**

2 **The first name Angelos appears in two different forms. First find the two forms. Can you work out when each form would be used?**

## 1 GREEK VERBS

Verbs are words used to express an action or state of being. [íme] **είμαι** *I am* and [periméno] **περιμένω** *I wait* are both examples of verbs. In English, verbs are usually preceded by words such as *I, you, they*, etc.; these are called subject or personal pronouns and indicate the subject, that is, who or what is carrying out the action of the verb. These words are generally omitted in Greek because, unlike in English, the ending of the verb changes to indicate the subject, and so there is no need to mention the subject explicitly. The exception to this is if special emphasis is required. Compare, for example, the following two sentences:

| [íme kalá] | **είμαι καλά** | *I am fine.* (neutral statement; no subject required) |
| [egó íme kalá] | **εγώ είμαι καλά** | *I am fine.* (The emphasis is that I am fine and not somebody else.) |

The subject pronouns [egó] **εγώ** *I* and [esí] **εσύ** *you* are introduced in Unit 2.

> **LANGUAGE TIP**
> There is no difference in Greek between *I wait* and *I am waiting*. For both you say [periméno] **περιμένω** or [egó periméno] **εγώ περιμένω**.

## 2 THE VERB *TO BE*

The verb [íme] **είμαι** *to be* is the most commonly used verb in both English and Greek. Learn the different forms of this verb and be sure to return to this section for the next few weeks of your studies until you know the verb by heart.

| [íme] | **είμαι** | *I am* |
| [íse] | **είσαι** | *you are* (sing/infml) |
| [íne] | **είναι** | *he/she/it is* |
| [ímaste] | **είμαστε** | *we are* |
| [ísaste]/[íste] (both forms are correct) | **είσαστε/είστε** | *you are* (pl/fml) |
| [íne] | **είναι** | *they are* |

NOTES

**1** [pos íse]? **Πώς είσαι;** or [pos íste]? **Πώς είστε;** can both be used to say *How are you?* The first is used when you know someone well and the second in more formal situations.

**2** *he/she/it is* and *they are* are the same in Greek: [íne] **είναι**. This is, however, an exception to the rule as Greek verbs normally have two different forms for the third person singular and third person plural.

**3** The *'I* form' of Greek verbs is also the form found when you look up a verb in a dictionary, that is to say that the verb *to be* and its *'I* form' (*I am*) are both [íme] **είμαι** in Greek.

### 3 ONE WORD, MANY FORMS

Greek is an inflected language. This means that many words change their form to show, for example, that they are singular or plural; formal or informal; masculine, feminine or neuter. English also inflects in this way; for example, the word *girl* becomes *girls* in the plural; the verb *to do* changes to *did* in the past tense, and so on.

An example of Greek inflection you have already encountered is the first name *Angelos*, which appeared as both [ángelos] **Άγγελος** and [ángele] **Άγγελε** in the conversation. Verbs in Greek, as is sometimes the case in English, change their endings depending on the subject and the tense. You will learn more about this in coming units, but for the time being, you simply need to focus on the forms found in the conversations, grammar sections and exercises.

# Conversation 2 Χαίρω πολύ!
*Pleased to meet you!*

Greeks shake hands only in formal situations. Informally, good friends and relatives – both men and women – kiss each other when they meet or depart. The notion of personal space is different in Greek culture. Greeks usually allow less distance between themselves and the other person when introducing themselves or being introduced, talking to others or standing in a queue. Stepping back in a face-to-face conversation might only invite the other person to move forward and try to get closer to you! In general, Greeks are much more physically demonstrative than north Europeans.

 **NEW WORDS AND EXPRESSIONS 2**

 **01.04 Listen to the words and expressions that are used in the conversation and note their meaning. Then listen again and repeat after the speaker.**

| | | |
|---|---|---|
| [na] [sas] [sistíso] | να σας συστήσω | *Let me introduce you.* |
| [ke] | και | *and* |
| [héro] [polí] | χαίρω πολύ | *Pleased to meet you.* |
| [kalós orísate] | καλώς ορίσατε | *welcome* |
| [stin] | στην | *to/in/at (used with nouns)* |
| [eláTHa] | Ελλάδα | *Greece* |
| [efharistoóme] | ευχαριστούμε | *thank you (lit. we thank you)* |
| [pos se léne]? | πώς σε λένε; | *What's your name?* |
| [me léne] | με λένε … | *My name is … (lit. they call me)* |

 01.05 *Angelos introduces John and Mary to Anna.*

**1 Listen to the conversation a couple of times. Without looking at the text, can you identify which phrase means *Welcome to Greece!*?**

| | | |
|---|---|---|
| **Angelos** | [na sas sistíso]. [apo'THó] [o John] [ke i Mary]. | *Let me introduce you. This is John and Mary.* |
| **Anna** | [yiásas]. [héro polí]. [kalós orísate] [stin eláTHa]. | *Hello. Pleased to meet you. Welcome to Greece!* |
| **John** | [efharistó]. | *Thanks.* |
| **Mary** | [efharistoóme]. [pos se léne]? | *Thank you. What's your name?* |
| **Anna** | [ána]. [me léne ána]. | *Anna. My name is Anna.* |

| Άγγελος | Να σας συστήσω! Από'δω ο John και η Mary. |
| Άννα | Γεια σας. Χαίρω πολύ. Καλώς ορίσατε στην Ελλάδα! |
| John | Ευχαριστώ. |
| Mary | Ευχαριστούμε! Πώς σε λένε; |
| Άννα | Άννα. Με λένε Άννα. |

**2 Now read the conversation and answer the questions.**
  **a** What is the difference between **Ευχαριστώ** and **Ευχαριστούμε**?
  **b** What is the difference between the words **Από** and **Πώς**?

 **3 Listen to the conversation again and pay attention to the words which run together. Practise speaking the parts of Anna and Mary or Angelos and John and pay particular attention to your pronunciation.**

 # Language discovery 2

**Read the conversation again and find the Greek word for** *the* **in three different forms preceding the following words. How is it different from English?**
  **a** John       **b** Mary       **c** Greece

## 1 THE GREEK ARTICLE *THE*

Greek has several different forms for the word *the* (called the definite article) because it changes according to gender (masculine, feminine or neuter), number (singular or plural) and function in the sentence of the noun it accompanies. You can read more about this in the Grammar summary. In the two conversations in this unit the Greek word for *the* appeared in the following instances:

| [sto aeroTHrómio] | **στο αεροδρόμιο** | *at the airport* (n) |
| [to lonTHíno] | **το Λονδίνο** | *London* (n) (lit. *the London*) |
| [o John] | **ο John** | *John* (m) (lit. *the John*) |
| [i méri] | **η Mary** | *Mary* (f) (lit. *the Mary*) |
| [stin eláTHa] | **στην Ελλάδα** | *in Greece* (f) (lit. *the Greece*) |

The words [sto] **στο** and [stin] **στην** are a combination of the preposition [se] **σε** *to/in/at* plus the word for *the*. Notice also that the Greek word for *the* is used before names, i.e. [i méri] **η Mary** *Mary* and not simply [méri] **Mary**. It is also used in front of other proper nouns, e.g. **στην Ελλάδα** *in Greece*.

## 2 GREEK NOUNS

Nouns are words that typically refer to a person, thing or abstract concept (such as friend, airport, happiness). English nouns have two forms, the singular and the plural (*friend – friends*). In Greek, however, nouns usually have several forms, depending on their gender, number and function in the sentence. Two examples from this unit are the name **Άγγελ-ος** or **Άγγελ-ε** and the word **φίλ-ος or φίλ-ους**. You will learn more about this in the next few units and in the Grammar summary at the back of the book.

## 3 CONTRACTED FORMS

Angelos introduced John and Mary with the contracted phrase [apo'THó] **από'δω** instead of the complete phrase [apó eTHó] **από εδώ**. In Greek, contracted forms are used extensively in everyday informal language, and occur especially when the first word ends in a vowel and the second word starts with a vowel. English uses similar contracted forms in everyday speech (e.g. *what is > what's; I am > I'm*).

 # Practice

1 **What greeting would you use at these times?**
   **a**  10:00      **b**  18:00      **c**  23:00

2 **Match the words on the left with the words on the right to form word pairs.**
   **a**  [yiásoo]              **1**  [hárika]
   **b**  [kalispéra]          **2**  [parakaló]
   **c**  [héro polí]          **3**  [yia]
   **d**  [efharistó]          **4**  [kalós sas vríka]
   **e**  [kalós orísate]      **5**  [kaliníhta]

3 **Match each question with its corresponding answer.**
   **a**  [yiatí íse eTHó]?      **1**  [periméno fíloos]
   **b**  [ti kánis]?           **2**  [eléni]
   **c**  [pos se léne]?        **3**  [kalá]
   **d**  [pos íste]?          **4**  [ímaste polí kalá]

**4 Rearrange these lines to make a dialogue.**

   **a** [apo'THó] [o yiánis]
   **b** [kalá, kalá] [yiatí íse eTHó]?
   **c** [yiásoo yiáni]! [ti kánis]?
   **d** [eTHó stin eláTHa]?
   **e** [kalá efharistó]. [esí ti kánis]?

**5 You have learned that the definite article (*the*) has many forms in Greek. Choose the correct one from the three options given in each of the following examples.**

   **a** [méno] _____ [lonTHíno]     **1** [sto]     **2** [stin]     **3** [to]
   **b** [íme apó] _____ [lonTHíno]   **1** [sto]     **2** [stin]     **3** [to]
   **c** [íme apó] _____ [eláTHa]     **1** [tin]     **2** [stin]     **3** [i]
   **d** [méno] _____ [athína]        **1** [tin]     **2** [stin]     **3** [i]

**6 Someone introduces you to several Greek friends of theirs. Choose the correct form, [o] or [i], in each case.**

   **a** [apo'THó] _____ [ioána]
   **b** [apo'THó] _____ [vasílis]
   **c** [apo'THó] _____ [yiánis]
   **d** [apo'THó] _____ [ángelos]
   **e** [apo'THó] _____ [ána]
   **f** [apo'THó] _____ [eléni]

**7  01.06 Listen again to Conversation 2 and fill in the blanks with one of the words from the box. Alternatively, complete the missing words first and then listen to the conversation to check your answers.**

|   |   |   |   |
|---|---|---|---|
| [o] | [i] | [sas] | [stin] |
| [poli] | [se] | [me] |  |

| | |
|---|---|
| **Angelos** | [na] **a** _____ [sistíso]. [apóTHo] **b** _____ [John] [ke] **c** _____ [Mary]. |
| **Anna** | [yiásas]. [héro] **d** _____. [kalós orísate] **e** _____ [eláTHa]. |
| **John** | [efharistó]. |
| **Mary** | [efharistoóme]. [pos] **f** _____ [léne]? |
| **Anna** | [ána]. **g** _____ [léne ána]. |

**8** **How many Greek words can you find in this word search? There are nine to be found! The words read across, down, up, backwards and diagonally.**

| k | a | l | i | m | e | r | a |
|---|---|---|---|---|---|---|---|
| a | p | o | p | s | t | i | n |
| l | o | o | o | t | h | i | o |
| a | y | i | a | s | o | o | t |
| p | e | r | i | m | e | n | o |

**9** **Now go back to the previous exercise and rewrite the words you found in the word search using the Greek alphabet.**

a _____        f _____

b _____        g _____

c _____        h _____

d _____        i _____

e _____

**10** **Greek pronunciation. Read the two adverts and answer these questions:**

   **a** Is the pronunciation of the letters **ω** and **o** different in the first advert?

   **b** Is the pronunciation of the letters **αι** and **ε** different in the second advert?

ΚΩΤΣΟΒΟΛΟΣ

ΡΑΔΙΟΑΘΗΝΑΙ

Νέο !

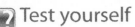

# Test yourself

**1** What would you say in the following situations?
   **a** You meet your friend Anna. Say hello to her.
   **b** Ask her how she is.
   **c** Ask her why she is at the airport.
   **d** Say *thank you* to a friend.
   **e** Say *goodbye* to your teacher.
   **f** How would you say *good morning* and *goodnight*?
   **g** Say *Pleased to meet you* when you are introduced to Mr X.

**2** What are the people in the pictures saying?

**3** How many words can you translate into English from the word search in exercise 8 of the Practice section?

You will find the answers to the Practice and Test yourself exercises in the Key to the exercises. If most of your answers are correct, you are ready to move on to Unit 2. If not, go back and revise this unit before moving on.

| SELF CHECK | |
|---|---|
| **I CAN...** | |
| ⚪ | . . . say *hello* and *goodbye*. |
| ⚪ | . . . exchange greetings. |
| ⚪ | . . . ask and say how people are. |
| ⚪ | . . . introduce myself and my family. |
| ⚪ | . . . address people when I meet them. |

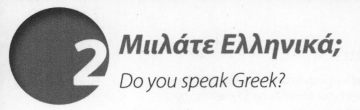

# Μιλάτε Ελληνικά;

*Do you speak Greek?*

**In this unit you will learn how to:**
▶ *ask and say where someone comes from and where he/she lives now.*
▶ *ask which languages someone speaks.*
▶ *say where you come from and where you live.*
▶ *say which languages you speak.*
▶ *say the names of some cities and countries.*

**CEFR: (A1)** *Can produce simple questions and statements regarding where people come from and where they currently live; Can ask which languages people speak.*

## Η Ελλάδα *Greece*

[eláTHa] **Ελλάδα** *Greece* occupies an area of 132,000 km², approximately 4 per cent of the European Union. The country is around 800 km from north to south and 1,000 km from east to west. Around 81 per cent of the country is on the European mainland with the remaining 19 per cent made up of islands. [athína] **Αθήνα** *Athens* is the capital and largest city, with more than 4 million inhabitants, and [thesaloníki] **Θεσσαλονίκη** *Thessaloniki* the second largest, with roughly 1,200,000. The total population is around 10 million, with another 4 million Greeks living abroad. Mount [ólimbos] **Όλυμπος** *Olympus* is the highest mountain (2,920 m). [kríti] **Κρήτη** *Crete* is the biggest island with an area of 8,380 km² and [évia] **Εύβοια** *Euboea* (or *Evvoia*) the second largest (3,800 km²). [lézvos] **Λέσβος** *Lesbos* (or *Lesvos*) and [róTHos] **Ρόδος** *Rhodes* cover an area of 1,630 km² and 1,400 km² respectively. Greece is divided into nine large geographical areas: [stereá eláTHa] **Στερεά Ελλάδα** *Sterea* (population 4.5 million), [makeTHonía] **Μακεδονία** *Macedonia* (2.3 million), [pelopónisos] **Πελοπόννησος** *Peloponnese* (1 million), [thesalía] **Θεσσαλία** *Thessaly* (750,000), [kríti] **Κρήτη** *Crete* (550,000), [nisiá eghéu] **Νησιά Αιγαίου** *the Aegean Islands* (500,000), [ípiros] **Ήπειρος** *Epirus* (350,000), [thráki] **Θράκη** *Thrace* (350,000) and [nisiá ioníu] **Νησιά Ιονίου** *the Ionian Islands* (200,000). You can see these areas on the map.

 Can you name Greece's largest city, highest mountain and biggest island?

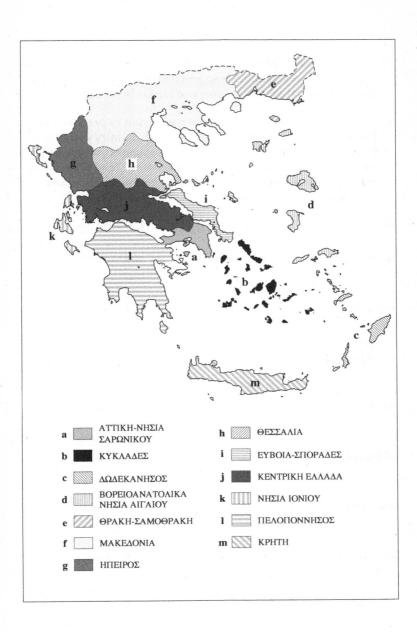

| | | | | |
|---|---|---|---|---|
| a | ΑΤΤΙΚΗ-ΝΗΣΙΑ ΣΑΡΩΝΙΚΟΥ | h | | ΘΕΣΣΑΛΙΑ |
| b | ΚΥΚΛΑΔΕΣ | i | | ΕΥΒΟΙΑ-ΣΠΟΡΑΔΕΣ |
| c | ΔΩΔΕΚΑΝΗΣΟΣ | j | | ΚΕΝΤΡΙΚΗ ΕΛΛΑΔΑ |
| d | ΒΟΡΕΙΟΑΝΑΤΟΛΙΚΑ ΝΗΣΙΑ ΑΙΓΑΙΟΥ | k | | ΝΗΣΙΑ ΙΟΝΙΟΥ |
| e | ΘΡΑΚΗ-ΣΑΜΟΘΡΑΚΗ | l | | ΠΕΛΟΠΟΝΝΗΣΟΣ |
| f | ΜΑΚΕΔΟΝΙΑ | m | | ΚΡΗΤΗ |
| g | ΗΠΕΙΡΟΣ | | | |

Vocabulary builder

 **1** **02.01** **Listen a couple of times to the names of the geographical areas while looking at the map and familiarizing yourself with their location. Then listen again and repeat them out loud.**

 **2** **02.02** **When you meet someone new and want to practise your Greek, you will probably want to say which country you come from, which city you live in and which languages you speak. Listen to the audio and study the chart below. Then listen once again and repeat the names of the countries, cities and languages after the speaker.**

| City | Country | Language |
|---|---|---|
| [i athína] | [i eláTHa] | [ta eliniká] |
| **η Αθήνα** | **η Ελλάδα** | **τα Ελληνικά** |
| *Athens* | *Greece* | *Greek* |
| [to lonTHíno] | [i anglía] | [ta angliká] |
| **το Λονδίνο** | **η Αγγλία** | **τα Αγγλικά** |
| *London* | *England* | *English* |
| [to parísi] | [i galía] | [ta galiká] |
| **το Παρίσι** | **η Γαλλία** | **τα Γαλλικά** |
| *Paris* | *France* | *French* |
| [i rómi] | [i italía] | [ta italiká] |
| **η Ρώμη** | **η Ιταλία** | **τα Ιταλικά** |
| *Rome* | *Italy* | *Italian* |
| [to verolíno] | [i yermanía] | [ta yermaniká] |
| **το Βερολίνο** | **η Γερμανία** | **τα Γερμανικά** |
| *Berlin* | *Germany* | *German* |
| [i maTHríti] | [i ispanía] | [ta ispaniká] |
| **η Μαδρίτη** | **η Ισπανία** | **τα Ισπανικά** |
| *Madrid* | *Spain* | *Spanish* |
| [i néa iórki] | [i amerikí] | [ta angliká] |
| **η Νέα Υόρκη** | **η Αμερική** | **τα Αγγλικά** |
| *New York* | *America* | *English* |
| [to síTHnei] | [i afstralía] | [ta angliká] |
| **το Σίδνεϋ** | **η Αυστραλία** | **τα Αγγλικά** |
| *Sydney* | *Australia* | *English* |

Did you notice that all city names, country names and languages are preceded by the definite article in Greek? The three articles used here are:

► [i] **η** before feminine nouns
► [to] **το** before neuter nouns.
► [ta] **τα** before neuter nouns in the plural – the words for languages are plural in Greek.

**3 02.03 Here are some typical questions and answers about where someone is from and where he/she lives now. Listen to the audio as you read the text. Then listen once again and repeat after the speaker.**

| | | |
|---|---|---|
| [apó poo íse]? | **Από πού είσαι;** | *Where are you from?* |
| [apó pia póli]? | **Από ποια πόλη;** | *From which city?* |
| [apó pia hóra]? | **Από ποια χώρα;** | *From which country?* |
| [íme apó tin néa iórki]. | **Είμαι από τη Νέα Υόρκη.** | *I'm from New York.* |
| [apó to parísi]. | **Από το Παρίσι.** | *From Paris.* |
| [íme apó tin anglía]. | **Είμαι από την Αγγλία.** | *I'm from England.* |
| [apó to lonTHíno]. | **Από το Λονδίνο.** | *From London.* |
| [íme apó tin athína]. | **Είμαι από την Αθήνα.** | *I'm from Athens.* |
| [íme apó tin eláTHa]. | **Είμαι από την Ελλάδα.** | *I'm from Greece.* |

Did you notice that the feminine article takes a new form, either **τη** or **την**, after the preposition *from*? If you are from *Scotland* [i skotía] you can say [íme apó tin skotía] **Είμαι από την Σκωτία** *I'm from Scotland.* [íme apó tin oo-alía] **Είμαι από την Ουαλία** means *I'm from Wales* and [íme apó tin irlanTHía] **Είμαι από την Ιρλανδία** means *I'm from Ireland.* The neuter article **το** remains unchanged.

**4 02.04 In these early stages when you cannot yet express yourself fluently in Greek you may well want to ask people if they speak English. Here are some questions and answers relating to speaking and understanding. Listen and repeat each one after the speaker. If you want to challenge yourself a little more, read each example out loud first and then listen to the audio to check your pronunciation.**

| [milás/miláte anliká]? | Μιλάς/Μιλάτε Αγγλικά; | *Do you (infml/fml)*<br>*speak English?* |
| [katalavénis/<br>katalavénete]? | Καταλαβαίνεις/<br>Καταλαβαίνετε; | *Do you understand?* |
| [xéris/xérete eliniká]? | Ξέρεις/Ξέρετε Ελληνικά; | *Do you (infml/fml)*<br>*know Greek?* |
| [ne], [miláo anliká]. | Ναι, μιλάω Αγγλικά. | *Yes, I speak English.* |
| [THen katalavéno]. | Δεν καταλαβαίνω. | *I don't understand.* |
| [óchi] [THén xéro<br>elliniká]. | Όχι, δεν ξέρω Ελληνικά. | *No, I don't know Greek.* |

# Conversation 1 **Μιλάτε Ελληνικά;** *Do you speak Greek?*

 **NEW WORDS AND EXPRESSIONS 1**

 **02.05** **Listen to the words and expressions that are used in the conversation. Note their meaning.**

| [po-po]! | πω, πω! | *wow!* |
| [ne] | ναι | *yes* |
| [líga] | λίγα | *a little* |
| [esí] | εσύ | *you* |
| [egó] | εγώ | *I* |
| [brávo] | Μπράβο | *bravo* |

 **02.06** *Anna is surprised at how well John and Mary speak Greek.*

**1** **Listen to the conversation once or twice without looking at the text. Can you list the languages you hear?**

| **Anna** | [efharistó], [efharistoóme],<br>[po-po]! [miláte eliniká]? | *Thanks, thank you! Wow!*<br>*Do you speak Greek?* |
| **John** | [ne], [anliká] [ke líga]<br>[eliniká]. [esí]? | *Yes, English and some Greek.*<br>*You?* |

18

| Mary | [egó miláo eliniká], [angliká] [ke líga] [yermaniká]. | _I speak Greek, English and some German._ |
| Anna | [brávo]! | _Bravo!_ |

| Άννα | Ευχαριστώ, ευχαριστούμε! Πω, πω! Μιλάτε Ελληνικά; |
| John | Ναι. Αγγλικά και λίγα Ελληνικά. Εσύ; |
| Mary | Εγώ μιλάω Ελληνικά, Αγγλικά και λίγα Γερμανικά. |
| Άννα | Μπράβο! |

**2 Now read the conversation and answer the questions.**
   **a** What languages does John speak?
   **b** What languages does Mary speak?

 **3 Listen again and pay special attention to the words which run together. Practise speaking the part of the part of John or Mary and pay particular attention to your pronunciation.**

# Language discovery 1

**1 There are two personal pronouns in this conversation. Can you find the Greek words for the following?**
   **a** I                    **b** you

**2 Find the Greek words for the following three languages that are mentioned in the conversation. Do you notice anything special about the endings of the words?**
   **a** Greek       **b** English       **c** German

### 1 PERSONAL PRONOUNS

Personal pronouns are important building blocks for any conversation. Two of them [egó] **εγώ** _I_ and [esí] **εσύ** _you_ were used in the conversation. See the table below for the rest of the personal pronouns speaker.

| [egó] | **εγώ** | _I_ |
| [esí] | **εσύ** | _you_ (sing/infml) |
| [aftós] | **αυτός** | _he_ |
| [aftí] | **αυτή** | _she_ |

| | | |
|---|---|---|
| [aftó] | **αυτό** | *it* |
| [emís] | **εμείς** | *we* |
| [esís] | **εσείς** | *you* (pl/fml) |
| [aftí] | **αυτοί** | *they* (m or m + f) |
| [aftés] | **αυτές** | *they* (f only) |
| [aftá] | **αυτά** | *they* (n) |

## 2 THE VERB *TO SPEAK*

Another useful verb you met in the conversation above is [miláo] **μιλάω** *I speak*. The table gives you all the forms of the verb. Remember you learned in Unit 1 that you do not usually need to use personal pronouns such as *I, you* and *they* before the verb because the different verb endings tell you which person is being referred to. Here, however, the personal pronouns are given in brackets before the verb to give you a little extra help.

| | | |
|---|---|---|
| [egó] [miláo/miló] | **(εγώ) μιλάω/μιλώ** | *I speak* |
| [esí] [milás] | **(εσύ) μιλάς** | *you speak* |
| [aftós/-tí/-tó] [milái/milá] | **(αυτ-ός/-ή/-ό) μιλάει ι/ μιλά** | *he/she/it speaks* |
| [emís] [miláme] | **(εμείς) μιλάμε** | *we speak* |
| [esís] [miláte] | **(εσείς) μιλάτε** | *you speak* |
| [aftí/-és/tá] [milán(e)/ miloón(e)] | **(αυτ-οί/-ές/-ά) μιλάν(ε)/ μιλούν(ε)** | *they speak* |

> **LANGUAGE TIP**
> You can see that some parts of the verb [miláo] **μιλάω** *I speak* have alternative forms. There is no difference between them in meaning and native speakers often use both forms interchangeably.

# Conversation 2 Είστε από το Λονδίνο;
*Are you from London?*

 **NEW WORDS AND EXPRESSIONS 2**

 **02.07 Listen to the words and expressions that are used in the conversation and note their meaning. Then listen again and repeat after the speaker.**

| [íste]? | Είστε; | Are you? (pl/fml) |
| [tin] [afstralía] | την Αυστραλία | Australia |
| [óhi] | όχι | no |
| [ki] | κι | and |
| [amerikí] | Αμερική | America |
| [íse]? | Είσαι; | Are you? (sing/infml) |
| [ton] [póro] | τον Πόρο | Poros |
| [alá] | αλλά | but |
| [tóra] | τώρα | now |
| [méno] | μένω | I live |

 **02.08** *Anna is trying to find out where John and Mary come from.*

**1  Listen to their conversation a couple of times without looking at the text. Which countries do John and Mary come from?**

| **Anna** | [íste] [apó to lonTHíno]? | *Are you from London?* |
| **John** | [óhi], [íme] [apó tin afstralía]. | *No, I'm from Australia.* |
| **Mary** | [ki egó] [apó tin amerikí]. [esí]? [íse] [apó tin athína]? | *And I am from America. And you? Are you from Athens?* |
| **Anna** | [óhi], [íme] [apó ton póro], [alá tóra] [méno stin athína]. | *No, I'm from Poros but I live in Athens now.* |
| | | |
| **Άννα** | Είστε από το Λονδίνο; | |
| **John** | Όχι, είμαι από την Αυστραλία. | |
| **Mary** | Κι εγώ, από την Αμερική. Εσύ; Είσαι από την Αθήνα; | |
| **Άννα** | Όχι. Είμαι από τον Πόρο, αλλά τώρα μένω στην Αθήνα. | |

**2  Now read the conversation and answer the questions.**
   **a**  Where does Anna come from?
   **b**  Where does she live now?

 **3  Listen again and pay special attention to the words which run together. Practise speaking the part of John or Mary and pay particular attention to your pronunciation.**

# Language discovery 2

1 **The conversation has three different forms of the definite article (*the*) following the preposition *from*. Can you find them and work out why the different forms are used?**

2 **All the verbs were used without personal pronouns in the conversation. Can you add the corresponding pronouns for each verb form?**
   a *you are* (sing) _____
   b *you are* (pl) _____
   c *I am* _____
   d *I live* : _____

## THE ARTICLE *THE*

You learned in Unit 1 that there are different forms for the word *the* in Greek, depending on the gender and number of the word it precedes. The word also changes depending on what is called the 'case' of the word that follows the article, which may be nominative, genitive or accusative. You will learn more about this in future units. For now, all you need to know is that after words such as **από** *from* and **σε** *in* (called prepositions) the word for *the* becomes **τον** (masculine), **την** (feminine) or **το** (neuter). This is called the accusative case in Greek and is similar to the difference in English between *who* and *whom*.

Note too that the definite article is often used with proper names, such as names of cities (**το Λονδίνο**), names of countries (**η Ελλάδα**) and people's first names (**η Άννα**).

So, sentences expressing *I'm from …* and *I live in …* will have three different forms of the definite article:

| | | |
|---|---|---|
| [íme apó ton póro]. | **Είμαι από τον Πόρο.** | *I'm from Poros.* |
| [íme apó tin afstralía]. | **Είμαι από την Αυστραλία.** | *I'm from Australia.* |
| [íme apó to lonTHíno]. | **Είμαι από το Λονδίνο.** | *I'm from London.* |
| [méno ston póro]. | **Μένω στον Πόρο.** | *I live in Poros.* |
| [méno stin afstralía]. | **Μένω στην Αυστραλία.** | *I live in Australia.* |
| [méno sto lonTHíno]. | **Μένω στο Λονδίνο.** | *I live in London.* |

# Practice

**1** **You are in Patras, a bustling harbour in the Western Peloponnese, where many visitors arrive by boat from Italy. You see some cars with the following nationality stickers. Complete the table using transliteration and/or Greek script with the correct country and language relating to each sticker.**

| Symbol | Country | Language |
|--------|---------|----------|
| **GR** | a _____ | _____ |
| **E** | b _____ | _____ |
| **I** | c _____ | _____ |
| **F** | d _____ | _____ |
| **GB** | e _____ | _____ |

**2** **Match each question with the most appropriate answer.**

   **a** [apó poo íse]? Από πού είσαι;          **1** [stin athína]. Στην Αθήνα.
   **b** [apó pia póli]? Από ποια πόλη;          **2** [lonTHino]. Λονδίνο.
   **c** [miláte italiká]? Μιλάτε Ιταλικά;          **3** [óhi]. Όχι.
   **d** [poo ménete]? Πού μένετε;          **4** [apó tin anglía]. Από την Αγγλία.

**3** **Monster words! The following sentences have not been separated into their individual words. Insert spaces in the appropriate places to make proper sentences. Use capital letters if necessary. Then translate each sentence into English.**

   **a** [íneapótinthesaloníki]. είναιαπότηνθεσσαλονίκη
   **b** [alátóraménostinpátra]. αλλάτώραμένειστηνπάτρα
   **c** [miláoitalikákelígaispaniká]. μιλάωιταλικάκαιλίγαισπανικά
   **d** [iathínaínestineláTHa]. ηαθήναείναιστηνελλάδα
   **e** [ketoparísistingalía]. καιτοπαρίσιστηνγαλλία

4  **The six largest cities and towns in Greece are listed below, with their populations in brackets. Can you find them on the map and then translate each one into English?**

a  [i athína] η Αθήνα (4,000,000)
b  [i thesaloniki] η Θεσσαλονίκη (1,000,000)
c  [i pátra] η Πάτρα (170,000)
d  [to iráklio] το Ηράκλειο (125,000)
e  [i lárisa] η Λάρισα (120,000)
f  [o vólos] ο Βόλος (80,000)

5  **Choose the correct form of the Greek word for** *the* **in each of the following cases. Then rewrite each sentence using Greek script.**

a  [íme apó] _____ [lonTHíno].       1 [o]   2 [to]   3 [sto]
b  [méno] _____ [lonTHíno].          1 [o]   2 [to]   3 [sto]
c  [íme apó] _____ [amerikí].        1 [i]   2 [tin]  3 [stin]
d  [apó] _____ [néa iórki].          1 [i]   2 [tin]  3 [stin]
e  _____ [néa iórki íne stin amerikí].  1 [i]   2 [tin]  3 [stin]
f  _____ [lonTHíno íne stin anglía].     1 [o]   2 [to]   3 [sto]

**6** **Look at the names of the following European capitals then write each one in the correct place on the map. Next, write in transliteration and/or Greek script the names of the corresponding countries.**

 **a** [i rómi] η Ρώμη
 **b** [to lonTHíno] το Λονδίνο
 **c** [i maTHríti] η Μαδρίτη
 **d** [to parísi] το Παρίσι
 **e** [to verolíno] το Βερολίνο

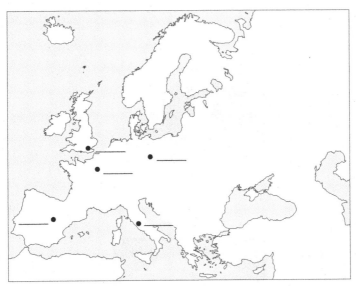

 **7** **02.09 Listen again to Conversation 2 without reading the text then fill in the missing words using the words in the box. Note that one of the words is used twice! Finally, can you write out each sentence using Greek script?**

| [alá] | [apó] | [esí] | [egó] | [óhi] |

| | |
|---|---|
| **Anna** | [íste] **a** _____ [to lonTHíno]? |
| **John** | **b** _____. [íme] [apó tin afstralía]. |
| **Mary** | [ki] **c** _____ [apó tin amerikí]. **d** _____? [íse] [apó tin athína]? |
| **Anna** | **e** _____. [íme] [apó ton póro]. **f** _____ [tóra] [méno stin athína]. |

**8** 02.10 **Look at the three business cards, then listen to the dialogue and decide which business card it relates to.**

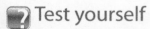

# ❓ Test yourself

1 How would you ask which country someone is from?
2 How do you ask someone *Where do you live now?* in Greek?
3 How would you say *I'm from Cardiff but I live in Manchester now*?
4 Give the Greek words for three European languages.
5 Give the names of three European cities in Greek.

## SELF CHECK

**I CAN. . .**

. . . ask where someone comes from and where he/she lives now.

. . . ask which languages someone speaks.

. . . give personal information about where I come from and where I live.

. . . say which languages I speak.

. . . say the names of some cities and countries.

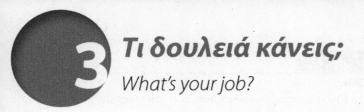

# 3 Τι δουλειά κάνεις;

*What's your job?*

**In this unit you will learn how to:**
▶ **talk about different jobs and professions.**
▶ **ask someone what their job is and say what your own job is.**
▶ **say the names of different professions.**
▶ **make sentences negative and turn a statement into a question.**

**CEFR: (A1)** *Can and ask and answer simple questions, initiate and respond to simple statements;* **(A2)** *Can understand sentences and frequently used expressions related to areas of most immediate relevance. Can describe aspects of his/her environment, e.g. people, work, interests.*

##  Εργασία στην Ελλάδα *Employment in Greece*

Many Greeks are [iTHiotikós ipálilos] **ιδιωτικός υπάλληλος** *self-employed* and run anything from small one-man businesses to large companies. Others become [THimósios ipálilos] **δημόσιος υπάλληλος** *civil servants* in the hope of long-term job security. Shipping has a long tradition in Greece and employs a large number of [erghátris-erghátria] **εργάτης-εργάτρια** *workers*. Equally important for the Greek economy is the tourist industry, which generates around one-eighth of the gross national income. Last but not least, Greece is also an agricultural country, producing olive oil, wine, milk products, fruit, vegetables and cereals, and this sector also creates many part-time and full-time jobs.

Many foreigners come to work in Greece, often as employees for large multinational companies or as economic migrants hoping for a better future. Unfortunately the major economic recession that began in 2010 caused vast numbers of job losses, leaving many Greeks and foreigners unemployed. Working in the civil service no longer provides the job security it once did and job prospects are not very promising for the near future.

 Read the text once again. Can you guess what the Greek verb **εργάζομαι** means?

Vocabulary builder

 **1** 03.01 **Listen as you look at the following list of professions and complete the English translations in your book. Then listen again and try to imitate the speakers.**

| Masculine | Feminine |
|---|---|
| [o arhitéktonas] | [i arhitéktonas] |
| **ο αρχιτέκτονας** | **η αρχιτέκτονας** |
| *architect* | *architect* |
| [o moosikós] | [i moosikós] |
| **ο μουσικός** | **η μουσικός** |
| *musician* | _____ |
| [o pianístas] | [i pianístria] |
| **ο πιανίστας** | **η πιανίστρια** |
| *pianist* | *pianist* |
| [o servitóros] | [i servitóra] |
| **ο σερβιτόρος** | **η σερβιτόρα** |
| *waiter* | _____ |
| [o yiatrós] | [i yiatrós] |
| **ο γιατρός** | **η γιατρός** |
| *doctor* | *doctor* |
| [o THáskalos] | [i THaskála] |
| **ο δάσκαλος** | **η δασκάλα** |
| *teacher* | *teacher* |
| [o sigraféas] | [i sigraféas] |
| **ο συγγραφέας** | **η συγγραφέας** |
| *writer* | *writer* |
| [o ithopi-ós] | [i ithopi-ós] |
| **ο ηθοποιός** | **η ηθοποιός** |
| *actor* | _____ |
| [o trapezítis] | [i trapezítria] |
| **ο τραπεζίτης** | **η τραπεζίτρια** |
| *banker* | *banker* |

[o chrimatistís]
**ο χρηματιστής**
*stockbroker*
[o nosokómos]
**ο νοσοκόμος**
*nurse*

[i chrimatístria]
**η χρηματίστρια**
*stockbroker*
[i nosokóma]
**η νοσοκόμα**
*nurse*

## ΜΙΛΩΝΤΑΣ ΓΙΑ ΔΟΥΛΕΙΑ  QUESTIONS AND ANSWERS ABOUT WORK

 **2  03.02 Without looking at the text, listen to the recording in which people ask and answer questions to do with work. Then, listen again and repeat after the speaker, concentrating on your pronunciation.**

| | | |
|---|---|---|
| [ti THooliá kánis/ kánete]? | Τι δουλειά κάνεις/ κάνετε; | *What's your job?* |
| [pu THoolévis/ THoolévete]? | Πού δουλεύεις/ δουλεύετε; | *Where do you work?* |
| [ergházese/ergházeste]? | Εργάζεσαι/Εργάζεστε; | *Do you work?* |
| [THoolévo se énan yiatró/mía tavérna/ éna ghrafío]. | Δουλεύω σε έναν γιατρό/μία ταβέρνα/ ένα γραφείο. | *I work in a doctor's surgery/a traditional Greek restaurant/an office.* |
| [THe THoolévo tóra]. | Δε δουλεύω τώρα. | *I'm not working at the moment.* |
| [THoolévo ston kípo/stin koozína/sto nosokomío]. | Δουλεύω στον κήπο/ στην κουζίνα/στο νοσοκομείο. | *I work in the garden/ kitchen/hospital.* |
| [ergházome gia ton kósta/tin etería ion]. | Εργάζομαι για τον Κώστα/την εταιρία ΙΟΝ. | *I work for Kostas/the ION company.* |
| [íme THaskála sto skolío tis aghías ánas]. | Είμαι δασκάλα στο σχολείο της Αγίας Άννας. | *I am a teacher at St Anna's School.* |

# Conversation 1 Είμαι δασκάλα
## *I'm a teacher*

 **NEW WORDS AND EXPRESSIONS 1**

 **03.03** Listen to the following words and expressions that will be used in the next conversation. Then listen again and repeat after the speaker.

| | | |
|---|---|---|
| [ménete] | μένετε | *you live (pl/fml)* |
| [sto] | στο | *in the* |
| [THoolévo] | δουλεύω | *I work* |
| [gráfo] | γράφω | *I write* |
| [pediká] | παιδικά | *children's* |
| [vivlía] | βιβλία | *books* |
| [THooliá] | δουλειά | *work* |

 **03.04** *Anna finds out about John's and Mary's professions.*

**1** Listen to their conversation a couple of times without looking at the text. What does Anna do for a living?

| | | |
|---|---|---|
| **Anna** | [ti]? [afstralía]? [amerikí]? [ke tóra] [ménete sto lonTHíno]? | *What? Australia? America? And now you live in London?* |
| **John** | [ne]. [THoolévo] [sto lonTHíno]. [íme arhitéktonas]. | *Yes. I work in London. I'm an architect.* |
| **Mary** | [ki' egó] [íme sigraféas]. [gráfo pediká vivlía]. [esí]? [ti THooliá kánis]? | *And myself, I'm a writer. I write children's books. How about you? What do you do for a living?* |
| **Anna** | [íme THaskála]. | *I'm a teacher.* |
| | | |
| **Άννα** | Τι; Αυστραλία; Αμερική; Και τώρα μένετε στο Λονδίνο; | |
| **John** | Ναι. Δουλεύω στο Λονδίνο. Είμαι αρχιτέκτονας. | |
| **Mary** | Κι εγώ είμαι συγγραφέας. Γράφω παιδικά βιβλία. Εσύ; Τι δουλειά κάνεις; | |
| **Άννα** | Είμαι δασκάλα. | |

**2 Now read the conversation and answer the questions.**

   **a** Where does John live now?

   **b** What does he do for a living?

   **c** What is Mary's job?

   **d** Is Anna a writer?

 **3 Listen again and pay special attention to the words which run together. Practise speaking the part of Mary or Anna and pay particular attention to your pronunciation.**

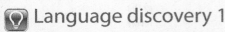

## Language discovery 1

**1 The following three professions are all mentioned in the conversation. Find the Greek words for them and write them in Greek script.**

   **a** architect

   **b** writer

   **c** teacher

> **LANGUAGE TIP**
> Unlike in English, when you say what your job is in Greek you do not use the indefinite article *a/an*. *I am an architect* = [íme arhitéktonas].

**2 Look at the list of professions earlier in the unit. You will see that some have the same word for both male and female (e.g.** [o servitóros]/[i servitóra] **ο σερβιτόρος/η σερβιτόρα** *waiter/waitress*) **while others have the same word for both forms (e.g.** [o yiatrós]/[i yiatrós] **ο γιατρός/η γιατρός** *doctor*).

   **Go back to the three professions mentioned in Conversation 1. For each one, decide if a different word is used for the male and female forms or if the same word is used. If the forms are different, write out the female form.**

**3 Read the conversation once again. There are four main verbs in this conversation. Find the Greek words for them and write them in Greek script.**

   **a** I live

   **b** I work

   **c** I write

   **d** I am

## 1 PROFESSIONS

As you have seen, professions may have different forms for masculine and feminine, or the same word may be used for both sexes. Compared to English, Greek tends to have many more professions with two words instead of one. The list at the beginning of the unit gives a good overview regarding most words for professions in Greek. Here are some examples from that list as a reminder, divided into two groups.

| Group I (same word for both sexes) | Group II (two different words) |
|---|---|
| ο αρχιτέκτον-ας/η αχιτέκτον-ας *architect* | ο πιανίστ-ας/η πιανίστ-ρια *pianist* |
| ο γιατρ-ός/η γιατρ-ός *doctor* | ο φοιτητ-ής/η φοιτήτ-ρια *student* |
| ο δικηγόρος/η δικηγόρος *lawyer* | ο δάσκαλ-ος/η δασκάλ-α *teacher* |

**Go back through all the professions mentioned so far and decide whether they belong to Group I or Group II.**

## 2 VERB GROUPS

As you have seen, Conversation 1 features four common verbs: **μένω** *I live*, **δουλεύω** *I work*, **γράφω** *I write* and **είμαι** *I am*. If you look at the verb endings, you will see that the verb **είμαι** has a different ending from the other three and therefore belongs to a different verb group. Verbs in the same group have the same endings. If you look back at the Vocabulary builder you will see another verb with similar endings to **είμαι** and which is therefore part of the same group: **εργάζομαι** *I work*.

> **LANGUAGE TIP**
> There are two words for *work* in Greek: **δουλεύω** is informal and **εργάζομαι** is formal.

The first three of these verbs are part of the most important verb group, referred to as Group 1 in this book, which accounts for around 65 per cent of all Greek verbs. The other two verbs are part of another group (Group 5), which comprises around 15 per cent of all Greek verbs. The remaining 20 per cent of verbs fall into one of three other verb groups (Group 2, 3 or 4).

Here are conjugations for the three Group 1 verbs and the two Group 5 verbs mentioned. The endings are underlined in each case and can be applied to any other verb from that group. Bear in mind, however, that the verb **είμαι** is irregular and therefore its endings are not exactly the same as those of other verbs from that group.

## Group 1 verbs

| | | |
|---|---|---|
| [méno] | **μένω** | I live |
| [ménis] | **μένεις** | you live (sing/infml) |
| [méni] | **μένει** | he/she/it lives |
| [ménume] | **μένουμε** | we live |
| [ménete] | **μένετε** | you live (pl/fml) |
| [ménun(e)] | **μένουν(ε)** | they live |

| | | |
|---|---|---|
| [THulévo] | **δουλεύω** | I work |
| [THulévis] | **δουλεύεις** | you work (sing/infml) |
| [THulévi] | **δουλεύει** | he/she/it works |
| [THulévume] | **δουλεύουμε** | we work |
| [THulévete] | **δουλεύετε** | you work (pl/fml) |
| [THulévun(e)] | **δουλεύουν(ε)** | they work |

| | | |
|---|---|---|
| [ghráfo] | **γράφω** | I write |
| [ghráfis] | **γράφεις** | you write (sing/infml) |
| [ghráfi] | **γράφει** | he/she/it writes |
| [gráfume] | **γράφουμε** | we write |
| [ghráfete] | **γράφετε** | you write (pl/fml) |
| [gráfun(e)] | **γράφουν(ε)** | they write |

## Group 5 verbs

| | | |
|---|---|---|
| [íme] | **είμαι** | I am |
| [íse] | **είσαι** | you are (sing/infml) |
| [íne] | **είναι** | he/she/it is |
| [ímaste] | **είμαστε** | we are |
| [ísaste/íste] | **είσαστε/είστε** | you are (pl/fml) |
| [íne] | **είναι** | they are |

| | | |
|---|---|---|
| [ergázome] | **εργάζομαι** | I work |
| [ergházese] | **εργάζεσαι** | you work (sing/infml) |

| [ergházete] | **εργάζεται** | *he/she/it works* |
| [erghazómaste] | **εργαζόμαστε** | *we work* |
| [erghazósaste/ ergházeste] | **εργαζόσαστε/ εργάζεστε** | *you work* (pl/fml) |
| [ergházonde] | **εργάζονται** | *they work* |

## Conversation 2 Πού μένεις;
*Where do you live?*

 **NEW WORDS AND EXPRESSIONS 2**

 **03.05 Listen to the words and expressions that are used in the next conversation and note their meaning.**

| [kséris] | ξέρεις | *you know* (sing/infml) |
| [THen] | δεν | *not* |
| [kséro] | ξέρω | *I know* |
| [poo] | πού | *where* |
| [kondá] | κοντά | *near, close to* |

 **03.06** *John and Mary now ask Anna some questions.*

**1 Listen to their exchange a couple of times without looking at the text. Does Anna live close to Angelos?**

| **John** | [ána], [kséris to lonTHíno]? | *Anna, do you know London?* |
| **Anna** | [óhi] [THen kséro to lonTHíno]. [kséro móno tin athína]. | *No, I don't know London. I only know Athens.* |
| **Mary** | [poo ménis]? [ménis] kondá ston ángelo]? | *Where do you live? Do you live near Angelos?* |
| **Anna** | [ne]. [méno] [kondá ston ángelo]. | *Yes. I live near Angelos.* |

| **John** | Άννα, ξέρεις το Λονδίνο; |
| **Άννα** | Όχι, δεν ξέρω το Λονδίνο. Ξέρω μόνο την Αθήνα. |
| **Mary** | Πού μένεις; Μένεις κοντά στον Άγγελο; |
| **Άννα** | Ναι. Μένω κοντά στον Άγγελο. |

**2 Now read the conversation and answer the questions.**

    **a** Does Anna know London or Athens better?

    **b** Did you pick up the two words for *yes* and *no* in Greek?

 **3 Listen again and pay special attention to the words which run together. Practise speaking the part of Anna and pay particular attention to your pronunciation.**

 ## Language discovery 2

**1 Can you find the Greek for the following English phrases in the conversation? Do the Greek questions also contain two verbs? Why do you think that is?**

    **a** … do you know?  **b** Where do you live?    **c** Do you live … ?

**2 The last two conversations include two words with a double γγ: συγγραφέας and Άγγελο. Would you guess that these two words have a similar or different sound for this double letter? To help you decide, listen to both conversations once again and just focus on the pronunciation of these two words.**

## 1 Asking questions

Asking questions in Greek in very simple: all you do is raise the intonation of your voice at the end of the sentence to make it sound like a question. There is no equivalent in Greek of the English *do …?* or *does …?*, and nor is there inversion of subject and verb, e.g. *you are well* ⟶ *are you well?* The written form, therefore, is exactly the same whether it is a statement or a question, apart from the question mark at the end.

| [ménis stin athína]. | **Μένεις στην Αθήνα.** | *You live in Athens.* |
|---|---|---|
| [ménis stin athína]? | **Μένεις στην Αθήνα;** | *Do you live in Athens?* |
| [íste THaskála]. | **Είστε δασκάλα.** | *You are a teacher.* |
| [íste THaskála]? | **Είστε δασκάλα;** | *Are you a teacher?* |

Listen carefully once again to the conversations in the past three units, paying particular attention to how the questions are formulated and the intonation of the speaker.

## 2 Question words

You already know four question words in Greek: [poo]? **πού;** *where?*, **[ti]?**
**τι;** *what?*, [pos]? **πώς;** *how?* and [pia]? **ποια;** *who?/which?/what?* Practise
using these words with the verbs that you have learned in order to form
questions in Greek. For instance:

| | | |
|---|---|---|
| [poo ménis]? | **Πού μένεις;** | *Where do you live?* |
| [ti grafis]? | **Τι γράφεις;** | *What do you write?/ What are you writing?* |
| [pos íse]? | **Πώς είσαι;** | *How are you?* |
| [pia kséris]? | **Ποια ξέρεις;** | *Who (female) do you know?* |

## 3 Negative statements

To make a sentence negative in Greek, simply put the negative word
[THen] **δεν** (or [THe] **δε** depending on the first letter of the following
word) before the verb.

| | | |
|---|---|---|
| [ménoome stin athína]. | **Μένουμε στην Αθήνα.** | *We live in Athens.* |
| [THe] [ménoome stin thesaloníki]. | **Δε μένουμε στην Θεσσαλονίκη.** | *We don't live in Thessaloniki.* |
| [íme sigraféas]. | **Είμαι συγγραφέας.** | *I am a writer.* |
| [THen] [íme arhitéktonas]. | **Δεν είμαι αρχιτέκτονας.** | *I am not an architect.* |
| [kséri angliká] | **Ξέρει Αγγλικά.** | *He knows English.* |
| [THen] [kséri italiká]. | **Δεν ξέρει Ιταλικά.** | *He doesn't know Italian.* |

# Practice

**1 Complete each sentence using one of the words from the box. In some cases there is more than one possible correct answer. The first one has been done for you. Once you have completed all the sentences, try to write them out in Greek script.**

> [egó]  [esí]  [aftós]  [aftí]
> [aftó]  [emís]  [esís]  [aftés]  [aftá]

**a** [esís] [poo ménete]?
**b** _____ [kséris eliniká]?
**c** _____ [ménoon stin pátra].
**d** _____ [THen periméno].
**e** _____ [íne o thomás].
**f** _____ [íne i ána].
**g** _____ [ímaste apó tin eláTHa].
**h** _____ [periménoon THío fíloos].

**2 Change the following positive statements into negative ones by replacing the words after each verb with the alternatives given in the second brackets. Once you have finished, translate each of the negative sentences into English.**

**Look at the example: [miláo galiká]. [eliniká] [THen miláo eliniká].**

**Now do the same to the following:**

**a** [miláme angliká]. [yermaniká]
**b** [kséro ton yiáni]. [ángelo]
**c** [ksérete tin ioána]. [ána]
**d** [periméni THío fíloos]. [tris fíloos]
**e** [ménoon stin athína]. [sta yánena]
**f** [íme apó tin anglía]. [amerikí]
**g** [íne apó tin eláTHa]. [italía]

**3 Change the following sentences into questions and then write them in Greek script, as in the example:**

[kséro yermaniká]. [esí] [esí kséris yermaniká]? Εσύ ξέρεις Γερμανικά;

**a** [ménoome stin yermanía]. [esís]
**b** [aftós íne apó tin afstralía]. [aftí]
**c** [kséroon líga eliniká]. [esí]
**d** [aftí periménoon THío fíloos]. [aftés]
**e** [miláo angliká]. [esí]

**f** [THen miláme ispaniká]. [esís]

**g** [ímaste apó tin anglía]. [esís]

**4** **Look at the pictures and write down the appropriate jobs in transliteration and Greek script. The third one has been done for you.**

**a** _____

**b** _____

**c** [nosokóma] νοσοκόμα _____

**d** _____

**e** _____

**f** _____

**5** **Read the following sentences. According to the pictures in the previous exercise, is each one true or false?**

**a** Αυτός δεν είναι γιατρός.

**b** Αυτή είναι δασκάλα.

**c** Αυτή δεν είναι νοσοκόμα.

**d** Αυτή είναι γραμματέας.

**e** Αυτός δεν είναι σερβιτόρος.

**f** Είναι αρχιτέκτονας.

**6** 03.07 **Listen to this short conversation between two people in which they talk about what they do for a living. Match their jobs or professions with two of the six cartoons.**

a The man's job _____

b The woman's job _____

**7 Match each question with the most appropriate answer.**

a [íse arhitéktonas]?      **1** [óhi], [íne pianístas].

b [íste yiatrós]?      **2** [óhi], [íne servitóra].

c [o yiánis íne servitóros]?      **3** [ne, íne THáskalos].

d [i ána íne sigraféas]?      **4** [óhi, íme moosikós].

e [o ángelos íne THáskalos]?      **5** [ne, íme yiatrós].

**8 Decide which of the three options is correct in each case. Then, translate the statements into English.**

a [kséro] _____ [lonTHíno kalá].    **1** [o]    **2** [to]    **3** [sto]

b _____ [thomás íne yiatrós].    **1** [o]    **2** [i]    **3** [to]

c _____ [ioána íne arhitéktonas].    **1** [o]    **2** [i]    **3** [to]

d [méno]_____ [pátra tóra]:    **1** [i]    **2** [tin]    **3** [stin]

e [alá íme apó] _____ [yiánena].    **1** [to]    **2** [ta]    **3** [sta]

**9 Monster words! The following sentences have not been separated into their individual words. Insert spaces in the appropriate places to make proper sentences. Then write out each sentence in Greek script.**

a [ímeservitóraTHenímepianístria].

b [THenímesigraféas].

c [ísteyiatrósóhiímemoosikós].

d [ménokondástinthesaloníki].

e [THenímasteapótinanglía].

**10** 03.08 **Listen again to Conversation 2 and fill in each blank using one of the words in the box. Then write out the conversation in Greek script.**

| [ne] | [óhi] | [poo] |
| --- | --- | --- |
| [móno] | [kondá] | [kséris] |

**John**    [ána], **a** _____ [to lonTHíno]?

**Anna**    **b** _____ [THen kséro to lonTHíno]. [kséro] **c** _____ [tin athína].

**Mary**    **d** _____ [ménis]? [ménis] **e** _____ [ston ángelo]?

**Anna**    **f** _____ [méno] **e** _____ [ston ángelo].

**11 Read the two business cards and decide which two Greek letters represent the following sounds.**

  **a** /u/ as in *put*       **b** /i/ as in *pin*       **c** /g/ as in *get*

Αγγελική Κουκουλά
*ΕΠΙΜΕΛΕΙΑ ΥΛΗΣ*

Εκδοτική **ΑΛΦΑ** ΕΠΕ

ΕΚΔΟΣΕΙΣ • ΒΙΒΛΙΟΠΩΛΕΙΟ

# Test yourself

1  How would you ask someone in Greek what their job is?

2  How would you say *I'm a teacher*?

3  If someone tells you [íme sigraféas] what is their job?

4  What is the difference between [méno sto Manchester] and [méno kondá sto Manchester]?

5  What is the difference between [íse apó tin anglía]? and [íste apó tin anglía]?

6  How would you translate these question words: [ti], [pos], [poo], [pia]?

## SELF CHECK

| I CAN... |
| --- |
| . . . talk about different jobs and professions. |
| . . . ask someone what their job is and say what my own job is. |
| . . . say the names of different professions. |
| . . . say which languages I speak. |
| . . . make sentences negative and turn a statement into a question. |

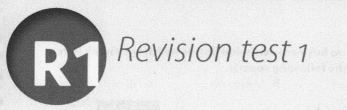

# R1 Revision test 1

**1** **Which greeting would you use at the following times?** *(5 points)*
   **a** 8:30            **d** 21:00
   **b** 12:30           **e** 23:40
   **c** 16:10

**2** **Which greeting should go in each of the speech bubbles?**
*(10 points)*

**3** **Take part in the following conversation using the English as a prompt.** *(6 points)*

**Από εδώ ο Νίκος!**
**You**        Say *Hello Nikos! Nice to meet you!*
**Καλώς όρισες στη Ελλάδα!**
**You**        Say *Thanks. Nice to be here!*
**Είσαι από την Ελλάδα;**
**You**        Say *No, I'm from Liverpool.*

**4** **Can you come up with the appropriate question for each of the following answers?** *(10 points)*
   **a** Περιμένω δύο φίλους.
   **b** Είμαι καλά. Εσύ;
   **c** Με λένε Άρη. Εσένα;
   **d** Μιλάω λίγο Ελληνικά.
   **e** Τώρα μένω στην Αθήνα.

**5** **Match each question with the most appropriate answer. Then translate each profession mentioned into English.** *(10 points)*

a Είσαι αρχιτέκτονας;           **1** Όχι, είναι πιανίστας;
b Είστε γιατρός;                **2** Όχι, είναι σερβιτόρα.
c Ο Γιάννης είναι σερβιτόρος;   **3** Ναι, είναι δάσκαλος.
d Η Άννα είναι συγγραφέας;      **4** Όχι, είμαι μουσικός.
e Ο Άγγελος είναι δάσκαλος;     **5** Ναι, είμαι γιατρός.

**6** **Look at the car stickers and name the countries and their corresponding languages.** *(10 points)*

| Symbol | Country | Language |
|---|---|---|
| USA | a _____ | 1 _____ |
| D | b _____ | 2 _____ |
| F | c _____ | 3 _____ |
| IT | d _____ | 4 _____ |
| GR | e _____ | 5 _____ |

**7** **Choose the correct forms of the Greek word for** *the* **and** *in the* **to complete the following sentences.** *(10 points)*

a _____ [íme apó] [athína].              **1** [i]   **2** [tin]   **3** [stin]
b _____ [athína íne stin eláTHa].        **1** [i]   **2** [tin]   **3** [stin]
c _____ [lonTHíno íne stin anglía].      **1** [o]   **2** [to]   **3** [sto]
d [méno] _____ [lonTHíno].               **1** [o]   **2** [to]   **3** [sto]
e [méno] _____ [athína].                 **1** [i]   **2** [tin]   **3** [stin]

**8** **Look at the Greek words. What is their correct transliteration?** *(6 points)*

a ΑΕΡΟΛΙΜΕΝΑΣ
**1** [aepoliménas]   **2** [aeroTHiménas]   **3** [aeroliménas]

b ΑΘΗΝΩΝ
**1** [athinón]   **2** [aTHinón]   **3** [athnnón]

c ΕΛΕΥΘΕΡΙΟΣ
**1** [elefthérios]   **2** [elefthérios]   **3** [elethérios]

**d** ΒΕΝΙΖΕΛΟΣ
  **1** [benizélos]   **2** [venizélos]   **3** [venisélos]
**e** ΛΟΝΔΙΝΟ
  **1** [lonTHíno]   **2** [lonthíno]   **3** [loTHíno]
**f** ΠΑΡΙΣΙ
  **1** [parísi]   **2** [papísi]   **3** [parízi]

**9 Can you solve the crossword puzzle by translating the clues into Greek? The shaded vertical word spells out the word for architect.** *(13 points)*

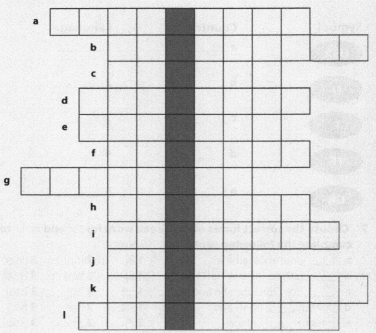

**a** writer
**b** waitress
**c** Athens
**d** good morning
**e** doctor
**f** USA

**g** musician
**h** father
**i** I work
**j** near
**k** pianist
**l** teacher

**10 Take part in the following conversation using the English as a prompt.** *(20 points)*

| | |
|---|---|
| **Maria** | [na sas sistíso] [apo'THó i maría]. |
| **You** | Say *Hi Maria! Pleased to meet you!* |
| **Maria** | [ki'egó]. [apó poo íse]? |
| **You** | Say *From the States. From New York. You?* |
| **Maria** | [apó ta yiánena] [alá tóra méno stin athína]. [esí]? |
| **You** | Say *I also live in Athens now. I am a children's author.* |

**TOTAL: 100 POINTS**

# Μένω σε διαμέρισμα

## I live in an apartment

**In this unit you will learn how to:**
▶ *talk about different types of accommodation.*
▶ *describe your own home.*
▶ *count from 0 to 10.*
▶ *use the plural forms of some Greek nouns.*

**CEFR: (A1)** *Can handle numbers;* **(A2)** *Can understand different types of accommodation; Can describe your own home; Can count from 0 to 10.*

##  Ένα σπίτι στην Ελλάδα *A Greek home*

Most Greeks used to own their home. Building one's own [spíti] **σπίτι** *house* or buying one's own [THiamérizma] **διαμέρισμα** *flat/apartment* is still a dream that many seek to fulfil, in spite of the increase in property taxes and the cost of land and building permits. More and more new families rent nowadays, rather than buying their own home.

Greek homes come in different architectural styles, with [sínhrona ktíria] **σύγχρονα κτίρια** *modern buildings* coexisting alongside [neoklasiká ktíria] **νεοκλασσικά κτίρια** *neoclassical buildings.* Modern apartments have fewer dividing walls, open-plan kitchens, more bathrooms, larger balconies and more colours. Building methods, however, are sometimes old-fashioned and not very time- or cost-effective. Construction companies have been known to build and un-build several times before a property is completed and create such an amount of [báza] **μπάζα** *rubble* that one wonders how anything gets finished! [betón] **μπετόν** *Concrete* is still the predominant building material compared to [xílo] **ξύλο** *wood*, [túvlo] **τούβλο** *brick*, [pétra] **πέτρα** *stone* or [métalo] **μέταλλο** *metal*. Flat roofs, sloping roofs and, increasingly, red-tiled roofs can be seen atop houses with white, pink, blue and other colourful facades. Local styles prevail in the countryside and on the islands, such as the famous whitewashed houses in the Cyclades or the stone houses built of grey slate in the Zagori villages in Epirus.

**1** Read the text and say if you live in a flat or a house.

Μένω σε ένα _____

**2** Give the Greek words for two building materials.

#  Vocabulary builder

**ΚΑΤΟΙΚΙΕΣ ΚΑΙ ΔΩΜΑΤΙΑ** *TYPES OF ACCOMMODATION AND ROOMS*

 **1** **04.01 Listen a couple of times to the recording while you read the list of types of accommodation. Then listen again and repeat them out loud.**

**Types of accommodation**

| | | |
|---|---|---|
| [i katikía] | η κατοικία | *residence* |
| [to spíti] | το σπίτι | *house/home* |
| [to THiamérizma] | το διαμέρισμα | *apartment/flat* |
| [i garsoniéra] | η γκαρσονιέρα | *studio/bedsit* |
| [to retiré] | το ρετιρέ | *penthouse* |
| [i monokatikía] | η μονοκατοικία | *detached house* |
| [i polikatikía] | η πολυκατοικία | *apartment building/ block of flats* |

 **2** **04.02 Now listen to the audio while you read the words for different rooms in a house. Then listen again and repeat each word out loud.**

**Rooms**

| | | |
|---|---|---|
| [to salóni] | το σαλόνι | *living room* |
| [to kathistikó] | το καθιστικό | *sitting room* |
| [i koozína] | η κουζίνα | *kitchen* |
| [i trapezaría] | η τραπεζαρία | *dining room* |
| [to ipnoTHomátio] | το υπνοδωμάτιο | *bedroom* |
| [to bánio] | το μπάνιο | *bathroom* |
| [i tzamaría] | η τζαμαρία | *conservatory* |

**3** **04.03** Listen carefully to the audio. You will hear different people telling you where they live. Now give each sentence a letter from a to d according to the order in which you heard the descriptions. Then listen again and repeat each sentence out loud.

\_\_\_\_\_ [eghó méno se mya monokatikía] Εγώ μένω σε μια μονοκατοικία.

\_\_\_\_\_ [eghó méno se éna THiamérizma] Εγώ μένω σε ένα διαμέρισμα.

\_\_\_\_\_ [eghó méno se éna spíti] Εγώ μένω σε ένα σπίτι.

\_\_\_\_\_ [eghó méno se mya polikatikía] Εγώ μένω σε μια πολυκατοικία.

## Conversation 1 Σε σπίτι;
### In a house?

 **NEW WORDS AND EXPRESSIONS 1**

 **04.04** Listen to the words and expressions that are used in the conversation. Note their meaning.

| [se] | σε | *in* |
| [mía] | μία | *a, an/one* |
| [éhi] | έχει | *it has* |
| [tésera] | τέσσερα | *four* |
| [THomátia] | δωμάτια | *rooms* |
| [éna] | ένα | *a, an/one* |
| [kéna] | κι ένα | *and a/an/one* |
| [mikró] | μικρό | *small* |
| [hol] | χωλ | *hallway* |
| [megálo] | μεγάλο | *big, large* |

**04.05** *Anna describes her flat to John and Mary.*

**1 Listen to the conversation a couple of times. How many rooms does Anna have?**

| | | |
|---|---|---|
| **Mary** | [ménis] [se spíti]? | *Do you live in a house?* |
| **Anna** | [óhi], [méno] [se THiamérizma] [se mía polikatikía]. [éhi] [tésera THomátia], [mía koozína], [éna bánio] [kéna mikró hol]. | *No, I live in an apartment in a block of flats. It has four rooms, a kitchen, a bathroom and a small hallway.* |
| **Mary** | [po-po], [íne megálo]! | *Wow, it's big!* |
| | | |
| **Mary** | Μένεις σε σπίτι; | |
| **Άννα** | Όχι, μένω σε διαμέρισμα σε μία πολυκατοικία. Έχει τέσσερα δωμάτια, μία κουζίνα, ένα μπάνιο, κι ένα μικρό χωλ. | |
| **Mary** | Πω, πω, είναι μεγάλο! | |

**2 Now read the conversation and answer the questions.**
  **a** Can you name two rooms in Anna's flat?
  **b** To help you memorize the new words and expressions, can you think of any English words that sound like the Greek words for *big* and *small*?

 **3 Listen again to the conversation and pay special attention to the words which run together. Practise speaking the part of Anna and pay particular attention to your pronunciation.**

## Language discovery 1

**1 In Conversation 1 there are different indefinite articles (*a* or *an*). Read or listen to the conversation again and decide which Greek article is used in each case.**
  **a** a hallway
  **b** a bathroom
  **c** a kitchen
  **d** a block of flats

**2** **The Greek words for** *a* **or** *an* **are also used to say the number**
**one. Read or listen to the conversation again and try to find the**
**numbers** *one* **and** *four* **as follows.**
   **a** one (for neuter nouns)
   **b** one (for feminine nouns)
   **c** four (for neuter nouns)

## 1 THE INDEFINITE ARTICLE

In Conversation 1 Anna says [mía koozína] **μία κουζίνα** *a kitchen* and
[éna bánio] **ένα μπάνιο** *a bathroom*. All you need to remember for now is
that [mía] **μία** goes with feminine nouns and [éna] **ένα** goes with neuter
nouns. The following table will give you an overview of the different forms
of the indefinite article:

|  | Masculine | Feminine | Neuter |
|---|---|---|---|
| Nominative | **ένας** | **μία/μια** | **ένα** |
|  | **Ένας κύριος σας μιλάει.** *A man is talking to you.* | **Μία κυρία σας θέλει.** *A woman is looking for you. (lit. A woman wants you.)* | **Ένα μεγάλο σπίτι δεν είναι για μένα.** *A big house is not for me.* |
| Accusative | **έναν** | **μία/μια** | **ένα** |
|  | **Θέλω έναν καφέ.** *I'd like a cup of coffee.* | **Μένω σε μία πολυκατοικία.** *I live in a block of flats.* | **Έχω ένα μεγάλο σαλόνι.** *I have a big living room.* |

In contrast to English, where *a* changes to *an* according to the sound of
the word that follows the article, in Greek the four different forms of the
indefinite article are used according to grammatical rules, i.e. the gender
and case of the noun that follows.

## 2 THE NUMBERS 1–10

**04.06** You are going to listen to the numbers 1–10. Listen carefully a
couple of times and pay special attention to the numbers *one*, *three* and
*four*, which have more than one form. Then listen again and repeat out
loud.

| [énas] | **ένας** (m) | *one* |
|---|---|---|
| [mía] | **μία** (f) |  |
| [éna] | **ένα** (n) |  |

| [THío] | **δύο** | *two* |
|---|---|---|
| [tris]<br>[tría] | **τρεις** (m/f)<br>**τρία** (n) | *three* |
| [téseris]<br>[tésera] | **τέσσερις** (m/f)<br>**τέσσερα** (n) | *four* |
| [pénde] | **πέντε** | *five* |
| [éksi] | **έξι** | *six* |
| [eptá]/[eftá] | **επτά/εφτά** | *seven* |
| [októ]/[ohtó] | **οκτώ/οχτώ** | *eight* |
| [enéa]/[eniá] | **εννέα/εννιά** | *nine* |
| [THéka] | **δέκα** | *ten* |

**LANGUAGE TIP**

The numbers *one*, *three* and *four* have more than one form because they have to agree with the gender (masculine, feminine or neuter) of the noun. The numbers *seven*, *eight* and *nine* have two different pronunciations; both are frequently used but the second is more informal than the first.

## Conversation 2 **Μεγάλο σπίτι!**
### *Big house!*

**NEW WORDS AND EXPRESSIONS 2**

**04.07 Listen to the words and expressions that are used in the conversation and note their meaning. Then listen again and repeat after the speaker.**

| [sálo] | σ'άλλο | *in a different* (lit. *another*) |
|---|---|---|
| [pósa] | πόσα | *how many* |
| [mazí me] | μαζί με | *along with* |
| [vesé] | WC | *toilet* |
| [pénde] | πέντε | *five* |

**04.08** *Angelos now describes his new house to his friends.*

**1** **Listen to the conversation a couple of times. Can you say how many bedrooms there are?**

| | | |
|---|---|---|
| **Angelos** | [ksérete] [egó méno] [sálo spíti tóra]. [íne mía monokatikía]. | *You know, I live in a different house now. It's a detached house.* |
| **Mary** | [pósa THomátia éhi]? | *How many rooms does it have?* |
| **Angelos** | [éhi] [éna megálo salóni], [mazí me mía trapezaría], [éna bánio] [kéna vesé], [ke pénde ipnoTHomátia]. | *It has one big living room, along with a dining room, a bathroom and a guest toilet, and five bedrooms.* |
| **Mary** | [megálo spíti]! | *Big house!* |
| **John** | [polí megálo spíti]! | *Very big house!* |
| | | |
| **Άγγελος** | Ξέρετε, εγώ μένω σ'άλλο σπίτι τώρα. Είναι μία μονοκατοικία. | |
| **Mary** | Πόσα δωμάτια έχει; | |
| **Άγγελος** | Έχει ένα μεγάλο σαλόνι, μαζί με μία τραπεζαρία, ένα μπάνιο κι ένα WC, και πέντε υπνοδωμάτια. | |
| **Mary** | Μεγάλο σπίτι! | |
| **John** | Πολύ μεγάλο σπίτι! | |

**2** **Now read the conversation and answer the questions.**
   **a** What kind of house is it?
   **b** Can you list all the rooms in the house?

 **3** **Listen again to the conversation and pay special attention to the words which run together. Practise speaking the part of Angelos and pay particular attention to your pronunciation.**

#  Language discovery 2

**1** **The two conversations in this unit include the following four phrases in which Greek adjectives are used. Find the Greek for these four phrases. What do you notice about the adjective endings?**

**a** big house
**b** different house
**c** small hallway
**d** big living room

**2 You have already learned the plural forms of two neuter nouns (δωμάτι-ο ⟶ δωμάτι-α and βιβλί-ο ⟶ βιβλί-α). Can you use what you have learned to work out the plural forms of the following neuter nouns in this unit?**

**a** μπάνι-ο
**b** κτίρι-ο
**c** ξύλ-ο
**d** μέταλ-ο

## 1 ADJECTIVES

If you look up an adjective in a Greek dictionary, you will find three different forms: masculine, feminine and neuter. This may seem like a lot to learn but you may find it easier if you learn each adjective as part of an adjective + noun combination, as in Language discovery exercise 1. Here is how you might find the adjectives for that exercise listed in a dictionary:

**άλλος, άλλη, άλλο** or **άλλ-ος/-η/-ο**

**μικρός, μικρή, μικρό** or **μικρ-ός/-ή/-ό**

**μεγάλος, μεγάλη, μεγάλο** or **μεγάλ-ος/-η/-ο**

## 2 PLURAL FORMS

As you completed Language discovery exercise 2 you will have learned that the ending **-ο** of singular adjectives changes to **-α** in the plural. Try to learn this as you will encounter it frequently. The **-α** ending usually either replaces the **-ο** ending or is added after the **-i** ending. Look at the following examples:

| | | |
|---|---|---|
| [ktíri-o/-a] | **κτίρι-ο/κτίρι-α** | *building/buildings* |
| [métal-o/-a] | **μέταλ-ο/μέταλ-α** | *metal/metals* |
| [spít-i/-a] | **σπίτ-ι/σπίτι-α** | *house/houses* |
| [salon-i/-a] | **σαλόν-ι/σαλόνι-α** | *living room/living rooms* |

Just as English does, Greek nouns have certain irregular plural endings. Look at the following examples, grouped according to gender.

## Masculine nouns

| [o fílos] | **ο φίλος** | friend | ⟶ | [i fíli] | **οι φίλοι** | friends |
| [o THáskalos] | **ο δάσκαλος** | teacher | ⟶ | [i THáskali] | **οι δάσκαλοι** | teachers |

## Feminine nouns

| [i THaskála] | **η δασκάλα** | teacher | ⟶ | [i THaskáles] | **οι δασκάλες** | teachers |
| [kuzína] | **η κουζίνα** | kitchen | ⟶ | [kuzínes] | **οι κουζίνες** | kitchens |

## Neuter nouns

| [to vivlío] | **το βιβλίο** | book | ⟶ | [ta vivlía] | **τα βιβλία** | books |
| [to spiti] | **το σπίτι** | house | ⟶ | [ta spítia] | **τα σπίτια** | houses |

## 3 ONE WORD, TWO MEANINGS?

It is easy to assume that every word has just one meaning but, as you will know from English, this is not always the case! There are two words in this unit which you met in Unit 1; here, however, they have a different meaning:

| [pos se léne]? | **Πώς σε λένε;** | What's your name? (lit. How do they call you?) |
| [méno se éna THiamérizma]. | **Μένω σε ένα διαμέρισμα.** | I live in an apartment. |
| [me léne ána]. | **Με λενε Άννα.** | My name is Anna (lit. They call me Anna). |
| [… me trapezaría] | **… με τραπεζαρία** | … with dining room |

These two words, **σε** and **με**, function both as pronouns, meaning *you* and *me* respectively, and as prepositions, meaning *in* and *with* respectively.

## 4 CONTRACTIONS

You will already be familiar with English contractions (such as *do not* ⟶ *don't; I have* ⟶ *I've*). These exist in Greek too and you have already encountered some in the previous units.

### Unit 1

| [sto] **στο** = [se] + [to] | at the |
| [stin] **στην** = [se] + [tin] | in the |

**Unit 2**

[kegó] or [ki egó] **κι εγώ** = [ke] + [egó]                    *and I*

**Unit 3**

[ston] **στον** = [se] + [ton]                                        *at the*

**Unit 4**

[kéna] or [ki éna] **κι ένα** = [ke] + [éna]                    *and one*

[sálo] **σ'άλλο** = [se] [álo]                                        *in another*

> **LANGUAGE TIP**
> It is not possible to use the uncontracted forms [se] + [to], [se] + [tin] and [se] + [ton].

> **INSIGHT**
> Before we move on to the Practice section it is worth reminding you of the importance of taking the vocabulary and grammar taught in each unit and making sure you can apply it to your own situation. Can you now describe your own home in Greek? Do you live in a house or a flat? How many rooms are there? Do you know the name of each room? Learn all the words in this unit, look up some more in a Greek dictionary and then try to construct a few sentences in Greek. Even better, find a Greek native speaker to practise them on!

 Practice

1  **Match each word on the left with a word that means either the same or the opposite on the right.**

   a  [kondá]                    1  [THiamérizma]
   b  [póli]                        2  [kathistikó]
   c  [spíti]                        3  [megálo]
   d  [salóni]                      4  [hóra] (*country*)
   e  [koozína]                    5  [makriá] (*far*)
   f  [mikró]                       6  [trapezaría]

2  **Now write the words in exercise 1 in Greek script and then translate each one into English.**

3  **Match each question with its corresponding answer.**

   a  [poo ménete]? Πού μένετε;          1  [óhi], [alá íne kondá]. Όχι,
                                                                αλλά είναι κοντά.

   b  [íne megálo]? Είναι μεγάλο;         2  [óhi], [íne mikró]. Όχι, είναι
                                                                μικρό.

**c** [íne] [stin athína]? Είναι στην Αθήνα;

**d** [poo íne]? Πού είναι;

**e** [ti íne] [i rafína]? Τι είναι η Ραφήνα;

**3** [i rafína] [íne] [éna limáni] Η Ραφήνα είναι ένα λιμάνι.

**4** [méno] [se THiamérizma]. Μένω σε διαμέρισμα.

**5** [íne stin rafína] Είναι στη Ραφήνα.

---

> **INSIGHT**
>
> [rafína] **Ραφήνα** is a [limáni] **λιμάνι** *port* on the Aegean coast. Boats leave from there to many islands in the Cyclades, such as Andros, Tinos and Mykonos.

---

**4 Put these sentences in the correct order to form a dialogue.**

**a** \_\_\_\_\_ [éna salóni] [kéna ipnoTHomátio]. Ένα σαλόνι κι ένα υπνοδωμάτιο.

**b** \_\_\_\_\_ [pósa THomátia éhi]? Πόσα δωμάτια έχει;

**c** \_\_\_\_\_ [éhis megálo spíti]? Έχεις μεγάλο σπίτι;

**d** \_\_\_\_\_ [móno THío THomátia]. Μόνο δύο δωμάτια.

**e** \_\_\_\_\_ [óhi polí megálo]. Όχι πολύ μεγάλο.

**f** \_\_\_\_\_ [ti THomátia]? Τι δωμάτια;

**5 Here is a plan of an apartment. Can you write the name of each room?**

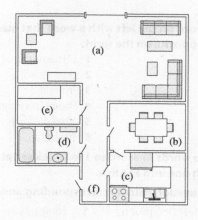

**a** _____     **d** _____

**b** _____     **e** _____

**c** _____     **f** _____

**6** Learning numbers is an essential part of studying a foreign language. Here is a list of emergency numbers in Greece. Can you read them out loud, number by number? The number 1 reads as [éna] ένα.

**a** 100 – Police
**b** 112 – European Emergency Number
**c** 134 – Telephone Operator
**d** 166 – Medical Assistance
**e** 169 – International Operator
**f** 171 – Tourist Police
**g** 199 – Fire Department

**7** The answers to the following puzzle are different types of home and room. Can you solve it? The vertical shaded word spells out the Greek for living room.

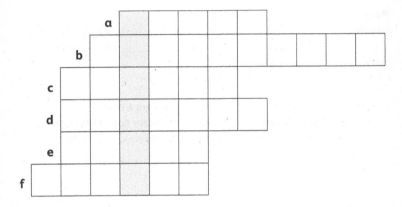

**a** home
**b** home
**c** room
**d** room
**e** room
**f** home

**8** Now write each word from the puzzle in Greek script.

a _____

b _____

c _____

d _____

e _____

f _____

g (shaded word) _____

**9** **04.09** Listen again to Conversation 2 of this unit. Choose a word from the box to complete each line of the conversation.

| [megálo] [sálo] [polí] |
| [mazí] [pénde] [pósa] |

**Angelos** [ksérete] [egó méno] **a** _____ [spíti tóra]. [íne mía monokatikía].

**Mary** **b** _____ [THomátia éhi]?

**Angelos** [éhi] [éna] **c** _____ [salóni], **d** _____ [me mía trapezaría], [éna bánio]/[kéna vesé], [ke] **e** _____ [ipnoTHomátia].

**Mary** [megálo spíti]!

**John** **f** _____ [megálo spíti]!

**10** Here is an advertisement for ΔΕΗ (Δημόσια Εταιρία Ηλεκτρισμού), Greece's state-run electricity company. Can you find the Greek words for *electricity* and *programmes* in this advertisement?

Σύγχρονα Προγράμματα Εξυπηρέτησης

# Test yourself

**You are now at the end of Unit 4. Let's see how easy the following questions are for you.**

1 What are the three Greek words for *bathroom*, *toilet* and *guest toilet*?

2 Name four rooms in a house (not counting the words in question 1 above).

3 Name four different types of home.

4 How do you say *I live in a detached house in London*?

5 Give the opposites of [megálo], [kondá] and [monokatikía].

6 Give words that mean the same as [salóni], [bánio] and [spíti].

## SELF CHECK

| | I CAN... |
|---|---|
| ○ | . . . talk about different types of accommodation. |
| ○ | . . . describe my own home. |
| ○ | . . . count from 0 to 10. |
| ○ | . . . use the plural forms of some Greek nouns. |

# **5** *Μία μεγάλη οικογένεια*

## *A big family*

**In this unit you will learn how to:**
▶ *ask questions about family and children.*
▶ *describe your own family.*
▶ *ask how old someone is and say how old you are.*
▶ *count from 11 to 100.*

**CEFR: (A2)** *Can understand sentences and frequently used expressions related to personal and family information; Can describe in simple terms aspects of his/her background; Can give and receive information about numbers from 11 to 100.*

## **Ελληνικά ονόματα** *Greek names*

Greek names often have a particular meaning, e.g. [elpíTHa] **Ελπίδα** *Elpitha* means *hope*, [aghápi] **Αγάπη** *Aghapi* means *love*, [zoí] **Ζωή** *Zoe* means *life*, [sotíris] **Σωτήρης** *Sotiris* means *saviour* and [THikéos] **Δικαίος** *Thikeos* means *justified*.

When Greeks are named after saints, that saint's day becomes the person's name day. Name days are observed and celebrated more in Greece than people's actual birthdays. The dates of several name days are very widely known, such as [vasílis] **Βασίλης** *Basilius* on 1 January, [yiánis] **Γιάννης** *John the Baptist* on 7 January and [yioryía] **Γιωργία** *George* on 23 April. Most birthdays will pass by unnoticed except perhaps for children's birthdays, which are often celebrated at fast-food restaurants or special playgrounds.

It is still customary to name a child after its grandparents. Even the order of name giving is set, starting with the grandparents on the paternal side. Of course, there are always exceptions, which can lead to a serious objection from the grandparent concerned! Most Greek children are baptized, the majority in the Greek Orthodox faith. Greek saints' names are still dominant, in order to respect traditional name-giving conventions and to satisfy religious views. The words [moró] **μωρό** *baby* or [bébis] **μπέμπης** *baby boy* and [béba] **μπέμπα** *baby girl* are used for unbaptized children. So, any unbaptized child, whatever their age, will be addressed as *baby* until the holy day of baptism!

What are the Greek words for *love, hope* and *life?*

# Vocabulary builder

**ΟΙΚΟΓΕΝΕΙΑΚΟ ΔΕΝΤΡΟ** *FAMILY TREE*

**1  05.01 Anna describes her family. Read the words in the family tree as you listen carefully a couple of times and then listen once again and repeat.**

[ártemis] **Άρτεμις**
[i yiayiá] **η γιαγιά**
*grandmother*

[oTHiséas] **Οδυσσέας**
[o papoós] **ο παππούς**
*grandfather*

[elphiTHa] **Ελπίδα**
[i sízigos] **η σύζυγος**
*spouse* (f)
[ángelos] **Άγγελος**
[o sízigos] **ο σύζυγος**
*spouse* (m)

[aléxanTHros] **Αλέξανδρος**
[o ándras] **ο άνδρας**
*husband* (lit. *man*)
[elisávet] **Ελισάβετ**
[i yinéka] **η γυναίκα**
*wife* (lit. *woman*)

[níkos] **Νίκος**
[o yios] **ο γιος**
*son*

[nióvi] **Νιόβη**
[i kóri] **η κόρη**
*daughter*

[andónis] **Αντώνης**
[to agóri] **το αγόρι**
*boy*

[yioryía] **Γιωργία**
[to korítsi] **το κορίτσι**
*girl*

**2** 05.02 **Look at the words and complete the missing translations. Then listen and try to imitate the pronunciation of the speaker.**

| Masculine | Feminine | Neuter |
|---|---|---|
| [o patéras] | [i mitéra] | [to peTHí] |
| **ο πατέρας** | **η μητέρα** | **το παιδί** |
| father | _____ | child |
| [o papoós] | [i yiayiá] | |
| **ο παππούς** | **η γιαγιά** | |
| _____ | grandmother | |
| [o yios] | [i kóri] | [to moró] |
| **ο γιος** | **η κόρη** | **το μωρό** |
| son | daughter | baby |
| [o egonós] | [i egoní] | [to egóni] |
| **ο εγγονός** | **η εγγονή** | **το εγγόνι** |
| _____ | granddaughter | grandchild |
| [o aTHelfós] | [i aTHelfí] | |
| **ο αδελφός** | **η αδελφή** | |
| brother | _____ | |
| [o (e)ksáTHelfos] | [i (e)ksaTHélfi] | |
| **ο (ε)ξάδελφος** | **η (ε)ξαδέλφη** | |
| cousin (m) | cousin (f) | |

# Conversation 1 Έχεις οικογένεια; *Do you have a family?*

 **NEW WORDS AND EXPRESSIONS 1**

 05.03 **Read the words and expressions that are used in the next conversation and note their meanings. Then listen and repeat after the speaker.**

| [páme] | πάμε | *shall we go?* (lit. *we go*) |
|---|---|---|
| [misó leptó] | μισό λεπτό | *just a minute* (lit. *half a minute*) |
| [áli] | άλλη | *another* |
| [erótisi] | ερώτηση | *question* |
| [éhete] | έχετε | *do you have?* (pl/fml) |
| [peTHiá] | παιδιά | *children* |
| [éhoome] | έχουμε | *we have* |
| [agóri] | αγόρι | *boy* |

| | | |
|---|---|---|
| [pénde hronón] | πέντε χρονών | five years old (lit. five of years) |
| [trión hronón] | τριών χρονών | three years old (lit. three of years) |
| [éhis] | έχεις | do you have? (sing/infml) |
| [ikoyénia] | οικογένεια | family |
| [ého] | έχω | I have |
| [megáli] | μεγάλη | large, big |

05.04 Anna is trying to get some personal information about Mary and John.

**1 Listen to the conversation a couple of times. Do they have any children?**

| | | |
|---|---|---|
| **Angelos** | [páme spíti tóra]? | Shall we go home now? |
| **Anna** | [misó leptó]. [áli mía erótisi]: [éhete peTHiá]? | Just a minute. One more question: Do you have any children? |
| **Mary** | [ne]. [éhoome] [THío peTHiá]: [éna agóri], [pénde hronón], [kéna korítsi], [trión hronón]. | Yes. We have two children: one boy, five years old, and one girl, three years old. |
| **John** | [esí]? [éhis ikoyénia]? | How about you? Do you have a family? |
| **Anna** | [ne]. [ého] [mía megáli ikoyénia]. | Yes. I have a big family. |

| | |
|---|---|
| **Άγγελος** | Πάμε σπίτι τώρα; |
| **Άννα** | Μισό λεπτό. Άλλη μία ερώτηση: έχετε παιδιά; |
| **Mary** | Ναι. Έχουμε δύο παιδιά: ένα αγόρι, πέντε χρονών, κι ένα κορίτσι, τριών χρονών. |
| **John** | Εσύ; Έχεις οικογένεια; |
| **Άννα** | Ναι. Έχω μία μεγάλη οικογένεια. |

**2 Read the conversation and answer the questions.**
   **a** Find the Greek phrase that means Just a minute.
   **b** How old is Mary and John's son?
   **c** And how old is their daughter?

**3** Listen again and pay special attention to the words which run together. Practise speaking the part of Anna or Mary and pay particular attention to your pronunciation.

## Language discovery 1

**1** Find the following phrases in the conversation. What do you notice about the underlined words?

  **a** Do you have <u>a</u> family?

  **b** five years <u>old</u>

  **c** Just <u>a</u> moment.

  **d** Do you have <u>any</u> children?

**2** Find the following numbers in the conversation. Which one has something different about it compared to what you learned in Unit 4?

  **a** one

  **b** two

  **c** three

  **d** five

**3** Find the following neuter nouns in the conversation. Can you work out their plural form? One is already given in the plural.

  **a** house/home _____    houses/homes _____

  **b** boy _____    boys _____

  **c** girl _____    girls _____

  **d** children _____

### 1 WORD FOR WORD

When you learn a foreign language, it is natural to try to translate everything word for word and to find an equivalent for each word in the other language. As you may already have realized, language does not always work out as conveniently as that! In past units you have encountered extra Greek words that are not present in the English translation, e.g. [íme i ána] **Είμαι η Άννα** *I am (the) Anna* or [íme apó to lonTHíno] **Είμαι από το Λονδίνο** *I am from (the) London*. In this unit, you will learn structures containing extra English words that are not present in Greek, for instance in the four examples of the first Language discovery activity. Keep an eye open for more of these in future units and be aware that it will be easier to learn them as chunks of language rather than to attempt a word-for-word translation into English.

## 2 SAYING YOUR AGE

Be careful if you are saying an age that includes any of the numbers one, three or four. In these cases, you should use the words [enós] **ενός** *one*, [trión] **τριών** *three* and [tesáron] **τεσσάρων** *four* respectively. Only these numbers will change. Look at the following examples.

| | | |
|---|---|---|
| [íme triánda hronón] | **Είμαι τριάντα χρονών.** | *I'm 30 years old.* |
| [íme triánda enós hronón]. | **Είμαι τριάντα ενός χρονών.** | *I'm 31 years old.* |
| [íme triánda THÍo hronón]. | **Είμαι τριάντα δύο χρονών.** | *I'm 32 years old.* |
| [íme triánda trión hronón]. | **Είμαι τριάντα τριών χρονών.** | *I'm 33 years old.* |
| [íme triánda tesáron hronón]. | **Είμαι τριάντα τεσσάρων χρονών.** | *I'm 34 years old.* |
| [íme triánda pénde hronón]. | **Είμαι τριάντα πέντε χρονών.** | *I'm 35 years old.* |

> **LANGUAGE TIP**
> When saying your age, remember that the word *old*, as in *I'm 30 years old*, is not used in Greek. You simply say *I'm 30 years*.

## 3 NEUTER PLURAL

When you completed exercise 3 you will have seen that the plural of neuter nouns is formed by adding the ending **-α** to the noun. The four words used in this exercise are:

**σπίτι** ⟶ **σπίτια**

**αγόρι** ⟶ **αγόρια**

**κορίτσι** ⟶ **κορίτσια**

**παιδί** ⟶ **παιδιά**

Note that the sound of the letter **ι** changes when it becomes part of the plural ending. In the singular form it has an /i/ sound as in the word *pin*. When the letter **α** is added to make the plural form, it changes its sound to /y/. Look at the transliteration of the four words and their plural forms:

[spíti] ⟶ [spit-ya]

[aghóri] ⟶ [aghór-ya]

[korítsi] ——▶ [koríts-ya]

[peTHí] ——▶ [peTH-ya]

# Conversation 2 **Πόσων χρονών είναι;**
*How old are they?*

 **NEW WORDS AND EXPRESSIONS 2**

 **05.05 Read the words and expressions that are used in the next conversation and note their meanings. Then listen and repeat after the speaker.**

| | | |
|---|---|---|
| [ándras] | άντρας | *husband* |
| [moo] | μου | *my* |
| [servitóros] | σερβιτόρος | *waiter* |
| [ton léne] | τον λένε | *his name is* (lit. *they call him*) |
| [agória] | αγόρια | *boys* |
| [ta] | τα | *the* (used with neuter plural nouns) |
| [ta onómatá toos] | τα ονόματά τους | *their names* |
| [póso hronón] | πόσο χρονών | *how old* |
| [THóTHeka] | δώδεκα | *twelve* |
| [THéka] | δέκα | *ten* |
| [eptá] | επτά | *seven* |
| [ah]! | αχ! | *oh!* |
| [yiatí]? | γιατί; | *why?* |
| [févyete] | φεύγετε | *are you leaving?* (pl/fml) |
| [thélo na] | θέλω να | *I want to* |
| [sas] | σας | *you* |
| [ksanaTHó] | ξαναδώ | *see again* |
| [na sas ksanaTHó] | να σας ξαναδώ | *to see you* (pl) *again* |

**05.06** *Anna describes her family to Mary and John and hopes to see them again soon.*

**1  Listen to the conversation a couple of times. How many children does Anna have?**

| | | |
|---|---|---|
| **Anna** | [o ándras moo] [íne servitóros]. [ton léne] [yiórgo]. [éhoome] [tría peTHiá]: [THío agória] [kéna korítsi]. [ta onómata toos] [íne] [yiánis], [THéspina] [ke níkos]. | *My husband is a waiter. His name is Yiorgos. We have three children: two boys and one girl. Their names are Yiannis, Despina and Nikos.* |
| **Mary** | [póso hronón íne]? | *How old are they?* |
| **Anna** | [o yiánis] [íne THóTHeka], [I THéspina] [íne THéka] [ke o níkos] [íne eptá]. [ah]! [yiatí févyete]? [thélo] [na sas ksanaTHó]! | *Yiannis is twelve, Despina is ten and Nikos is seven. Oh! Why are you leaving? I want to see you again!* |
| **Άννα** | Ο άντρας μου είναι σερβιτόρος. Τον λένε Γιώργο. Έχουμε τρία παιδιά: δύο αγόρια κι ένα κορίτσι. Τα ονόματά τους είναι Γιάννης, Δέσποινα και Νίκος. | |
| **Mary** | Πόσο χρονών είναι; | |
| **Άννα** | Ο Γιάννης είναι δώδεκα, η Δέσποινα είναι δέκα κι ο Νίκος είναι επτά. Αχ! Γιατί φεύγετε; Θέλω να σας ξαναδώ! | |

**2  Read the conversation and answer the questions.**
   **a** What does Anna's husband do?
   **b** How old are the two sons?
   **c** And how old is Anna's daughter?

**3  Listen again and pay special attention to the words which run together. Practise speaking the part of Anna and pay particular attention to your pronunciation.**

# Language discovery 2

**1  Find the following phrases in the conversation. What do you notice about the word order? Is an article necessary in Greek?**
   **a** my husband
   **b** their names

**2** **Phrases a and c are from Conversation 2. One word has been replaced in each to create phrases b and d. Can you translate all four phrases? What role do the underlined words play?**

   **a** <u>Τον</u> λένε Γιώργο.

   **b** <u>Σας</u> λένε Γιώργο.

   **c** Θέλω να <u>σας</u> ξαναδώ!

   **d** Θέλω να <u>τον</u> ξαναδώ!

**3** **Find the following numbers in the conversation.**

   **a** seven

   **b** ten

   **c** twelve

## 1 POSSESSIVE PRONOUNS

You learned about subject or personal pronouns (*I, you, they*, etc.) in Unit 2. This unit introduces possessive pronouns, which are words such as *my, your, his, our*, etc. There are two important differences to note between Greek and English:

**a** In Greek, these words are pronouns and come after the noun they modify, whereas in English they are called possessive adjectives and come before the noun (for example, *my house, her car*).

**b** An article is used before the noun in Greek. Look at the following examples:

| Masculine | Feminine | Neuter |
|---|---|---|
| [o ándras moo] **ο άντρας μου** *my husband* | [i yinéka moo] **η γυναίκα μου** *my wife* | [to spíti moo] **το σπίτι μου** *my house* |
| [o papoós moo] **ο παππούς μου** *my grandfather* | [i yiayiá moo] **η γιαγιά μου** *my grandmother* | [to THomátió moo] **το δωμάτιό μου** *my room* |
| [o yios moo] **ο γιος μου** *my son* | [i kóri moo] **η κόρη μου** *my daughter* | [to peTHí moo] **το παιδί μου** *my child* |

Study the table and come back to it as often as you need to in order to become familiar with the full list of possessive pronouns. Note that the word for *his* and *its* is the same in Greek: [too] **του**.

| [moo] | **μου** | *my* |
| [soo] | **σου** | *your* (sing/infml) |

| [too] | **του** | *his* |
| [tis] | **της** | *her* |
| [too] | **του** | *its* |
| [mas] | **μας** | *our* |
| [sas] | **σας** | *your* (pl/fml) |
| [toos] | **τους** | *their* |

## 2 PERSONAL PRONOUNS

One of the first things you learned to say in Greek was the important question [pos se léne]? **Πώς σε λένε;** *What's your name?* (lit. *What do they call you?*) and its equally important answer [me léne] … **Με λένε …** *My name is …* (lit. *They call me …*). In this unit you met a similar phrase: [ton léne yiórgo] **Τον λένε Γιώργο** *His name is Yiorgos* (lit. *They call him Yiorgos*). The words **με**, **σε** and **τον** are personal pronouns. They precede only a very few verbs, and are different from the other personal pronouns you saw in Units 2 and 3. The following table shows the verbs *to go* and *to call* and the personal pronouns used for each one.

| [páo] **εγώ πάω** | *I go* | [me léne] **με λένε** | *they call me* |
|---|---|---|---|
| [pas] **εσύ πας** | *you go* | [se léne] **σε λένε** | *they call you* |
| [pái] **αυτός πάει** | *he goes* | [ton léne] **τον λένε** | *they call him* |
| [pái] **αυτή πάει** | *she goes* | [ti léne] **τη λένε** | *they call her* |
| [pái] **αυτό πάει** | *it goes* | [to léne] **το λένε** | *they call it* |
| [páme] **εμείς πάμε** | *we go* | [mas léne] **μας λένε** | *they call us* |
| [páte] **εσείς πάτε** | *you go* | [sas léne] **σας λένε** | *they call you* |
| [páne] **αυτοί πάνε** | *they go* (m, m/f) | [toos léne] **τους λένε** | *they call them* (m, m/f) |
| [páne] **αυτές πάνε** | *they go* (only f) | [tis léne] **τις λένε** | *they call them* (only f) |
| [páne] **αυτά πάνε** | *they go* (only n) | [ta léne] **τα λένε** | *they call them* (only n) |

### 3 THE NUMBERS 11–20

 **05.07** You are going to listen to the numbers 11 to 20. Try to listen a couple of times without looking at the numbers. Then listen once again and repeat after the speaker.

| [éndeka] | **έντεκα** | *eleven* |
|---|---|---|
| [THóTHeka] | **δώδεκα** | *twelve* |
| [THekatrís] | **δεκατρείς** (m/f) | *thirteen* |
| [THekatría] | **δεκατρία** (n) | |
| [THekatéseris] | **δεκατέσσερις** (m/f) | *fourteen* |
| [THekatésera] | **δεκατέσσερα** (n) | |
| [THekapénde] | **δεκαπέντε** | *fifteen* |
| [THekaéksi] | **δεκαέξι** | *sixteen* |
| [THekaeftá] | **δεκαεφτά** | *seventeen* |
| [THekaohtó] | **δεκαοχτώ** | *eighteen* |
| [THekaeniá] | **δεκαεννιά** | *nineteen* |
| [íkosi] | **είκοσι** | *twenty* |

The numbers 17, 18 and 19 have two interchangeable forms (like 7, 8 and 9). The alternative forms are [THekaeptá] **δεκαεπτά**, [THekaoktó] **δεκαοκτώ** and [THekaenéa] **δεκαεννέα** respectively.

### 4 THE NUMBERS 21–100

 **05.08** Now listen to the numbers 21–100. If you want, you can first say each number and then compare your pronunciation with the audio.

| [íkosi éna] | **είκοσι ένα** | *twenty-one* |
|---|---|---|
| [íkosi THío] | **είκοσι δύο** | *twenty-two* |
| [triánda] | **τριάντα** | *thirty* |
| [triánda éna] | **τριάντα ένα** | *thirty-one* |
| [saránda] | **σαράντα** | *forty* |
| [penínda] | **πενήντα** | *fifty* |
| [exínda] | **εξήντα** | *sixty* |
| [evTHomínda] | **εβδομήντα** | *seventy* |
| [oghTHónda] | **ογδόντα** | *eighty* |
| [enenínda] | **ενενήντα** | *ninety* |
| [ekató] | **εκατό** | *one hundred* |

# Practice

**1** **Angelos has a family photo which shows some family members and explains who is who. Match the following words with their English translation.**

**1**    **2**    **3**    **4**    **5**    **6**

| | | | |
|---|---|---|---|
| **a** | [o patéras moo] | **1** | my sister |
| **b** | [i mitéra moo] | **2** | my mother |
| **c** | [i aTHelfí moo] | **3** | my cousin |
| **d** | [o yios moo] | **4** | my father |
| **e** | [i kóri moo] | **5** | my daughter |
| **f** | [o exáTHelfos moo] | **6** | my son |

**2** **Now match the following six words with the correct people in Angelos's family photo. Then write the words in Greek.**

    **a** [yios]
    **b** [mitéra]
    **c** [patéras]
    **d** [exáTHelfos]
    **e** [kóri]
    **f** [aTHelfí]

**3** **Match each question with the most appropriate answer.**

| | | | |
|---|---|---|---|
| **a** | [éhete peTHiá]? | **1** | [ton léne yiórgo]. |
| **b** | [éhis ikoyénia]? | **2** | [íme THóTHeka]. |
| **c** | [pos léne ton ándra soo]? | **3** | [óhi], [THeného]. |
| **d** | [pos léne tin sízigo soo]? | **4** | [ne], [ého éna peTHí]. |
| **e** | [póso hronón íse]? | **5** | [tin léne ioána]. |

**4** **05.09 Some schoolchildren are asked how old they are. Listen to the audio and then work out how old each child is.**

    **a** [yiórgos] Γιώργος
    **b** [panayiótis] Παναγιώτης

**c** [kóstas] Κώστας

**d** [elpíTHa] Ελπίδα

**e** [ioána] Ιωάννα

**f** [ariána] Αριάννα

**5** 05.10 **Two friends are telling each other their telephone number**
[sto spíti] **στο σπίτι** *at home* **and** [stin THooliá] **στη δουλειά** *at work.*
**Listen to the audio and write down both numbers.**

**a** [spíti] στο σπίτι _____

**b** [THooliá] στη δουλειά _____

**6** **Translate the following phrases into Greek.**

**a** his flat

**b** our home

**c** their grandfather

**d** her mother

**e** my room

**f** your husband

**7** **Let's have some fun now! How many Greek words can you find in
this word search? There are twelve words to find and they read
across, up and down.**

| p | a | p | o | o | s | y |
|---|---|---|---|---|---|---|
| a | n | p | l | h | e | i |
| m | y | i | n | e | k | a |
| e | o | a | e | n | a | y |
| k | o | r | i | t | s | i |
| k | m | i | t | e | r | a |

**8** **Now write out the words from the word search in Greek.**

**9** 05.11 **Listen again to Conversation 2 and complete each
sentence below by choosing one word from the box.**

> [níkos] [ándras] [korítsi]
> [peTHiá] [ton] [hronón] [yiatí]
> [eptá] [THéka] [THóTHeka]

[ána]  [o **a** _____ moo] [íne servitóros]. **b** _____ [léne] [yiórgo].
[éhoome] [tría] **c** _____: [THío agória] [kéna] **d** _____ [ta
onómatá toos] [íne] [yiánis], [THéspina] [ke] **e** _____.

Mary  [póso] **f** _____ [íne]?

[ána]  [o yiánis [íne] **g** \_\_\_\_\_, [i THéspina] [íne] **h** \_\_\_\_\_ [ki-o] **e** \_\_\_\_\_
[íne] **i** \_\_\_\_\_. [ah]! **j** \_\_\_\_\_ [févyete]? [THélo] [na sas ksanaTHó] …

**10 Look at the two business cards and try to find words with the Greek letter –υ/Υ and the following pronunciation options:**

**a** /i/ as in *pin*
**b** /y/ as in *yellow*
**c** /v/ as in *vase*
**d** /u/ as in *pull*

## ❓ Test yourself

1  Give six Greek words for different members of the family.
2  How do you say the numbers 11, 12, 14, 17, 19 and 20 in Greek?
3  Can you describe your own family in Greek?
4  How do you ask someone how old they are?
5  *What is it called in Greek?* is an important question. How do you say it in Greek?

| SELF CHECK | |
|---|---|
| | **I CAN...** |
| ⬤ | . . . ask questions about family and children. |
| ⬤ | . . . describe my own family. |
| ⬤ | . . . ask how old someone is and say how old I am. |
| ⬤ | . . . count from 11 to 100. |

# Καλώς ορίσατε!

## Welcome!

**In this unit you will learn how to:**
▶ *welcome people and reply to people when they welcome you.*
▶ *ask for or offer drinks.*
▶ *read and understand items on a drinks menu.*
▶ *thank people and reply when they thank you.*

**CEFR: (A1)** *Can ask people for things and give people things;* **(A2)** *Can find specific, predictable information in simple everyday material such as menus; Can locate specific information in lists and isolate the information required; Can understand short, simple texts containing the highest frequency vocabulary, including a portion of shared international vocabulary items; Can establish social contact: greetings and farewells, introductions, giving thanks.*

 ## Παραγγελία ποτών  *Ordering drinks*

[frapés] **Φραπές** *iced coffee* is the most popular drink consumed during the summer months. You can always order [nes] **νες** or [nes kafés] **νες καφές**, which is a cup of hot instant coffee, or [elinikós kafés] **ελληνικός καφές** *Greek coffee* which is a small cup of strong black coffee. When ordering Greek coffee at a [kafenío] **καφενείο** *traditional café* or [kafetéria] **καφετέρια** *café*, you should specify how sweet you would like it to be: [skéto] **σκέτο** *no sugar*, [métrio] **μέτριο** *medium*, i.e., with one spoon of sugar or [glikó] **γλυκό** *sweet*, i.e., with two spoons of sugar. [frédo] **Freddo** *iced cappuccino*, regular cappuccino or espresso are other coffee options.

Some popular cold drinks are [lemonáTHa] **λεμονάδα** *lemonade*, [portokaláTHa] **πορτοκαλάδα** *orangeade* and, of course, all international soft drinks. You can always ask for [neró] **νερό** *water*, or more precisely [emfialoméno neró] **εμφιαλωμένο νερό** *bottled water*, or [éna potíri neró] **ένα ποτήρι νερό** *a glass of water*. Some drinks come in a [bookáli] **μπουκάλι** *bottle* and others in a [kootí] **κουτί** *can*, so you can always ask for [éna bookáli kóka kóla]/[éna kootí kóka kóla] **ένα μπουκάλι κόκα κόλα/ένα κουτί κόκα κόλα** *a bottle/can of Coke*.

**1** How many words can you find with the word *coffee* as a separate word or as a prefix in the text?

**2** What are the alternative ways that you can order a Greek coffee?

# Vocabulary builder

**ΚΑΤΑΛΑΒΑΙΝΩ ΤΟΝ/ΤΗΝ ΣΕΡΒΙΤΟΡ-Ο/-Α** *UNDERSTANDING THE WAITER OR WAITRESS*

**1** **06.01 Listen to some typical questions a waiter or waitress might ask and write down the order you hear them in. Then listen again and repeat.**

**a** Καλημέρα, τι θέλετε παρακαλώ;

**b** Καλημέρα, τι θα πάρετε παρακαλώ;

**c** Καλημέρα, τι θα πιείτε παρακαλώ;

**d** Καλημέρα, τι θα θέλατε παρακαλώ;

**ΔΙΝΩ ΠΑΡΑΓΓΕΛΙΑ** *PLACING AN ORDER*

**2** **06.02 Look at the following phrases you might need when you order a drink and fill in the missing English words. Then listen and try to imitate the pronunciation of the speakers.**

| | |
|---|---|
| Θέλω έναν σκέτο παρακαλώ. | *I'd like* (lit. *I want*) *a* _____, *please*. |
| Θα πάρω έναν φραπέ γλυκό με γάλα. | *I'm going to have an iced* _____ *with milk.* |
| Εγώ θα πιω μια πορτοκαλάδα. | *I'm going to have an* _____. |
| Θα'θελα μια λεμονάδα. | *I'd like a* _____. |
| Έναν μέτριο ελληνικό για μένα! | *A* _____ *Greek coffee for me!* |
| Μου φέρνετε ένα νες καφέ παρακαλώ; | *Could you bring me an* _____, *please?* |
| Φέρτε μου φραπέ σκέτο χωρίς γάλα. | *Can you bring me an iced coffee without sugar and* _____ *milk.* |

**ΚΑΤΑΛΟΓΟΣ** *MENU ITEMS AND PRICES*

**3** **06.03 Read the menu as you listen and repeat the words and expressions. Try to work out what the items mean in English. You can check your answers in the key.**

| ΖΕΣΤΑ ΡΟΦΗΜΑΤΑ | ΑΝΑΨΥΚΤΙΚΑ | ΠΟΤΑ |
|---|---|---|
| Ελληνικός καφές .......2,00 | Πορτοκαλάδα .........2,20 | Μπίρα ..............................3,20 |
| Φραπές .........................3,50 | Λεμονάδα ..................2,20 | Ποτήρι κρασί ...............4,30 |
| Τσάι ..............................2,40 | Χυμός (ανανάς) ......3,00 | Μπουκάλι Ρετσίνα....11,00 |
| Ζεστή σοκολάτα ......3,00 | Νερό (μικρό) ............1,00 | Καραφάκι Ούζο ..........6,00 |

## ΚΑΤΑΛΑΒΑΙΝΩ ΜΙΑ ΠΑΡΑΓΓΕΛΙΑ *UNDERSTANDING AN ORDER*

**4  06.04 Now listen to two friends ordering from the menu above. Listen carefully and decide which the correct option is in each case.**

**a  1** Φραπές μέτριος με γάλα     **2** Φραπές μέτριος χωρίς γάλα
**b  1** Νερό μικρό                **2** Νερό μεγάλο
**c  1** Ποτήρι Ρετσίνα            **2** Μπουκάλι Ρετσίνα

# Conversation 1 **Καλώς ορίσατε!** *Welcome!*

## NEW WORDS AND EXPRESSIONS 1

**06.05 Listen to the words and expressions that are used in the next conversation and note their meaning.**

| [hérome] | χαίρομαι | *I'm glad* |
|---|---|---|
| [poo] | που | *that* |
| [ksanavlépo] | ξαναβλέπω | *I see again* |
| [kalós se vríkame]. | Καλώς σε βρήκαμε. | *Glad to be here again* (lit. *Good to have found you*). |
| [kírie] | κύριε = κ. | *Mister = Mr* |
| [kiría] | κυρία = κα. | *Mistress = Mrs* |

**06.06** *Angelos drives them home now. Elpitha, his wife, and Andonis and Yioryía, his children, are there waiting for Mary and John.*

**1 Listen to the conversation a couple of times. What does John say in reply to Elpitha's welcome?**

| | | |
|---|---|---|
| **Elpitha** | [kalós orísate]! [hérome] [poo sas ksanavlépo]! | *Welcome! Glad to see you again!* |
| **John** | [yiásoo elpíTHa]. [kalós se vríkame]. | *Hi, Elpitha. Glad to be here again.* |
| **Mary** | [yiásoo elpíTHa], [yiásas peTHiá]. | *Hi, Elpitha, hi kids.* |
| **Andonis** | [yiásas] [kírie John]. [yiásas] [kiría Mary]. | *Hello, Mr John. Hello, Mrs Mary.* |
| **Yioryía** | [yiásas] | *Hello.* |
| **Ελπίδα** | Καλώς ορίσατε! Χαίρομαι που σας ξαναβλέπω! | |
| **John** | Γεια σου, Ελπίδα. Καλώς σε βρήκαμε. | |
| **Mary** | Γεια σου, Ελπίδα. Γεια σας, παιδιά. | |
| **Αντώνης** | Γεια σας, κύριε John. Γεια σας, κυρία Mary. | |
| **Γιωργία** | Γεια σας. | |

**2 Now read the conversation and answer the questions.**

    **a** What are the names of Angelos' children? Can you write the names in Greek?

    **b** What are the words for *Mr* and *Mrs* in Greek?

 **3 Listen again to the conversation and pay special attention to the words which run together. Practise speaking the parts of Elpitha and Mary.**

 ## Language discovery 1

**1 The conversation includes a phrase used when welcoming people. Find it and complete the list which gives another three phrases used to say *Welcome!*. Finally, decide which two phrases are appropriate when you informally welcome one friend or relative, and which two phrases you would use when you formally welcome a stranger or a customer.**

    **a** Καλώς ήλθες!

    **b** Καλώς ήλθατε!

    **c** Καλώς όρισες!

    **d** _____

**2 Mary, Andonis and Yioryía use the phrase Γεια σας four times, twice to address more than one person. Find the missing information: first, the name of the person who uses the phrase, and then the name of the person they are addressing.**

Who uses the phrase?                    Whom were they addressing?

_____                        _____

_____                        _____

_____                        _____

## WELCOMING SOMEONE

There are many expressions used in Greek to welcome someone. The phrases [kalós órises] **Καλώς όρισες** and [kalosórises] **Καλωσόρισες** both mean *welcome* and are used to address one person informally. The following expressions are used when addressing one person formally or more than one person: [kalós orísate]! **Καλώς ορίσατε!** or [kalosorísate]! **Καλωσορίσατε!** There are two alternative phrases which mean the same: [kalós ílthes]! **Καλώς ήλθες!** and [kalós ílthate]! **Καλώς ήλθατε!** The most typical replies to these expressions are [kalós se vríka]! **Καλώς σε βρήκα!**, used by one person to reply informally to another person, and [kalós sas vríka]! **Καλώς σας βρήκα!** when one person replies to more than one person or formally to one person. Finally, [kalós sas vríkame]! **Καλώς σας βρήκαμε!** is used when two or more people are replying to more than one person. The closest translation for all these phrases is *Nice to see/meet you* or *Nice to be here*.

# Conversation 2 Θέλετε έναν καφέ;
*Would you like a coffee?*

## NEW WORDS AND EXPRESSIONS 2

**06.07 Listen to the words and expressions that are used in the next conversation and note their meanings.**

| [eláte] | ελάτε | *come* |
|---|---|---|
| [kathíste] | καθίστε | *have a seat, sit down* |
| [kanapé] | καναπέ | *sofa* |
| [páre] | πάρε | *take* |
| [karékla] | καρέκλα | *chair* |
| [kondá] [moo] | κοντά μου | *close to me* |

| [efharistó] | ευχαριστώ | thanks |
|---|---|---|
| [oréo] | ωραίο | nice, beautiful |
| [pináte]? | πεινάτε; | Are you hungry? |
| [THipsáte]? | διψάτε; | Are you thirsty? |
| [thélete]? | θέλετε; | Would you like? (lit. Do you want?) (pl/fml) |
| [kafé] | καφέ | coffee |
| [kóka kóla] | κόκα κόλα | coke |
| [éhis] | έχεις | do you have? |
| [portokaláTHa] | πορτοκαλάδα | orangeade |
| [frapé] | φραπέ | iced coffee |
| [yia] [ména] | για μένα | for me |

**06.08** *Elpitha is trying to find out what her guests might like to drink.*

**1 Listen to the conversation a couple of times. What does she offer them first?**

| **Angelos** | [eláte], [kathíste ston kanapé]. [John], [pare mía karékla] [kondá moo]. | *Come on in, have a seat on the sofa. John, take a chair close to me.* |
|---|---|---|
| **John** | [efharistó]. | *Thanks.* |
| **Mary** | [oréo spíti], [polí oréo] [ke polí megálo]. | *Nice house, very nice and very big.* |
| **Elpitha** | [pináte]? [THipsáte]? [Thélete] [énan kafé], [mía kóka kóla]? | *Are you hungry? Are you thirsty? Would you like a coffee, a coke?* |
| **Mary** | [éhis portokaláTHa]? | *Do you have orangeade?* |
| **John** | [énan frapé] [yia ména]. | *An iced coffee for me.* |

| **Άγγελος** | Ελάτε, καθίστε στον καναπέ. John, πάρε μία καρέκλα κοντά μου. |
|---|---|
| **John** | Ευχαριστώ. |
| **Mary** | Ωραίο σπίτι, πολύ ωραίο και πολύ μεγάλο. |
| **Ελπίδα** | Πεινάτε; Διψάτε; Θέλετε έναν καφέ, μία κόκα κόλα; |
| **Mary** | Έχεις πορτοκαλάδα; |
| **John** | Έναν φραπέ για μένα. |

**2 Now read the conversation and answer the questions.**
  **a** What does Mary say about the house?
  **b** What would Mary and John like to drink?

**3** Listen again to the conversation and pay special attention to the words which run together. Practise speaking the parts of Angelos and Mary.

## Language discovery 2

**1** Angelos uses three verbs to request something from his guests. Find them and complete the gaps. Can you guess why there are two verb forms in Greek?

**a** έλα _____ **b** κάθισε _____ **c** _____

**2** Mary uses three verbs to ask her guests something. Find them and complete the gaps. Can you guess why there are two verb forms in Greek?

**a** πεινάς _____ **b** διψάς _____ **c** θέλεις _____

**3** The conversation includes the names of four drinks. Find them and decide whether you would use **έναν** or **μία** *a/an* for each one. Does the choice of article depend on the sound of the word that follows, as it does in English?

**a** Θέλω _____
**b** Θέλω _____
**c** Θέλω _____
**d** Θέλω _____

### 1 IMPERATIVES

When giving orders or making requests, a special verb form is used. This is called the imperative. Imperative verb forms should be learned by heart as they are not usually the same as the infinitive form, as they are in English. Look at the answers you gave to the first exercise. If they are correct you will see the singular verb form (used when speaking informally to one person) and the plural verb form (used when speaking to more than one person, or formally to one person) of the imperative. Here are the main verb forms and the corresponding imperatives of these three verbs:

| Main verb form: | **έρχομαι** *to come* | **κάθομαι** *to sit* | **παίρνω** *to take* |
| --- | --- | --- | --- |
| Imperative form: | **έλα-ελάτε** | **κάθισε-καθίστε** | **πάρε-πάρτε** |

### 2 THE GREEK VERB ΘΕΛΩ

When addressing someone directly in Greek, remember always to decide on the appropriate form of the word for *you* (**εσύ** or **εσείς**) when using any verb regardless of verb form. For example, *Do you want …?* would be **θέλεις** (or **θες**) if asking a friend and **θέλετε** if asking a stranger or someone you have a more formal relationship with. Remember too that the personal pronouns **εσύ** and **εσείς** will be usually left out.

[thélo] **Θέλω** is a very common verb in Greek. Although it essentially means *want*, it is used to express all manner of nuances including *I want it here and now!, I want it if possible, I would like* or even *I'd love to!* Pay attention to the speaker's intonation if you hear this verb in order to understand which nuance of meaning is implied. Look at the forms of the verb:

| [thélo] | **Θέλω** | *I want* |
| [thélis] | **Θέλεις** | *you want* (sing/infml) |
| [théli] | **Θέλει** | *he/she/it wants* |
| [théloome] | **Θέλουμε** | *we want* |
| [thélete] | **Θέλετε** | *you want* (pl/fml) |
| [théloon(e)] | **Θέλουν(ε)** | *they want* |

### 3 THE INDEFINITE ARTICLE

The Greek indefinite article has different forms used to correspond to the noun it accompanies. The following are forms used when ordering something or making a request.

| (masculine) έναν | (feminine) μία/μια | (neuter) ένα |
|---|---|---|
| **Θέλω έναν καφέ.** *I'd like a (cup of) coffee.* | **Θέλω μία πορτοκαλάδα.** *I'd like an orangeade.* | **Θέλω ένα ποτήρι νερό.** *I'd like a glass of water.* |

> **LANGUAGE TIP**
> When ordering or requesting items which are masculine in gender, then the final [s] **ς** is dropped from the noun:
> **Θέλω έναν καφέ/φραπέ/χυμό.** *I'd like a coffee/iced coffee/juice.*
> The main form of these three nouns is **ο καφές/ο φραπές/ο χυμός**.

### 4 THANKING SOMEONE

No matter how little you can converse in a foreign language, being able to exchange pleasantries will go a long way. If you can thank someone or respond when they *thank you*, native speakers will appreciate your courtesy. [efharistó] **ευχαριστώ** *thanks*, [efharistó polí] **ευχαριστώ πολύ** *thanks a lot,* [parakaló] **παρακαλώ** *you're welcome* (lit. *please*) and [típota] **τίποτα** *don't mention it* (lit. *nothing*) will all be useful phrases when making simple conversation with Greeks.

 ## Practice

1 **Mary has taken out a family photo and talks about the people in it. In each case, match the words with the correct person in the photo.**

**a** [o papoós moo]       **d** [i eksaTHélfi moo]
**b** [i yiayiá moo]       **e** [o yios moo]
**c** [o aTHelfós moo]       **f** [o ándras moo]

2 **Can you match these six words mentioned in Activity 1 with their correct English translation?**

**a** [papoós]       **1** son
**b** [yiayiá]       **2** husband
**c** [aTHelfós]       **3** grandfather
**d** [eksaTHélfi]       **4** brother
**e** [yios]       **5** grandmother
**f** [ándras]       **6** cousin

3 **Match each question with the most appropriate answer.**

**a** [éhis oréo spíti]?       **1** [óhi], [mía lemonáTHa].
**b** [thélis énan kafé]?       **2** [éna tsái], [efharistó].
**c** [thélis mía portokaláTHa]?       **3** [óhi], [pináme]!
**d** [THipsáte]?       **4** [polí oréo ke polí megálo].
**e** [ti thélis]?       **5** [ne], [éna frapé parakaló].

## 4 Rearrange these lines to make a dialogue.

**a** [ti thélis] [na pyis]? Τι θέλεις να πιεις;

**b** [éna himó] [se parakaló] Ένα χυμό σε παρακαλώ.

**c** [ángele], [THipsás]? Άγγελε, διψάς;

**d** [THe kséro]. [ti éhi]? Δε ξέρω. Τι έχει;

**e** [ne polí] [mitéra]. Ναι πολύ, μητέρα.

**f** [éhi himó lemonáTHa] [ke fisiká kafé]. Έχει χυμό, λεμονάδα και φυσικά καφέ.

## 5 Translate your part of the conversation to complete the following dialogue.

| | |
|---|---|
| **[fílos]** | [páre mía karékla] [kondá moo]. |
| **You** | Say *Close to you? Why?* |
| **[fílos]** | [yiatí] [thélo na miláme] [angliká]. |
| **You** | Say *English? I want to speak Greek!* |
| **[fílos]** | [eliniká]? [oréa]! [kafé stin arhí]? |
| **You** | Say *Why not? Coffee to start with* (lit. *in the beginning*). *An iced coffee for me.* |

## 6 Can you solve the following crossword puzzle? The shaded vertical word means *butter.*

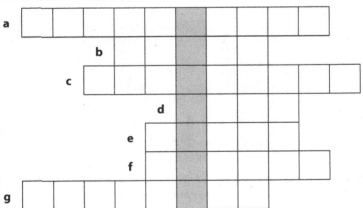

**a** I see again
**b** bread
**c** lemonade
**d** tea
**e** juice
**f** iced coffee
**g** coke

**7** 06.09 **Listen again to Conversation 2 of this unit and fill in the blanks using the words from the box. Then try to write out the whole conversation in Greek script.**

| [pináte] | [kanapé] | [énan] |
|----------|----------|--------|
| [ména] | [eláte] | [mía] |
| [yia] | [karékla] | [éhis] |

**Angelos**     **a** _____. [kathíste ston] **b** _____. [John], [páre mía]
                **c** _____ [kondá moo].
**John**        [efharistó].
**Mary**        [oréo spíti], [polí oréo] [ke polí megálo].
**Elpitha**     **d** _____? [THipsáte]? [thélete] **e** _____. [kafé],
                **f** _____ [kóka kóla]?
**Mary**        **g** _____ [portokaláTHa]?
**John**        [éna frapé] **h** _____ **i** _____.

**8** **Look at the label and use it to help you ask for the following.**
  **a** I'd like a small bottle of water.
  **b** I'd like a big bottle of water.
  **c** I'd like a bottle of mineral water.
  **d** Do you have tap water?

**9** **You are in a café and would like to order the following drinks. Fill in the missing words to complete your order.**

  **a** Θέλω _____ παρακαλώ.                    *I'd like a Greek coffee without sugar, please.*

  **b** _____ έναν φραπέ γλυκό με γάλα.   *I'm going to have an iced coffee with sugar and milk.*

  **c** _____ μια πορτοκαλάδα.                   *I'm going to have an orangeade.*

  **d** Θα'θελα _____.                                  *I'd like a lemonade.*

  **e** Έναν μέτριο ελληνικό _____!          *A Greek coffee with one sugar for me!*

**f** _____ ένα νες καφέ παρακαλώ;    *Could you bring me a filter coffee, please?*

**g** Φέρτε μου έναν φραπέ _____;    *Can you bring me an iced coffee without sugar or milk?*

**10** **Read the menu and order the following drinks. Remember what you have learned about the use of the indefinite article έναν/μία/ένα.**

**a** a sweet Greek coffee
**b** an iced coffee with milk but no sugar
**c** a small bottle of water
**d** a small carafe of ouzo
**e** a beer
**f** a hot chocolate.

| ΖΕΣΤΑ ΡΟΦΗΜΑΤΑ | ΑΝΑΨΥΚΤΙΚΑ | ΠΟΤΑ |
|---|---|---|
| Ελληνικός καφές .....2,00 | Πορτοκαλάδα .........2,20 | Μπίρα ...............................3,20 |
| Φραπές ......................3,50 | Λεμονάδα ..................2,20 | Ποτήρι κρασί .................4,30 |
| Τσάι ...........................2,40 | Χυμός (ανανάς) .......3,00 | Μπουκάλι Ρετσίνα ....11,00 |
| Ζεστή σοκολάτα ....3,00 | Νερό (μικρό) ............1,00 | Καραφάκι Ούζο ...........6,00 |

#  Test yourself

**1** Give the names of five drinks in Greek. [kóka kóla] doesn't count!

**2** How do you say *Come and sit next to me?*

**3** Ask *Do you have an orangeade or a juice?*

**4** How do you say *Have a seat!*

## SELF CHECK

| | I CAN... |
|---|---|
| ○ | . . . welcome people and reply to them when they welcome me. |
| ○ | . . . ask for and offer drinks. |
| ○ | . . . read and understand items on a drinks menu. |
| ● | . . . thank people and reply when they thank me. |

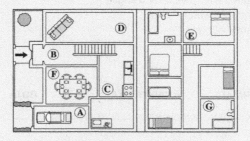

# R2 *Revision test 2*

**1  Here is the layout of a house. Do you remember the words for each room? The first one has been done for you.** *(6 points)*

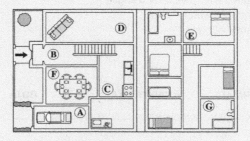

| | | | |
|---|---|---|---|
| **a** | [párkin] | **e** | _____ |
| **b** | _____ | **f** | _____ |
| **c** | _____ | **g** | _____ |
| **d** | _____ | | |

**2  A friend is showing you some family pictures hanging on the wall. Match each phrase to the correct pictures.** *(10 points)*

**1** [o yiórgos] [ke i maría]. Ο Γιώργος και η Μαρία.
**2** [i ikoyenía papá]. Η οικογένεια Παππά.
**3** [i elpíTHa] [íne i aTHelfí moo]. Η Ελπίδα είναι η αδελφή μου.

**4** [o papoós moo] [o yiánis]. Ο παππούς μου ο Γιάννης.

**5** [o ksáTHelfos ke i ksaTHélfi moo]. Ο ξάδελφος και η ξαδέλφη μου.

**3** **Some numbers are missing in the grid. Can you write them out in words?** *(10 points)*

| a |    | 1  | 2  |    | 4  |    |
|---|----|----|----|----|----|----|
| b | 6  |    |    | 8  | 9  |    |
| c |    |    |    | 13 |    | 15 |
| d |    |    | 17 | 18 |    |    |

**4** **Can you match each image to the correct English heading? There are at least five words that you should be able to translate into English. Can you find them and translate them?** *(10 points)*

1 underground
2 closed
3 restaurant

4 ticket
5 pastry shop

**5 Read the text and check whether the statements after the text are true or false.** *(10 points)*

Ο Γιώργος μένει σε ένα μικρό διαμέρισμα σε μια μεγάλη πολυκατοικία. Έχει μόνο ένα δωμάτιο και το μπάνιο είναι μικρό αλλά βολικό. Αυτό είναι μεγάλο πρόβλημα γιατί η Άννα, η φίλη του, θέλει να μείνει με τον Γιώργο και ο Γιώργος δε δουλεύει τώρα.

**a** Το διαμέρισμα είναι μεγάλο.
**b** Η πολυκατοικία είναι μικρή.
**c** Το διαμέρισμα έχει δύο δωμάτια.
**d** Το μπάνιο δεν είναι βολικό.
**e** Ο Γιώργος δουλεύει τώρα.

**6 Match each Greek word in the left-hand column to its correct translation in the right-hand column. Then add the correct article to each Greek word.** *(14 points)*

**a** _____ κατοικία
**b** _____ σπίτι
**c** _____ διαμέρισμα
**d** _____ γκαρσονιέρα
**e** _____ ρετιρέ
**f** _____ μονοκατοικία
**g** _____ πολυκατοικία

1 studio/bedsit
2 detached house
3 residence
4 apartment building
5 house/home
6 penthouse
7 apartment/flat

**7 Nikos is showing you a family photo and explains who everyone is. Read the phrases and translate them into English.** *(20 points)*

**a** Από εδώ η γιαγιά μου η Άρτεμις και ο παππούς μου ο Οδυσσέας.
**b** Τη σύζυγο μου τη λένε Ελπίδα.
**c** Έχουμε δύο παιδιά. Ένα αγόρι και ένα κορίτσι.
**d** Τον γιο μας τον λένε Άγγελο και την κόρη μας τη λένε Νιόβη.
**e** Μένουμε σε μία μεγάλη μονοκατοικία.

## 8 Can you come up with an appropriate question for each of the following answers? *(10 points)*

a Ο άντρας μου δε δουλεύει τώρα.

b Έχουμε τρία παιδιά.

c Ναι, έχω μία μεγάλη οικογένεια.

d Τη γυναίκα μου τη λένε Άννα.

e Ναι, μιλάω λίγο Ελληνικά!

## 9 Take part in the following conversation using the English as a prompt. *(10 points)*

| | |
|---|---|
| **Maria** | Ελάτε, καθίστε στον καναπέ. |
| **You** | Say *Thanks. That's a nice big house!* |
| **Maria** | Πεινάτε; Διψάτε; Θέλετε έναν καφέ; |
| **You** | Say *That's a good idea. A coffee for me please!* |
| **Maria** | Τι καφέ θέλετε; Ένα φραπέ ίσως; |
| **You** | Say *Yes. An iced coffee, medium without milk. And some water, please.* |
| **Maria** | Ένα ποτήρι ή ένα μπουκάλι; |
| **You** | Say *A glass of water, please.* |
| **Maria** | Με ή χωρίς ανθρακικό; |
| **You** | Say *I don't understand! What is that in English?* |

**TOTAL: 100 POINTS**

# 7 Τι ωραία πολυθρόνα!

## What a nice armchair!

**In this unit you will learn how to:**
▶ *agree or disagree with someone.*
▶ *say if you like or dislike something.*
▶ *use more Greek nouns in singular and plural form.*
▶ *use adjectives.*
▶ *use words for colour and furniture.*

**CEFR: (A2)** *Can describe in simple terms aspects of his/her immediate environment; Can write about everyday aspects of his/her environment; Can explain what he/she likes or dislikes; Can agree or disagree.*

##  Ελληνική φιλοξενία *Greek hospitality*

People often talk about Greek [filoxenía] **φιλοξενία** *hospitality.* This is a compound word from [fílos] **φίλος** *friend* and [xénos] **ξένος** *guest/stranger/foreigner.* Generally speaking, Greeks are hospitable people; they open their homes to friends and acquaintances and entertain generously. Of course, hospitality in its broad sense can be interpreted differently among people in different situations. You need to experience it in order to realize what it is like and what lies between the reality and the myth. What is generally unthinkable for many of us, e.g. sleeping three or four people in one [THomátio] **δωμάτιο** *room,* in the [avlí] **αυλή** *yard* or on the [tarátsa] **ταράτσα** *roof,* used to be offered as part of the Greek hospitality in the past. Nowadays things have changed and the financial crisis makes many people reserved. Many tourists and visitors in Greece have experienced a combination of hospitality and [evghénia] **ευγένεια** *kindness* as well as impoliteness and [aghénia] **αγένεια** *rudeness.* We should not over-generalize though and make stereotypes. Be prepared for both, though, and have a pleasant [paramoní/THiamoní] **παραμονή/διαμονή** *(longer/shorter) stay.*

---

There are some Greek compound words (two words together) in the text which come with different prefixes, e.g. **φίλ-, ευ-, α-, παρα-,** and **δια-.** Can you come up with a couple of words which have one of these prefixes from past units?

---

# Έπιπλα στο σπίτι *Furniture*

You learned about different types of houses in Unit 4. Now it's time to learn the words for the different items found inside houses. When you learn the name of a room, try to learn the words for items that may be found in that room. Certain associations can be made as follows: [koozína] **κουζίνα** *kitchen* with [pángos] **πάγκος** *counter*, [trapézi] **τραπέζι** *table*, [nerochítis] **νεροχύτης** *sink*, [karékla] **καρέκλα** *chair*, [psighío] **ψυγείο** *refrigerator* and [fúrnos] **φούρνος** *stove*; [ipnoTHomátio] **υπνοδωμάτιο** *bedroom* with [kathréftis] **καθρέφτης** *mirror*, [kreváti] **κρεβάτι** *bed* and [doolápa] **ντουλάπα** *wardrobe*; [bánio] **μπάνιο** *bathroom* with [baniéra] **μπανιέρα** *bathtub* and [niptíras] **νιπτήρας** *washbasin*; and [salóni] **σαλόνι** *living room* with [polithróna] **πολυθρόνα** *armchair* and [kanapés] **καναπές** *sofa*. Some other useful words are [balkóni] **μπαλκόνι** *balcony/ porch*, [paráthiro] **παράθυρο** *window*, [pórta] **πόρτα** *door* and [avlí] **αυλή** *courtyard*.

---

 Now look at the picture and see how many items of furniture you can label in Greek.

---

Vocabulary builder

ΣΕ ΕΝΑ ΣΑΛΟΝΙ *IN A LIVING ROOM*

 **1** **07.01 The following table includes all the items that you can see in the picture. Listen carefully to Nikos as he will list only what he has in his living room. Tick the items you hear. Then listen again and repeat the sentences after the speaker.**

| Το παράθυρο | | Η κουρτίνα | | Το κάδρο | |
| Η βιβλιοθήκη | | Η καρέκλα | | Η πόρτα | |
| Το τηλέφωνο | | Η πολυθρόνα | | Ο καναπές | |
| Το τραπεζάκι | | Η μπρίζα | | Η τηλεόραση | |

 **2** **07.02 Without using a dictionary, can you work out which words on the list in exercise 1 correspond to the English words? Decide which is the correct word in each case and then listen and compare your answers.**

 **a** curtain
 **b** television
 **c** telephone
 **d** coffee table
 **e** door
 **f** sofa

ΕΠΙΠΛΑ *FURNITURE*

 **3** **07.03 Look at the following items of furniture and sort them according to their gender (masculine, feminine or neuter). Then listen to the audio and compare your answers. Finally, listen again and repeat after the speaker.**

> πάγκος  τραπέζι  νεροχύτης
> καρέκλα  καθρέφτης  κρεβάτι
> ντουλάπα  μπανιέρα  τραπεζάκι
> νιπτήρας  πολυθρόνα  κάδρο

| Masculine | Feminine | Neuter |
| --- | --- | --- |
| | | |

## ΗΛΕΚΤΡΙΚΕΣ ΣΥΣΚΕΥΕΣ *ELECTRICAL APPLIANCES*

**4  07.04 Look at the list of electrical appliances and complete the missing English expressions. Then listen and try to imitate the pronunciation of the speaker.**

| | |
|---|---|
| Το ψυγείο | _____ |
| Το πλυντήριο πιάτων | *dishwasher* |
| Το πλυντήριο ρούχων | *washing* _____ |
| Ο φούρνος | _____ |
| Ο φούρνος μικροκυμάτων | _____ |
| Η καφετιέρα | _____ *machine* |
| Ο βραστήρας νερού | *kettle* |
| Η τηλεόραση | *television* |

# Conversation 1 Εδώ είναι η κουζίνα
*Here's the kitchen*

**NEW WORDS AND EXPRESSIONS 1**

**07.05 Listen to the words and expressions that are used in the next conversation and note their meanings.**

| | | |
|---|---|---|
| [éla na soo THíkso] | έλα να σου δείξω | *let me show you* (lit. *come to show you*) |
| [páme] | Πάμε | *Let's go* |
| [oréa] | ωραία | *beautiful* |
| [polithróna] | πολυθρόνα | *armchair* |
| [hóro] | χώρο | *space, area* |
| [karékles] | καρέκλες | *chairs* |
| [vlépo] | βλέπω | *I see* |

**07.06** *Elpitha is proud of their new house and shows Mary around.*

**1  Listen to the conversation a couple of times. Which room does she take Mary to first?**

| | | |
|---|---|---|
| **Elpitha** | Mary [éla na soo THíkso] [to spíti]. | *Mary, let me show you the house.* |
| **Mary** | [ne] [to thélo polí]. [páme]. | *Yes, I'd like that a lot. Let's go.* |
| **Elpitha** | [eTHó íne to ipnoTHomátio mas]. | *Here's our bedroom.* |
| **Mary** | [ti oréa polithróna] [ke ti megálo kreváti]! | *What a beautiful armchair and what a big bed!* |

| Elpitha | [eTHó íne i koozína]. [éhi megálo pángo] [ke hóro yia megálo trapézi] [ke polés karékles]. | *Here's the kitchen. It has a long worktop and space for a big table and many chairs.* |
| Mary | [vlépo], [vlépo]. [brávo, elpíTHa]. | *I see, I see. Bravo, Elpitha.* |
| Ελπίδα | Mary, έλα να σου δείξω το σπίτι. | |
| Mary | Ναι, το θέλω πολύ. Πάμε. | |
| Ελπίδα | Εδώ είναι το υπνοδωμάτιό μας. | |
| Mary | Τι ωραία πολυθρόνα και τι μεγάλο κρεβάτι! | |
| Ελπίδα | Εδώ είναι η κουζίνα. Έχει μεγάλο πάγκο και χώρο για μεγάλο τραπέζι και πολλές καρέκλες. | |
| Mary | Βλέπω, βλέπω. Μπράβο, Ελπίδα. | |

**2 Now read the conversation and answer the questions.**

  **a** What items of furniture did Mary see in the bedroom?

  **b** Can a big table fit into the kitchen without a problem?

**3 Listen again and pay special attention to the words which run together. Practise speaking the part of Mary and pay particular attention to your pronunciation.**

 # Language discovery 1

**1 The conversation includes five adjectives. Find them and fill in the gaps.**

| | | |
|---|---|---|
| **a** | many chairs | _____ karékles |
| **b** | long worktop | _____ pángo |
| **c** | beautiful armchair | _____ polithróna |
| **d** | big table | _____ trapézi |
| **e** | big bed | _____ kreváti |

**2 Are you a good word detective? Read the conversation again carefully and try to find the following words hidden as words or parts of a word in the text.**

  **a** bravo

  **b** mega-

  **c** hypno-

  **d** cuisine

  **e** poly-

  **f** trapezoid

## 1 ADJECTIVES

Adjectives are words which describe people or things, giving more information about the noun they modify. Greek adjectives, like nouns, have a gender (masculine, feminine or neuter) and different singular or plural forms, which makes them a little more challenging to learn. If you look up a Greek adjective in the dictionary you will see it listed with all three gender forms in the singular, e.g. **μεγάλ-ος/μεγάλ-η/μεγάλ-ο**.

When you learn a new adjective, try to learn the word for its opposite at the same time. This is a good way of expanding your vocabulary. Try, for example, to learn these three word pairs by heart:

| | | |
|---|---|---|
| [polí – líghes] | **πολλές – λίγες** | *many – few* |
| [meghálo – mikró] | **μεγάλο – μικρό** | *big – small* |
| [oréa – áschimi] | **ωραία – άσχημη** | *beautiful – ugly* |

## 2 BEING A GOOD DETECTIVE!

Did you manage to do exercise 2? Being a good word detective, which means observing words and their sounds carefully, can help your understanding when you are having a real conversation with a native speaker. Remember too the influence Greek has had on English – you will recognize many Greek words that have become part of the English language, often as prefixes or suffixes. Two of the words above have given us *oligarchy* (*government from a few*) and *microscope* (*small + see*).

# Conversation 2 **Σου αρέσει;** *Do you like it?*

### NEW WORDS AND EXPRESSIONS 2

**07.07 Listen to the words and expressions that are used in the next conversation. Note their meanings.**

| | | |
|---|---|---|
| [praktikó] | πρακτικό | *practical* (with neuter noun) |
| [ótan] | όταν | *when* (not as a question) |
| [anángi] | ανάγκη | *necessity; necessary* |
| [vévea] | βέβαια | *of course, naturally* |
| [lootró] | λουτρό | *bath; bathroom* |
| [soo arési]? | Σου αρέσει; | *Do you like?* (sing/infml) |
| [hrómata] | χρώματα | *colours* |
| [strongilós] | στρογγυλός | *round* |
| [kathréftis] | καθρέφτης | *mirror* |

| [mávro] | μαύρο | *black* |
| [áspro] | άσπρο | *white* |
| [antíthesi] | αντίθεση | *contrast* |
| [simfonó] | συμφωνώ | *I agree* |
| [THíkio] | δίκιο | *right* |

 **07.08** *Elpitha takes Mary further around the house.*

**1  Listen to the conversation a couple of times. Which is the next room that she takes Mary to?**

| Elpitha | [eTHó] [íne to vesé]. [íne lígo mikró] [alá polí praktikó] [ótan íne anángi]. | *Here's the toilet. It's a little bit small but very practical when necessary.* |
| Mary | [ne], [vévea]. | *Yes, of course.* |
| Elpitha | [apo'THó to lootró]. [soo arési]? | *This is the bathroom. Do you like it?* |
| Mary | [moo arési polí]. [moo arésoon] [ta hrómata polí] [ke o strongilós kathréftis]. | *I like it a lot. I like the colours and the round mirror.* |
| Elpitha | [ne] [to mávro ke áspro] [kánoon] [megáli antíthesi] [alá moo arésoon]. | *Yes, black and white create a great contrast and I like them.* |
| Mary | [simfonó]. [éhis THíkio]. | *I agree. You're right.* |
| Ελπίδα | Εδώ είναι το WC. Είναι λίγο μικρό αλλά πολύ πρακτικό όταν είναι ανάγκη. | |
| Mary | Ναι, βέβαια. | |
| Ελπίδα | Από'δω το λουτρό. Σου αρέσει; | |
| Mary | Μου αρέσει πολύ. Μου αρέσουν τα χρώματα πολύ και ο στρογγυλός καθρέφτης. | |
| Ελπίδα | Ναι, το μαύρο και άσπρο κάνουν μεγάλη αντίθεση αλλά μου αρέσουν. | |
| Mary | Συμφωνώ. Έχεις δίκιο. | |

**2  Now read the conversation and answer the questions.**
   **a**  What does Mary like in the bathroom?
   **b**  What colour theme is in the bathroom?

**3 Listen again and pay special attention to the words which run together. Practise speaking the part of Mary and pay particular attention to your pronunciation.**

## Language discovery 2

**1 The conversation includes four adjectives. Find them and fill in the gaps.**

a great contrast _____ antíthesi
b round mirror _____ kathréftis
c small toilet _____ vesé
d practical toilet _____ vesé

**2 The conversation includes four phrases which are used to express agreement with someone. How would you say them in Greek?**

a You're right.
b Yes, of course.
c I agree.
d I like it a lot.

**3 There are two phrases that use the verb *to like* in this conversation. Can you find how to say the following in Greek? Why are two different verb forms used?**

a I like it a lot.
b I like the colours a lot.

### 1 MORE ADJECTIVES

Conversation 2 also includes another four adjectives. Read them and try to memorize them. As you saw earlier in this unit, with each adjective you learn it is useful to learn its opposite too, so these are also listed.

| | | |
|---|---|---|
| [meghál-os/-i/-o] | **μεγάλ-ος/-η/-ο** | *big* |
| [mikr-ós/-í/-ó] | **μικρ-ός/-ή/ό** | *small* |
| [stroghil-ós/-í/-ó] | **στρογγυλ-ός/-ή/-ό** | *round* |
| [tetraghón-os/-i/-o] | **τετράγων-ος/-η/-ο** | *square* |
| [mikr-ós/-í/-ó] | **μικρ-ός/-ή/ό** | *small* |
| [meghál-os/-i/-o] | **μεγάλ-ος/-η/-ο** | *big* |
| [praktik-ós/-í/-ó] | **πρακτικ-ός/-ή/-ό** | *practical* |
| [ávol-os/-i/-o] | **άβολ-ος/-η/-ο** | *uncomfortable* |

## 2 EXPRESSING LIKES, DISLIKES, PREFERENCE AND AGREEMENT

 **07.09** Being able to say that you like or dislike something, that you prefer something or that you agree with someone is useful in many conversations. Read the expressions as you listen to the audio.

| Liking and agreement | Disliking and disagreement |
|---|---|
| [moo arési] **μου αρέσει** I like | [antipathó] **αντιπαθώ** I dislike |
| [moo arésoon] **μου αρέσουν** I like | [THen marési] **δεν μ'αρέσει** I don't like |
| [simfonó] **συμφωνώ** I agree | [THiafonó] **διαφωνώ** I disagree |
| [ého THíkio] **έχω δίκιο** I'm right | [ého áTHiko] **έχω άδικο** I'm wrong |
| [protimó] **προτιμώ** I prefer | [THen protimó] **δεν προτιμώ** I don't prefer |

Now read the following examples:

| | | |
|---|---|---|
| [ého THíkio i áTHiko]? | **Έχω δίκιο ή άδικο;** | Am I right or wrong? |
| [simfonó mazí soo]. | **Συμφωνώ μαζί σου.** | I agree with you. |
| [moo arési i maría]. | **Μου αρέσει η Μαρία.** | I like Maria. |
| [protimó kafé ke óhi tsái]. | **Προτιμώ καφέ και όχι τσάι.** | I prefer coffee to tea. |
| [THen moo arésoon o THimítris ke i María]. | **Δε μου αρέσουν ο Δημήτρης και η Μαρία.** | I don't like Dimitris and Maria. |

## 3 THE VERB *TO LIKE*

The verb forms [moo arési] **μου αρέσει** I like (used with only one person or thing) and [moo arésoon] **μου αρέσουν** I like (used with more than one person or thing) are common ways of expressing *liking*. The structure of this verb is different from the English verb *to like* as instead of saying *I like X*, you say instead *Me is pleasing X*. The two different forms are necessary because what is liked becomes the subject of the verb and so the verb will change according to whether the subject is singular or plural. Look at the different forms:

| I like (only one person or thing) | | | I like (more than one person or thing) | | |
|---|---|---|---|---|---|
| [moo arési] | **μου αρέσει** | I like | [moo arésoon] | **μου αρέσουν** | I like (sing/infml) |
| [soo arési] | **σου αρέσει** | you like (sing/infml) | [soo arésoon] | **σου αρέσουν** | you like |
| [too arési] | **του αρέσει** | he/it likes | [too arésoon] | **του αρέσουν** | he/it likes |
| [tis arési] | **της αρέσει** | she likes | [tis arésoon] | **της αρέσουν** | she likes |

| [mas arési] | μας αρέσει | we like | [mas arésoon] | μας αρέσουν | we like |
|---|---|---|---|---|---|
| [sas arési] | σας αρέσει | you like (pl/fml) | [sas arésoon] | σας αρέσουν | you like (pl/fml) |
| [toos arési] | τους αρέσει | they like | [toos arésoon] | τους αρέσουν | they like |

The first two forms in each case have an alternative contracted form:
[marési] **μ'αρέσει** and [sarési] **σ'αρέσει**, and [marésoon] **μ'αρέσουν** and [sarésoon] **σ'αρέσουν**.

Look at the following examples:

| [moo arési o kanapés]. | **Μου αρέσει ο καναπές.** | I like the sofa. |
|---|---|---|
| [moo arésoon i karékles]. | **Μου αρέσουν οι καρέκλες.** | I like the chairs. |
| [THen too arési o kathréftis]. | **Δεν του αρέσει ο καθρέφτης.** | He doesn't like the mirror. |
| [the mas arésoon ta hrómata]. | **Δε μας αρέσουν τα χρώματα.** | We don't like the colours. |

## 4 PLURAL NOUNS

As in English, there are different ways to form plural nouns in Greek. Two endings are used in particular: [-es] **-ες** for masculine and feminine nouns and [-a] **-α** for neuter nouns. Look at the list. You don't have to try to memorize everything at once; instead come back to it as often as necessary.

**Masculine**

| [o kanapés] | **ο καναπές** | sofa |
|---|---|---|
| [i kanapéTHes] | **οι καναπέδες** | sofas |
| [o pángos] | **ο πάγκος** | counter |
| [i pángi] | **οι πάγκοι** | counters |
| [o kathréftis] | **ο καθρέφτης** | mirror |
| [i kathréftes] | **οι καθρέφτες** | mirrors |

**Feminine**

| [i karékla] | **η καρέκλα** | chair |
|---|---|---|
| [i karékles] | **οι καρέκλες** | chairs |
| [i polithróna] | **η πολυθρόνα** | armchair |
| [i polithrónes] | **οι πολυθρόνες** | armchairs |
| [i koozína] | **η κουζίνα** | kitchen |
| [i koozínes] | **οι κουζίνες** | kitchens |

**Neuter**

| | | |
|---|---|---|
| [to THomátio] | **το δωμάτιο** | *room* |
| [ta THomátia] | **τα δωμάτια** | *rooms* |
| [to kreváti] | **το κρεβάτι** | *bed* |
| [ta krevátia] | **τα κρεβάτια** | *beds* |
| [to trapézi] | **το τραπέζι** | *table* |
| [ta trapézia] | **τα τραπέζια** | *tables* |

## 5 COLOURS

This unit has introduced the words for two colours: [mávro] **μαύρο** *black* and [áspro] **άσπρο** *white*. Here are some more.

| | | | | | |
|---|---|---|---|---|---|
| [mov] | **μωβ** | *purple* | [ble] | **μπλε** | *blue* |
| [prásino] | **πράσινο** | *green* | [kítrino] | **κίτρινο** | *yellow* |
| [portokalí] | **πορτοκαλί** | *orange* | [kókino] | **κόκκινο** | *red* |

 Practice

**1 How well do you know your flags? Look at the pictures of the six flags. What colours should each of them be?**

a [eláTHa]   d [elvetía] *Switzerland*

b [italía]   e [galía]

c [yermanía]   f [ispanía]

**2 Somebody wants more than one of everything. Can you change the sentences from singular to plural, following the example?**

[moo arési to trapézi] ⟶ [moo arésoon ta trapézia]

   **a** [moo arési o kathréftis]
   **b** [moo arési o kanapés]

**c** [moo arési i karékla]
**d** [moo arési i polithróna]
**e** [moo arési to bánio¹]
**f** [moo arési to kreváti]

**3** It is useful to learn some words in pairs (either opposites or words that mean similar things). Match each word in the left-hand column with one in the right-hand column to make pairs of words.

| | | | |
|---|---|---|---|
| **a** [strongilós] στρογγυλός | | **1** [áshimos] άσχημος |
| **b** [mikrós] μικρός | | **2** [polís] πολύς |
| **c** [oréos] ωραίος | | **3** [áTHikos] άδικος |
| **d** [THíkeos] δίκαιος | | **4** [megálos] μεγάλος |
| **e** [lígos] λίγος | | **5** [tetrágonos] τετράγωνος |

**4** In the previous exercise all words were given in the masculine form. Can you change the endings to neuter following the example?

[strongilós] ⟶ [strongiló]

**a** [mikrós]
**b** [oréos]
**c** [THíkeos]
**d** [lígos]
**e** [áshimos]
**f** [polís]
**g** [áTHikos]
**h** [megálos]
**i** [tetrágonos]

**5** Rearrange these lines to make a dialogue.

**a** [egó protimó ta mikrá spítia]. Εγώ προτιμώ τα μικρά σπίτια.
**b** [ne], [alá íne polí megálo]. Ναι, αλλά είναι πολύ μεγάλο.
**c** [THen éhis THíkio]. Δεν έχεις δίκιο.
**d** [moo arésoon ta megála spítia]. Μου αρέσουν τα μεγάλα σπίτια.
**e** [soo arési to spíti mas]? Σου αρέσει το σπίτι μας;
**f** [óhi]! [óhi]! [antipathó ta mikrá spítia]! Όχι, όχι! Αντιπαθώ τα μικρά σπίτια!

---

¹ The word [bánio] not only means *bathroom* but also *bathtub* and *swimming*.

**6** 07.10 **Listen again to Conversation 2 of this unit and fill in the blanks using a word from the box. If you prefer, fill in the blanks first and then listen and check your answers.**

> [vévea]   [alá]   [THíkio]
> [kathréftis]   [áspro]   [arésoon]
> [praktikó]   [lootró]

| | |
|---|---|
| **Elpitha** | [eTHó] [íne to vesé]. [íne lígo mikró] [alá polí] **a** _____ [ótan íne anángi]. |
| **Mary** | [ne], **b** _____. |
| **Elpitha** | [apó'THo to] **c** _____ [soo arési]? |
| **Mary** | [moo arési polí]. [moo] **d** _____ [ta hrómata polí] [ke o strongilós] **e** _____ |
| **Elpitha** | [ne] [to mávro ke] **f** _____ [kánoon] [megáli antíthesi]. **g** _____ [moo arésoon]. |
| **Mary** | [simfonó]. [éhis] **h** _____. |

**7** **Read the following conversation between Mary and Elpitha about Greece. Then say whether each of the sentences is true or false.**

| | |
|---|---|
| **Mary** | [moo arési i eláTHa] [yiatí íne mikrí]. |
| **Elpitha** | [THen simfonó]. [THen íne polí mikrí]. |
| **Mary** | [THiafonó] [alá] … [moo arési] [o kerós¹] [stin eláTHa]. |
| **Elpitha** | [eTHó] [simfonó mazí soo]. [éhis THíkio]. |
| **Mary** | [vévea], [yiatí THen protimó] [tin vrohí²] [sto lonTHíno]. |
| **Elpitha** | [THen éhis áTHiko] |

¹[kerós] **καιρός** weather; ² [vrohí] **βροχή** rain

 **a** They both believe Greece is a small country.
 **b** They both agree that Greece has nice weather.
 **c** Mary dislikes rainy days in London.
 **d** Mary dislikes the weather in Greece.
 **e** Elpitha likes the weather in Greece.

**8** **Now can you translate the conversation in exercise 7?**

**9** **07.11** **Listen to Nikos describing his house. Look at the plan and decide whether or not it is Nikos' house.**

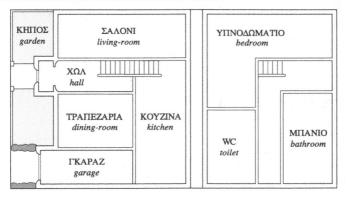

KHΠOΣ *garden*

ΣΑΛΟΝΙ *living-room*

ΥΠΝΟΔΩΜΑΤΙΟ *bedroom*

XΩΛ *hall*

ΤΡΑΠΕΖΑΡΙΑ *dining-room*

KOYZINA *kitchen*

WC *toilet*

ΜΠΑΝΙΟ *bathroom*

ΓΚΑΡΑΖ *garage*

 ## Test yourself

**How did you find Unit 7? It introduced some important new vocabulary – let's see how much of it you remember.**

1 Can you name four of your favourite colours?
2 What are the opposites of *I like, I agree* and *I'm right* in Greek?
3 How would you say *I like, I agree* and *I'm right* in Greek?
4 What are the two Greek words for *dislike*?
5 Can you name five items of furniture?
6 What are the opposites of *square, big* and *black* in Greek?
7 How would you say *square, big* and *black* in Greek?
8 Name three electrical appliances.

## SELF CHECK

| I CAN... |
| --- |
| ...agree or disagree with someone. |
| ...say if I like or dislike something. |
| ...use more Greek nouns in singular and plural form. |
| ...use adjectives. |
| ...use words for colour and furniture. |

# 8 *Πώς περνάς την ημέρα;*

## How do you spend the day?

**In this unit you will learn how to:**

▶ *talk about daily routines.*
▶ *tell the time.*
▶ *count from 101 to 1,000.*
▶ *use Greek adverbs of frequency.*

**CEFR: (A2)** *Can use a series of phrases and sentences to describe daily routines; Can give and receive information about numbers; Can indicate time.*

##  Πρωινό, μεσημεριανό και βραδινό
### *Breakfast, lunch and dinner*

[proinó] **πρωινό** *breakfast* is almost non-existent in Greece. Very few people actually sit down at the breakfast table and have a full breakfast; instead they usually have [kafé] **καφέ** *coffee*, [tsái] **τσάι** *tea* or [gála] **γάλα** *milk* with perhaps a [kooloóri] **κουλούρι** *sesame breadstick*, a [krooasán] **κρουασάν** *croissant* or [dimitriaká] **δημητριακά** *cereal*. Continental and cooked breakfasts are available in hotels and restaurants in summer resorts.

As a mid-morning snack, Greek people might buy a [tirópita] **τυρόπιτα** *cheese pie*, [spanakópita] **σπανακόπιτα** *spinach pie* or [tost] **τοστ** *toasted sandwich*. [mesimerianó] **μεσημεριανό** *lunch* is often a full and at times heavy meal, which definitely requires an afternoon siesta! [vraTHinó] **βραδινό** *dinner*, on the other hand, when eaten at home, is usually just a light snack or leftovers from lunch. Many people go out for dinner with friends or colleagues, however, and this is usually an occasion for another heavy meal which often lasts for several hours and continues late into the night. All three words for the different meals derive from the time of day they are eaten: [proinó] **πρωινό** from [proí] **πρωί** *morning*; [mesimerianó] **μεσημεριανό** from [mesiméri] **μεσημέρι** *midday/afternoon* and [vraTHinó] **βραδινό** from [vráTHi] **βράδυ** *evening*.

 Name three things Greek people might have for breakfast.

# Vocabulary builder

**ΣΠΟΡ ΚΑΙ ΧΟΜΠΙ** *SPORTS AND HOBBIES*

**1 08.01 Look at the phrases and complete the missing English expressions. Then listen and try to imitate the pronunciation of the speakers.**

| | |
|---|---|
| Μ'αρέσει να κάνω γυμναστική συχνά. | *I often like to work out.* |
| Δε μ'αρέσει το τένις καθόλου. | *_____ tennis at all.* |
| Ένα χόμπι μου είναι το περπάτημα. | *Walking is one _____ of mine.* |
| Βλέπω ποδόσφαιρο πάντα. | *I always watch football.* |
| Μαγειρεύω σχεδόν κάθε μέρα. | *I cook almost every _____.* |
| Δε έχω πολύ ελεύθερο χρόνο. | *_____ much free time.* |
| Σπάνια βλέπω τηλεόραση. | *I seldom watch TV.* |
| Το αγαπημένο μου σπορ είναι | *Basketball is my favourite _____.* |
| το μπάσκετ. | |

**ΚΑΘΗΜΕΡΙΝΕΣ ΡΟΥΤΙΝΕΣ** *DAILY ROUTINES*

**2 08.02 Listen a couple of times to two people talking about their daily routines. Then read the phrases and decide whether each one is true or false. Finally, listen again and try to imitate the pronunciation of the speakers.**

| Man | Woman |
|---|---|
| **Σηκώνομαι πολύ νωρίς.** | **Σηκώνομαι πολύ αργά.** |
| **Μαθαίνω Ελληνικά κάθε μέρα.** | **Δε μαθαίνω Ελληνικά.** |
| **Κάνω ντους κάθε πρωί.** | **Κάνω μπάνιο κάθε βράδυ.** |
| **Πίνω λίγο καφέ.** | **Πίνω πολύ τσάι.** |
| **Επιστρέφω στο σπίτι αργά.** | **Επιστρέφω στο διαμέρισμα νωρίς.** |
| **Τελειώνω τη δουλειά στις τρεις.** | **Τελειώνω τη δουλειά στις τέσσερις.** |

**3** 08.03 **Now read about some more daily routines and match them with the pictures. The first has been done for you. Then listen again and try to imitate the pronunciation of the speakers.**

[ftáno sti THooliá].
Φτάνω στη δουλειά.     *I arrive at work.*     e

[sikónome argá].
Σηκώνομαι αργά.     *I get up late.*     _____

[epistréfo sto spíti argá].
Επιστρέφω στο σπίτι αργά.     *I get home late.* _     _____

[mathéno eliniká].
Μαθαίνω Ελληνικά.     *I study Greek.*     _____

[páo sto kreváti argá].
Πάω στο κρεβάτι αργά.     *I go to bed late.*     _____

[páo sti THooliá].
Πάω στη δουλειά.     *I go to work.*     _____

[tró-o vraTHinó].
Τρώω βραδινό.     *I eat dinner.*     _____

[THen tró-o proinó].
Δεν τρώω πρωινό.     *I don't eat breakfast.*     _____

[tró-o mesimerianó norís].
Τρώω μεσημεριανό νωρίς.     *I eat lunch early.*     _____

[káno dooz].
Κάνω ντους.     *I take a shower.*     _____

[píno polí kafé].
Πίνω πολύ καφέ.     *I drink a lot of coffee.*     _____

[telióno ti THooliá].
Τελειώνω τη δουλειά.     *I finish work.*     _____

[pérno to asansér].
Παίρνω το ασανσέρ.     *I use the lift.*     _____

[vlépo lígo tileórasi].
Βλέπω λίγο τηλεόραση.     *I watch some TV.*     _____

# Conversation 1 Τι ώρα είναι;
*What time is it?*

## NEW WORDS AND EXPRESSIONS 1

**08.04** **Listen to the words and expressions that are used in the next conversation. Note their meanings.**

| | | |
|---|---|---|
| [óra] | ώρα | *time* |
| [ti óra íne tóra]? | τι ώρα είναι τώρα; | *what time is it now?* |
| [akrivós] | ακριβώς | *exactly* |
| [pes moo] | πες μου | *tell me (sing/infml)* |
| [pernás] | περνάς | *you spend (sing/infml)* |
| [norís] | νωρίς | *early* |
| [siníthos] | συνήθως | *usually* |
| [sikónome] | σηκώνομαι | *I get up* |
| [etimázo] | ετοιμάζω | *I prepare* |
| [pérno] | παίρνω | *I take* |
| [sholío] | σχολείο | *school* |
| [épita] | έπειτα | *then, after that* |
| [páo] | πάω | *I go, I am going* |
| [psónia] | ψώνια | *shopping* |
| [teliká] | τελικά | *finally* |
| [mayirévo] | μαγειρεύω | *I cook* |
| [THistihós] | δυστυχώς | *unfortunately* |

**08.05** *Elpitha tells Mary about her daily routine.*

**1** **Listen to the conversation a couple of times. What time does Elpitha usually get up?**

| | | |
|---|---|---|
| **Mary** | [ti óra íne tóra]? | *What time is it now?* |
| **Elpitha** | [íne mía akrivós]. [yiatí ti thélis]? | *It's one o'clock exactly. Why, what do you want?* |
| **Mary** | [pes moo], [pos pernás tin iméra soo]? [ti kánis] [norís to proí]? | *Tell me, how do you spend your day? What do you do early in the morning?* |
| **Elpitha** | [siníthos] [sikónome stis eptá], [etimázo proinó] [ke pérno ta peTHiá] [sto sholío]. [épita páo yia psónia]. [teliká mayirévo] … [THistihós]. | *I usually get up at seven, I prepare breakfast and I take the children to school. Afterwards I go shopping. Finally, I cook … unfortunately.* |

| Mary | Τι ώρα είναι τώρα; |
|---|---|
| Ελπίδα | Είναι μία ακριβώς. Γιατί, τι θέλεις; |
| Mary | Πες μου, πώς περνάς την ημέρα σου; Τι κάνεις νωρίς το πρωί; |
| Ελπίδα | Συνήθως σηκώνομαι στις επτά. Ετοιμάζω πρωινό και παίρνω τα παιδιά στο σχολείο. Έπειτα πάω για ψώνια. Τελικά, μαγειρεύω … δυστυχώς. |

**2 Now read the conversation and answer the questions.**

   **a** Which Greek phrase means *Afterwards I go shopping*?

   **b** Does Elpitha sound happy about her daily routine? Which word helps your decision here?

 **3 Listen again and pay special attention to the words which run together. Practise speaking the part of Elpitha.**

#  Language discovery 1

**1 The conversation includes some words that relate to when or how often something happens. Can you find the Greek words for the following?**

   **a** finally

   **b** afterwards

   **c** usually

   **d** early

   **e** exactly

**2 There are also some expressions relating to telling the time. Find the Greek for the following:**

   **a** What's the time?

   **b** It's one o'clock exactly.

   **c** I usually get up at seven.

## 1 TELLING THE TIME

**08.06** Telling the time in Greek is not very difficult. The most important thing, of course, is to remember the numbers from 1 to 60! If you are unsure, go back to Unit 5 and refresh your memory before continuing. There are two different ways of telling the time: the easy way and the more challenging way! Let's start with the easy way. Read each example first before you listen to the audio, and check that you have the correct pronunciation. Alternatively, you can always listen to the audio first and then repeat after the speaker.

| [mía ke triánda pénde] | **μία και τριάντα πέντε** | *one thirty-five* |
| [THío ke íkosi] | **δύο και είκοσι** | *two twenty* |
| [tris ke triánda] | **τρεις και τριάντα** | *three thirty* |
| [téseris ke THekapénde] | **τέσσερις και δεκαπέντε** | *four fifteen* |
| [pénde ke saránda pénde] | **πέντε και σαράντα πέντε** | *five forty-five* |

The more challenging way requires you to remember some important words:

| [ke] | **και** | *past* (you already know this word as *and*) |
| [pará] | **παρά** | *to, before* |
| [tétarto] | **τέταρτο** | *quarter, quarter past* |
| [misí] | **μισή** | *half, half past* |

Remember that the *hour* [óra] **ώρα** comes before the *minutes* [leptá] **λεπτά**. The word [ke] **και** *past* comes after the hours and before the minutes. Once again, say the times that you see and then listen to the audio and check your pronunciation.

| [THío pará íkosi pénde] | **δύο παρά είκοσι πέντε** | *twenty-five to two* |
| [THío ke íkosi] | **δύο και είκοσι** | *twenty past two* |
| [tris ke misí] | **τρεις και μισή** | *half past three* |
| [téseris ke tétarto] | **τέσσερις και τέταρτο** | *quarter past four* |
| [éksi pará tétarto] | **έξι παρά τέταρτο** | *quarter to six* |

**π.μ.** means *a.m.* and **μ.μ.** means *p.m.* The two letters stand for [pro mesimvrías] **προ μεσημβρίας** and [metá mesimvrías] **μετά μεσημβρίας** respectively. You should use the full forms when saying the expressions in Greek and not just the two letters, as in English.

Note too that as [óra] **ώρα** *hour* is feminine, the feminine form of [mía] **μία**, [tris] **τρεις** and [téseris] **τέσσερις** is needed.

Finally, [stis] **Στις** means *at* when telling the time, as the number is plural, except for [sti mía i óra] **στη μία η ώρα** *at one o'clock*, which uses the singular [sti] **στη**.

## 2 THE NUMBERS 101–1,000

 08.07 Talking of numbers, let's continue from where we left off in Unit 5. Note and study the new numbers from 101 to 1,000. Then listen and repeat after the speakers.

| [ekatón éna] | **εκατόν ένα** | *one hundred and one* |
| [ekatón pénde] | **εκατόν πέντε** | *one hundred and five* |

| | | |
|---|---|---|
| [ekatón ev THomínda] | **εκατόν εβδομήντα** | one hundred and seventy |
| [THiakósia] | **διακόσια** | two hundred |
| [triakósia] | **τριακόσια** | three hundred |
| [tetrakósia] | **τετρακόσια** | four hundred |
| [pendakósia] | **πεντακόσια** | five hundred |
| [eksakósia] | **εξακόσια** | six hundred |
| [eptakósia] or [eftakósia] | **επτακόσια/εφτακόσια** | seven hundred |
| [oktakósia] or [ohtakósia] | **οκτακόσια/οχτακόσια** | eight hundred |
| [eniakósia] | **εννιακόσια** | nine hundred |
| [hílji], [hílies], [hília] | **χίλιοι** (m), **χίλιες** (f), **χίλια** (n) | one thousand |

## Conversation 2 **Πάω στη δουλειά** I go to work

 **NEW WORDS AND EXPRESSIONS 2**

 **08.08 Listen to the words and expressions that are used in the next conversation. Note their meanings.**

| | | |
|---|---|---|
| [iméra] | ημέρα | day |
| [óli tin iméra] | όλη την ημέρα | all day |
| [ksipnáo] | ξυπνάω | I wake up |
| [dooz] | ντους | shower |
| [tró-o] | τρώω | I eat |
| [metá] | μετά | then, afterwards |
| [pérno] | παίρνω | I take |
| [tréno] | τρένο | train |
| [epistréfis] | επιστρέφεις | you return (sing/infml) |
| [méhri] | μέχρι | to, until |
| [tróte] | τρώτε | you eat (pl/fml) |
| [vraThinó] | βραδινό | dinner (n) |
| [yíro] | γύρω | around, about |
| [stis] | στις | at |
| [ékso] | έξω | out, outside |

**08.09** *Now Mary tells Elpitha about her daily routine.*

**1  Listen to the conversation a couple of times. When does Mary usually wake up?**

| | | |
|---|---|---|
| **Elpitha** | [esí ti kánis] [óli tin iméra]? | *What do you do all day?* |
| **Mary** | [ksipnáo stis eptámisi] [káno éna dooz] [ke tró-o proinó]. [metá pérno to tréno] [ke páo sti THooliá]. | *I wake up at 7:30, I take a shower and have breakfast. Then I take the train and go to work.* |
| **Elpitha** | [ti óra epistréfis spíti]? | *What time do you get back home?* |
| **Mary** | [THoolévo siníthos] [apó tis THéka] [méhri tis téseris] [epistréfo spíti] [stis pendémisi]. | *I usually work from ten o'clock to four o'clock. I get back home at 5:30.* |
| **Elpitha** | [ti óra] [tróte vraTHinó]? | *What time do you have (lit. eat) dinner?* |
| **Mary** | [yíro stis eptá] [sto spíti] [i stis októ ékso]. | *Around seven o'clock at home or at eight o'clock when eating out (lit. at eight o'clock out).* |
| **Ελπίδα** | Εσύ, τι κάνεις όλη την ημέρα; | |
| **Mary** | Ξυπνάω στις επτάμιση, κάνω ένα ντους και τρώω πρωινό. Μετά παίρνω το τρένο και πάω στη δουλειά. | |
| **Ελπίδα** | Τι ώρα επιστρέφεις σπίτι; | |
| **Mary** | Δουλεύω συνήθως από τις δέκα μέχρι τις τέσσερις. Επιστρέφω σπίτι στις πεντέμιση. | |
| **Ελπίδα** | Τι ώρα τρώτε βραδινό; | |
| **Mary** | Γύρω στις επτά στο σπίτι ή στις οκτώ έξω. | |

**2  Now read the conversation and answer the questions.**
  **a**  When does Mary usually work?
  **b**  When does she usually have dinner?

 **3  Listen again and pay special attention to the words which run together. Practise speaking the part of Mary.**

# Language discovery 2

**1 Which expressions have to do with telling the time in this conversation? Find the Greek phrases that correspond to the following.**

a around seven o'clock at home
b from ten o'clock to four o'clock
c I wake up at 7:30.

**2 The conversation also includes some useful verbs for describing daily activities. Try to give the Greek equivalents of the following English expressions without looking at the conversation. Then check and compare your answers.**

a I return home
b I usually work
c I go to work
d I take the train
e I take a shower
f I have breakfast

## 1 EXPRESSIONS OF TIME

The two conversations in this unit introduced you to a new group of words that express how often something happens. These words are called adverbs of frequency. Look at the following list:

| [pánda] | **πάντα** | *always* |
| [sheTHón pánda] | **σχεδόν πάντα** | *almost always* |
| [sihná] | **συχνά** | *often* |
| [merikés forés] | **μερικές φορές** | *sometimes* |
| [spánia] | **σπάνια** | *rarely* |
| [sheTHón poté] | **σχεδόν ποτέ** | *hardly ever* |
| [poté] | **ποτέ** | *never* |

Do not confuse the word [poté] **ποτέ** *never*, with the stress on the last syllable, with the word [póte] **πότε** *when*, which is a new word for you and has the stress on the first syllable.

In this unit you have also been introduced to more words relating to time. Study them here and come back to this list whenever you need to refresh your memory.

| [épita] | **έπειτα** | *then, later* |
| [teliká] | **τελικά** | *finally* |
| [méhri] | **μέχρι** | *until* |
| [yíro] | **γύρω** | *around, about* |
| [metá] | **μετά** | *afterwards, later* |
| [norís] | **νωρίς** | *early* |
| [argá] | **αργά** | *late* |

## THE DAILY ROUTINE

Daily routines are often pretty much universal, one way or another. A typical day at home would perhaps include cooking, cleaning, reading or watching TV, whereas a day at school involves learning and playing, and a day at work hopefully includes working, if nothing else! Some typical Greek activities during the summer are having an afternoon siesta, eating out late at night in outdoor tavernas, staying for hours in local coffee houses discussing everything from politics to football, watching or taking part in sport, and going to outdoor cinemas and open-air concerts. Here are some useful questions to ask people about how they spend their time, what hobbies they have and whether they like sport or not:

[pos pernás tin iméra]?/[échis hóbi]/[ti spor soo arésoon]

**Πώς περνάς την ημέρα/Έχεις χόμπι/Τι σπορ σου αρέσουν;**

*How do you spend the day?/Do you have any hobbies?/What kind of sports do you like?*

[ti kánis to proí/mesiméri/apóyevma/vráTHi]?

**Τι κάνεις το πρωί/μεσημέρι/απόγευμα/βράδυ;**

*What do you do in the morning/in the afternoon/in the evening/at night?*

There are, of course, no set answers to these questions. You might reply with one or more of the following:

[mayirévo]/[THoolévo]/[kimáme]/[tró-o]/[píno]/[perpató]/ [ého polá hóbi].

**μαγειρεύω/δουλεύω/κοιμάμαι/τρώω/πίνω/περπατώ/έχω πολλά χόμπι.**

*I cook/I work/I sleep/I eat/I drink/I walk/I have many hobbies.*

[marési to poTHósfero, to basket ke to kolímbi] .

**Μ'αρέσει το ποδόσφαιρο, το μπάσκετ και το κολύμπι.**

*I like football, basketball and swimming.*

 # Practice

**1** **The following sentences describe Maria's daily routine but in jumbled order. Rearrange the sentences into the correct order. To make it more of a challenge, cover up the transliteration column and work only with the Greek script!**

**a** [ftáno sti THooliá] [stis októ].  Φτάνω στη δουλειά στις οκτώ.

**b** [sikónome norís].  Σηκώνομαι νωρίς.

**c** [epistréfo sto spíti argá].  Επιστρέφω στο σπίτι αργά.

**d** [péfto sto kreváti argá].  Πέφτω στο κρεβάτι αργά.

**e** [páo sti THooliá].  Πάω στη δουλειά.

**f** [pérno vraTHinó stis eniá].  Παίρνω βραδινό στις εννιά.

**g** [THen tró-o proinó móno kafé].  Δεν τρώω πρωινό, μόνο καφέ.

**h** [tró-o mesimerianó sti THooliá].  Τρώω μεσημεριανό στη δουλειά.

**i** [káno dooz].  Κάνω ντους.

**j** [píno polí kafé sti THooliá].  Πίνω πολύ καφέ στη δουλειά.

**k** [telióno ti THooliá stis éksi].  Τελειώνω τη δουλειά στις έξι.

**l** [vlépo lígo tileórasi stis THéka].  Βλέπω λίγο τηλεόραση στις δέκα.

**2** **Can you translate the sentences in the previous exercise into English?**

**3** **How do you study Greek? Use a word from the box to answer each of the following questions about how frequently you do each task. Note that there are no correct answers as such, since every learner will have his/her own way of learning. To make the exercise more challenging, try to write each word in Greek script.**

> [pánda]   [sheTHón pánda]
> [siníthos]   [sihná]   [merikés forés]
> [spánia]   [sheTHón poté]   [poté]

**a** I listen to the recording.

**b** I speak to native speakers.

**c** I use a Greek dictionary.

**d** I revise past units.

**e** I make lists of important words.

**f** I listen to Greek music.

**g** I record myself speaking Greek.

**4** **08.10** Listen to some people saying at what time they do different activities. Match each time in the left-hand column with the correct activity in the right-hand column.

| | | | |
|---|---|---|---|
| **a** | 8:15 | **1** | [THen tró-o mesimerianó stis] |
| **b** | 9:15 | **2** | [pérno to tréno stis] |
| **c** | 13:30 | **3** | [tró-o proinó stis] |
| **d** | 16:20 | **4** | [ftáno sto spíti stis] |
| **e** | 16:41 | **5** | [ftáno sti THooliá stis] |
| **f** | 17:05 | **6** | [telióno ti THooliá stis] |

**5** **08.11** Listen to the people telling you what time it is. Can you put the times in the order you hear them?

| 8:30 | 7:05 | 10:30 | 11:45 | 1:45 | 8:05 |
|------|------|-------|-------|------|------|

**a** _____
**b** _____
**c** _____
**d** _____
**e** _____
**f** _____

**6** Can you identify which option is wrong in each case?

**a** [THoolévo]
  **1** [sto spíti]
  **2** [sto kókino]
  **3** [THistihós]
  **4** [stis THéka]

**b** [epistréfo]
  **1** [sto THiamérizma]
  **2** [sto vraTHinó]
  **3** [sti THooliá]
  **4** [sto aeroTHrómio]

**c** [telióno]
  **1** [ti THooliá]
  **2** [ton kafé]
  **3** [to mesimerianó]
  **4** [to asansér]

**d** [pérno]
  **1** [to asansér]
  **2** [to proinó moo]
  **3** [kreváti argá]
  **4** [THooliá sto spíti]

**7** 08.12 **Listen again to Conversation 2 and complete each sentence by choosing one word from the box.**

| [epistréfis] [óli] [tróte] [méhri] |
| [apó] [yíro] [tró-o] [ksipnáo] |
| [pérno] [ékso] |

| | |
|---|---|
| **Elpitha** | [esí ti kánis] **a** _____ [tin iméra]? |
| **Mary** | **b** _____ [stis eptámisi] [káno éna dooz] [ke] **c** _____ [proinó]. [metá] **d** _____ [to tréno] [ke páo sti THooliá]. |
| **Elpitha** | [ti óra] **e** _____ [spíti]? |
| **Mary** | [THoolévo siníthos] **f** _____ [tis THéka] **g** _____ [tis téseris] [epistréfo spíti] [stis pendémisi]. |
| **Elpitha** | [ti óra] **h** _____ [vraTHinó]? |
| **Mary** | **i** _____ [stis eptá] [sto spíti] [i stis októ] **j** _____. |

**8** 08.13 **Listen to three people talking about their hobbies. Look at the three pictures and match each one to the correct speaker.**

Speaker 1: _____

Speaker 2: _____

Speaker 3: _____

**a**

**b**

c

## ? Test yourself

**1** Can you say the following numbers in Greek?
- **a** 104
- **b** 184
- **c** 231
- **d** 456
- **e** 827
- **f** 951
- **g** 1,000

**2** Can you say the following times in Greek?
- **a** 7:20
- **b** 8:30
- **c** 9:00
- **d** 11:15
- **e** 1:30
- **f** 4:10
- **g** 5:45

**3** How do you say the following verbs in Greek?
- **a** get up
- **b** arrive
- **c** finish
- **d** come back
- **e** take

**4** Translate the following sentences into Greek:
- **a** I always get up at 6:15.
- **b** I never arrive at work early.
- **c** I sometimes finish my work late.
- **d** I seldom eat out.
- **e** I almost always take the train.

**5** Name three of your favourite hobbies.

## SELF CHECK

| | I CAN... |
|---|---|
| ○ | . . . talk about daily routines. |
| ○ | . . . tell the time. |
| ○ | . . . count from 101 to 1,000. |
| ○ | . . . use Greek adverbs of frequency. |

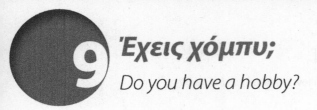

# 9 Έχεις χόμπυ;

## Do you have a hobby?

**In this unit you will learn how to:**
▶ *talk about your free time.*
▶ *ask others about their hobbies.*
▶ *name different kinds of Greek music and different types of books and films.*
▶ *use loanwords in Greek.*

**CEFR: (A2)** *Can understand sentences and frequently used expressions related to hobbies and free time; Can explain what he/she likes doing.*

## Μερικά χόμπυ και ελληνική μουσική *Hobbies and Greek music*

As with people in many other countries, Greeks tend to enjoy reading, television, cinema and theatre. Other favourite pastimes are watching and participating in sport, going to the gym, acquiring and using computer skills and travelling abroad. The national favourite sport has shifted in recent years from football to basketball. Outdoor activities such as [kiníghi] **κυνήγι** *hunting*, [psárema] **ψάρεμα** *fishing*, [pezoporía] **πεζοπορία** *hiking*, [orivasía] **ορειβασία** *mountain climbing* and of course [kolímbi] **κολύμπι** *swimming* are also popular. Most Greeks like listening to music and both Greek and international music can be heard every day on the radio or in bars and nightclubs. The most popular styles of traditional Greek music are [laïká] **λαϊκά** *pop music*, [elafrolaïká] **ελαφρολαϊκά** *soft pop music*, [rebétika] **ρεμπέτικα** *Greek blues*, [rok] **ροκ** *rock music* and [nisiótika] **νησιώτικα** *Greek island music*. Every region has its own traditional music, including both local melodies and instruments. Some popular Greek instruments are the [boozoóki] **μπουζούκι** *bouzouki*, the [baglamaTHáki] **μπαγλαμαδάκι** *small bouzouki* and the [líra] **λύρα** *lyre*.

The Greek words for some words relating to hobbies have not been provided in the text. The following are the Greek words for *television*, *gym*, *computer* and *travelling*. Can you work out which is which: **κομπιούτερ**, **γυμναστική**, **ταξίδι**, **τηλεόραση**?

# Vocabulary builder

**ΜΟΥΣΙΚΗ, ΦΙΛΜ, ΒΙΒΛΙΑ, ΣΠΟΡ** *MUSIC, FILMS, BOOKS, SPORT*

**1** 09.01 **Look at the words and complete the missing English expressions. Then listen and try to imitate the pronunciation of the speakers.**

> **LANGUAGE TIP**
> This unit can be used as a starting point for you to come up with different word lists in groups. For instance, if you like books, you should be able to say what kind of books you enjoy reading. If you like sport, you should be able to name a few different types, and if you like music, you should be able to mention some local or international kinds of music. You can personalize the following lists by highlighting all the words that are especially relevant to your own tastes. Remember too that if you have access to a dictionary you can look up some more words and add them to the four lists.

| **[moosikí]** | **Μουσική** | **Music** |
|---|---|---|
| [rok] | ροκ | _____ |
| [blooz] | μπλουζ | _____ |
| [laiká] | λαϊκά | *pop* |
| [tzaz] | τζαζ | _____ |
| [rebétika] | ρεμπέτικα | *Greek blues* |

| **[érga]** | **Έργα** | **Films** |
|---|---|---|
| [komoTHíes] | κωμωδίες | _____ |
| [THramatiká] | δραματικά | _____ |
| [thríler] | θρίλερ | *thriller* |
| [astinomiká] | αστυνομικά | *crime* |
| [epistimonikís fantasías] | επιστημονικής φαντασίας | *science fiction* |

| **[vivlía]** | **Βιβλία** | **Books** |
|---|---|---|
| [mithistorímata] | μυθιστορήματα | *novels* |
| [noovéles] | νουβέλες | _____ |
| [astinomiká] | αστυνομικά | *crime* |
| [istoríes agápis] | ιστορίες αγάπης | *love* _____ |
| [peripéties] | περιπέτειες | *adventure stories/thrillers* |

| [spor] | **Σπορ** | **Sports** |
|---|---|---|
| [poTHósfero] | ποδόσφαιρο | *football* |
| [ténis] | τένις | *tennis* |
| [vólei] | βόλεϋ | _____ |
| [ping pong] | πίνγκ πονγκ | *table tennis* |
| [básket] | μπάσκετ | _____ |

Many words in the lists are plural. The singular form is given here:

| [vivlío] | βιβλίο | *book* |
|---|---|---|
| [noovéla] | νουβέλα | *novel* |
| [mithistórima] | μυθιστόρημα | *novel* |
| [istoría] | ιστορία | *story; history* |
| [peripétia] | περιπέτεια | *adventure* |
| [komoTHía] | κωμωδία | *comedy* |

Two words are in the genitive singular. The base form, in the nominative case, is [agápi] **αγάπη** *love* and [fantasía] **φαντασία** *fiction* (lit. *fantasy*).

**2  Can you name the different types of films shown in the pictures?**

**3  09.02 Here are some questions and answers you might use when talking about hobbies. Complete the missing English words and then listen and try to imitate the speakers.**

| [soo arési i moosikí]? | Σου αρέσει η μουσική; | *Do you like _____?* |
|---|---|---|
| [sarési to sinemá]? | Σ'αρέσει το σινεμά; | *Do you like the _____?* |
| [soo arésoon ta spor]? | Σου αρέσουν τα σπορ; | *Do you like _____?* |
| [ti hóbi éhis/éhete]? | Τι χόμπυ έχεις/έχετε; | *What hobby do _____ have?* |

| | | |
|---|---|---|
| [marési polí/lígho] | Μ'αρέσει πολύ/λίγο. | I like it _____/a little bit. |
| [Then marésoon ta spor] | Δεν μ'αρέσουν τα σπορ. | I don't like sports. |
| [Then kano ghimnastikí] | Δεν κάνω γυμναστική. | I don't work out. |
| [écho polá hóbi] | Έχω πολλά χόμπυ. | I _____ many hobbies. |
| [marési na vlépo poTHósfero] | Μ'αρέσει να βλέπω ποδόσφαιρο. | I like to watch _____. |

## Conversation 1 **Τι κάνεις τον ελεύθερο χρόνο σου;** *What do you do in your free time?*

 **NEW WORDS AND EXPRESSIONS 1**

 **09.03 Listen to the words and expressions that are used in the next conversation. Note their meanings.**

| | | |
|---|---|---|
| [eléfthero] [hróno] | ελεύθερο χρόνο | *free time* |
| [marési] [nakoó-o] | μ'αρέσει ν'ακούω | *I like to listen to* |
| [moosikí] | μουσική | *music* |
| [kiríos] | κυρίως | *mainly* |
| [laïká] | λαϊκά | *popular music* |
| [eléftheres óres] | ελεύθερες ώρες | *free time* (lit. *free hours*) |
| [tileórasi] | τηλεόραση | *television* |
| [raTHiófono] | ραδιόφωνο | *radio* |

**09.04** *Angelos asks John about his free time.*

### 1 What does John like to do?

| Angelos | [John], [ti kánis] [ton eléfthero hróno soo]? | *John, what do you do in your free time?* |
|---|---|---|
| John | [marési nakoó-o moosikí]. | *I like to listen to music.* |
| Angelos | [ti moosikí sarési]? | *What kind of music do you like?* |
| John | [kiríos laïká] [alá ke rok]. [esí pos pernás] [tis eléftheres óres soo]? | *Mainly pop but rock too. How do you spend your free time?* |

| Angelos | [vlépo tileórasi] [i akoó-o raTHiófono]. | *I watch TV or listen to the radio.* |
|---|---|---|
| John | [polí oréa]. | *Very nice.* |
| Άγγελος | John, τι κάνεις τον ελεύθερο χρόνο σου; | |
| John | Μ'αρέσει ν'ακούω μουσική. | |
| Άγγελος | Τι μουσική σ'αρέσει; | |
| John | Κυρίως λαϊκά, αλλά και ροκ. Εσύ, πώς περνάς τις ελεύθερες ώρες σου; | |
| Άγγελος | Βλέπω τηλεόραση ή ακούω ραδιόφωνο. | |
| John | Πολύ ωραία. | |

**2 Now read the conversation and answer the following questions.**
  **a** What kind of music does John like?
  **b** What does Angelos do in his free time?

**3 Listen again and pay special attention to the words which run together. This time you can practise speaking the part of John.**

# Language discovery 1

**1 There are three expressions in the conversation which are used in a contracted form. Find these expressions using their English translations as a guide and and try to guess which letter or letters are missing in each case.**
  **a** I like
  **b** you like
  **c** to listen to

**2 What are the two ways of asking someone what they do in their free time?**

### 1 CONTRACTED FORMS

You have already seen that Greek uses many contracted forms, i.e. two words joined together into one in everyday speech. This unit includes the following contracted forms:

| Contracted form | Full form | English |
|---|---|---|
| [marési] **μ'αρέσει** | [moo] + [arési] **μου αρέσει** | I like |
| [marésoon] **μ'αρέσουν** | [moo] + [arésoon] **μου αρέσουν** | I like |
| [sarési] **σ'αρέσει** | [soo] + [arési] **σου αρέσει** | you like |
| [nakoó-o] **ν'ακούω** | [na] + [akoó-o] **να ακούω** | to listen to |

You can use either form. Simply remember that the contracted forms are more common.

## 2 QUESTION WORDS

In exercise 2, two different question words were used: [pos] **πώς** *how?* and [ti] **τι** *what?* Let's review some question words which you saw in previous units. If you cover the English translation, how many of these questions can you understand?

| | | |
|---|---|---|
| Unit 1: | **Πώς σε λένε; Γιατί είσαι εδώ;** | *What's your name? Why are you here?* |
| Unit 3: | **Πού μένεις;** | *Where do you live?* |
| Unit 4: | **Πόσα δωμάτια έχει;** | *How many rooms do you have?* |
| Unit 5: | **Πόσο χρονών είναι; Γιατί φεύγετε;** | *How old is he? Why are you leaving?* |
| Unit 8: | **Τι ώρα είναι; Γιατί, τι θέλεις;** | *What time is it? Why, what do you want?* |

# Conversation 2 **Έχεις χόμπυ;** *Do you have a hobby?*

 **NEW WORDS AND EXPRESSIONS 2**

 **09.05 Listen to the words and expressions that are used in the next conversation. Note their meanings.**

| | | |
|---|---|---|
| [enTHiaféron] | ενδιαφέρον | *interesting* |
| [troháTHin] | τροχάδην | *running* |
| [polés forés] | πολλές φορές | *often* (lit. *many times*) |
| [théatro] | θέατρο | *theatre* |
| [vóltes] | βόλτες | *walks, strolls; car rides* |

| [káthome spíti] | κάθομαι σπίτι | *I stay at home* (lit. *I sit home*) |
| [THiavázo] | διαβάζω | *I read; I study* |
| [vivlía] | βιβλία | *books* |
| [mithistorímata] | μυθιστορήματα | *novels* |

 **09.06** *Now Mary asks Elpitha about her hobbies.*

**1 What does Mary like to do?**

| Mary | [elpíTHa], [éhis hóbi]? | *Elpitha, do you have a hobby?* |
| Elpitha | [ne] [marésoon polí ta spor]. | *Yes, I like sports a lot.* |
| Mary | [enTHiaféron]. [ti spor]? | *Interesting. What sports?* |
| Elpitha | [marési to troháTHin] [to básket] [ke to ténis]. [polés forés páo sto théatro] [i sto sinemá]. [esí]? [ti hóbi éhis]? | *I like running, basketball and tennis. I often go to the theatre or the cinema. How about you? What are your hobbies?* |
| Mary | [marési na piyéno vóltes] [i na káthome spíti] [ke na THiavázo]. | *I like to go for a walk or stay at home and read.* |
| Elpitha | [ti vivlía siníthos THiavázis]? | *What kind of books do you usually read?* |
| Mary | [kiríos mithistorímata] [alá ke] [vivlía thríler]. | *Mainly novels but also thrillers.* |

| Mary | Ελπίδα, έχεις χόμπυ; |
| Ελπίδα | Ναι, μ'αρέσουν πολύ τα σπορ. |
| Mary | Ενδιαφέρον. Τι σπορ; |
| Ελπίδα | Μ'αρέσει το τροχάδην, το μπάσκετ και το τένις. Πολλές φορές πάω στο θέατρο ή στο σινεμά. Εσύ; Τι χόμπυ έχεις; |
| Mary | Μ'αρέσει να πηγαίνω βόλτες ή να κάθομαι σπίτι και να διαβάζω. |
| Ελπίδα | Τι βιβλία συνήθως διαβάζεις; |
| Mary | Κυρίως μυθιστορήματα αλλά και βιβλία θρίλερ. |

**2 Now read the conversation and answer the following questions.**
  **a** What kind of sports does Elpitha like?
  **b** What does Mary do in her free time?

**3 Listen again and pay special attention to the words which run together. This time you should practise speaking the part of Elpitha.**

## Language discovery 2

**1 You will already know that there are many words in English of Greek origin, but have you also begun to notice just how many English loan words there are in Greek? Read the conversation again and complete the table with the Greek words for the following, including the article where relevant.**

| Words of Greek origin | Words of English origin |
| --- | --- |
| theatre _____ | thriller _____ |
| book _____ | sports _____ |
| myth _____ | basket _____ |
| story _____ | tennis _____ |
| interesting _____ | hobby _____ |

**2 There are also five words in the plural form. Look at the English translations and find the corresponding Greek words in the conversation. Note down the singular and plural forms of these words. Does anything catch your attention?**
  **a** books
  **b** novels
  **c** sports
  **d** hobbies
  **e** walks

### 1 LOAN WORDS

How easy did you find exercise 1? By now you should be aware of the number of Greek words found in English and vice versa. New technologies have given several words to the Greek language, such as *computer*, *fax*, *tablet*, etc. Of course many other Greek words, such as *theatre*, *philosophy*, *athletics* and so on are found in several other languages, including English. Test yourself by covering the following English translations and guessing the meaning of each word.

## Words of Greek origin

| | | |
|---|---|---|
| [moosikí] | **η μουσική** | *music* |
| [théatro] | **το θέατρο** | *theatre* |
| [ráTHio] | **το ράδιο** | *radio* |
| [mithistórima] | **το μυθιστόρημα** | *novel* (lit. *myth story*) |
| [istoría] | **η ιστορία** | *history/story* |

## Words of English origin

| | | |
|---|---|---|
| *rock* | [rok] | **το ροκ** |
| *hobby* | [hóbi] | **το χόμπυ** |
| *sports* | [spor] | **το σπορ** |
| *basketball* | [básket] | **το μπάσκετ** |
| *tennis* | [ténis] | **το τένις** |

Of course, some words are not so obvious at first glance. In Conversation 2 the meaning of the word [vivlía] **βιβλία** is perhaps not so clear until you think of words like *bibliography* and *bibliophile*, then it becomes apparent that [vivlía] **βιβλία** and *books* are closely related.

## 2 THE SINGULAR AND PLURAL FORMS OF NOUNS

As mentioned in previous units, two common plural endings in Greek are **-ες** for masculine and feminine nouns and **-α** for neuter nouns. Of course, these are not the only two possible ways to form plurals forms although many words from this unit do take these forms. Look at the following examples:

| | | |
|---|---|---|
| [ι óra] ⟶ [ι óres] | **η ώρα ⟶ οι ώρες** | *hour ⟶ hours* |
| [ι forá] ⟶ [ι forés] | **ηφορά ⟶ οι φορές** | *time ⟶ times* |
| [i vólta] ⟶ [i vóltes] | **η βόλτα ⟶ οι βόλτες** | *walk ⟶ walks* |
| [to vivlío] ⟶ [ta vivlía] | **το βιβλίο ⟶ τα βιβλία** | *book ⟶ books* |
| [to théatro] ⟶ [ta théatra] | **το θέατρο ⟶ τα θέατρα** | *theatre ⟶ theatres* |

A little bit different, having an extra syllable in its plural form, is the following:

| [to mithistórima] ⟶ | **το μυθιστόρημα** | novel ⟶ novels |
| [ta mithistorímata] | **⟶ τα μυθιστορήματα** | |

There are also a lot of nouns in this unit that have only one form for both singular and plural. These are words that come from other languages, including English, and they are predominantly neuter nouns. Look at these examples:

| [to spor] ⟶ [ta spor] | **το σπορ ⟶ τα σπορ** | sport ⟶ sports |
| [to sinemá] ⟶ [ta sinemá] | **το σινεμά ⟶ τα σινεμά** | cinema ⟶ cinemas |
| [to hóbi] ⟶ [ta hóbi] | **το χόμπυ ⟶ τα χόμπυ** | hobby ⟶ hobbies |

### 3 THE VERB *TO SIT*

The verb [káthome] **κάθομαι**, which means *to sit* or *to stay*, depending on the context, belongs to a new group of verbs with special endings which you have not met before. The main ending of these verbs is **-μαι** (instead of **-ω** which signals most other Greek verbs). The verb [íme] **είμαι** *to be*, which you saw in Unit 1, has certain similarities that you can draw upon. Study the verb:

| [káthome] | **κάθομαι** | I sit/stay |
| [káthese] | **κάθεσαι** | you sit/stay (sing/infml) |
| [káthete] | **κάθεται** | he/she/it sits/stays |
| [kathómaste] | **καθόμαστε** | we sit/stay |
| [kathósaste] | **καθόσαστε/κάθεστε** | you sit/stay (pl/fml) |
| [káthonde] | **κάθονται** | they sit/stay |

This verb is one of a group known as reflexive verbs. Reflexive verbs all carry the idea of doing something to yourself. This is obvious in cases such as [plénome] **πλένομαι** *to wash oneself* but in other cases the notion of reflexivity is less apparent. The following are also reflexive verbs:

| [lipáme] | **λυπάμαι** | to be sorry |
| [kimáme] | **κοιμάμαι** | to sleep |
| [sikónome] | **σηκώνομαι** | to get up |

Practice

**1  09.07 Dimitris, Nikos and Maria are asked the questions [ti kánis ton eléfthero hróno soo]? and [pos pernás tis eléftheres óres soo]? Listen to the audio and tick the boxes corresponding to the activities or hobbies they enjoy.**

| Activities | Dimitris | Nikos | Maria |
|---|---|---|---|
| **1** smoke a | | | |
| **2** stay at | | | |
| **3** read a | | | |
| **4** play | | | |
| **5** drink | | | |
| **6** listen to | | | |
| **7** watch | | | |

You will find the new vocabulary at the end of exercise 2.

**2  Match each of the drawings in the previous activity with one of the following phrases. For more of a challenge, cover the transliteration column and work only with the Greek script!**

  **a**  [THiavázo efimeríTHa].      Διαβάζω εφημερίδα.

  **b**  [pézo poTHósfero].        Παίζω ποδόσφαιρο.

  **c**  [akoó-o raTHiófono].      Ακούω ραδιόφωνο.

  **d**  [kapnízo tsigáro].         Καπνίζω τσιγάρο.

**e** [vlépo tileórasi].      Βλέπω τηλεόραση.
**f** [káthome spíti].      Κάθομαι σπίτι.
**g** [píno kafé].      Πίνω καφέ.

---

**NEW WORDS**

| [kapnízo] | **καπνίζω** | *I smoke* |
| [tsigáro] | **τσιγάρο** | *cigarette* |
| [efimeríTHa] | **εφημερίδα** | *newspaper* |
| [pézo] | **παίζω** | *I play* |

---

**3** Combine one sentence fragment in a–e with another in 1–5 to make complete sentences. Note that in some cases more than one option is possible and so you should give all possible answers in each case.

**a** [sheTHón poté THen vlépo tileórasi ótan] …

**1** … [káthome spíti].

**b** [pánda kapnízo tsigára ótan] …

**2** … [éhi poTHósfero].

**c** [polés forés THiavázo vivlía ótan] …

**3** … [íme megálos].

**d** [spánia pézo poTHósfero ótan] …

**4** … [THen kséro ti álo na káno].

**e** [merikés forés akoó-o raTHiófono ótan] …

**5** … [píno kafé].

**4** The verbs are missing in these sentences. Can you fill them in? The English verbs in the box might help you a little, if you translate them first!

> listen   watch   read
> like   dislike   prefer

**a** [o níkos poté THen] _____ [tileórasi].
**b** [i maría ke o THimítris pánda] _____ [raTHiófono].
**c** _____ [ta laiká ke to rok].
**d** [emís stin eláTHa] _____ [polá vivlía].
**e** [egó] _____ [ta tsigára].

**5** Now translate each sentence in the previous exercise into English.

 **6** 09.08 Listen to the audio and tick the types of music Angelos, Despina and Arianna like.

|  | Άγγελος | Δέσποινα | Αριάννα |
|---|---|---|---|
| [laiká] |  |  |  |
| [elafrolaiká] |  |  |  |
| [rebétika] |  |  |  |
| [tzaz] |  |  |  |
| [rok] |  |  |  |
| [blooz] |  |  |  |

 **7** 09.09 Listen again to Conversation 2 and complete each sentence by choosing one word from the box.

> [forés]  [piyéno]  [siníthos]
> [marésoon]  [THiavázo]
> [enTHiaféron]  [thríler]  [troháTHin]

| Mary | [elpíTHa], [éhis hóbi]? |
|---|---|
| **Elpitha** | [ne] **a** _____ [polí ta spor]. |
| **Mary** | **b** _____ [ti spor]? |
| **Elpitha** | [marési to] **c** _____ [to básket] [ke to ténis]. [polés] **d** _____ [páo sto théatro] [i sto sinemá].[esí]? [ti hóbi éhis]? |
| **Mary** | [marési na] **e** _____ [vóltes] [i na káthome spíti] [ke na] **f** _____. |
| **Elpitha** | [ti vivlía] **g** _____ [THiavázis]? |
| **Mary** | [kiríos mithistorímata] [alá ke] [vivlía] **h** _____. |

# Test yourself

1 Name three different kinds of music (not including jazz, rock or blues!).
2 Name three different kinds of books.
3 Name three different kinds of films.
4 Ask someone how they spend their free time.
5 How do you spend your free time? Give three answers.
6 In Conversation 2 you were introduced to the new words [troháTHin], [vóltes], [enTHiaféron], [siníthos] and [kiríos]. Can you write them in Greek script and then translate them into English?
7 Can you give the opposites of the following words: [poté], [spánia], [marési], [komoTHíes]?

## SELF CHECK

| | I CAN... |
|---|---|
| ● | ...talk about my free time. |
| ● | ...ask others about their hobbies. |
| ● | ...name different kinds of Greek music and different types of books and films. |
| ● | ...use some loanwords in Greek. |

# 10 Στη λαϊκή αγορά

## At the fruit and vegetable market

**In this unit you will learn how to:**

▶ *ask for things in different amounts and quantities.*
▶ *ask how much something costs.*
▶ *say the names of different fruit, vegetables and herbs.*
▶ *describe different moods you are in.*
▶ *count from 1,000 to 10,000.*

**CEFR: (A2)** *Can understand sentences and frequently used expressions related to shopping; Can give and receive information about quantities, numbers, prices, etc.; Can make simple purchases by stating what is wanted and asking the price.*

## Στη λαϊκή αγορά *At the fruit and vegetable market*

Visitors to Greece will probably come across a [laikí agorá] **λαϊκή αγορά** *fruit and vegetable market* one way or another. Many local farmers sell their produce in different neighbourhoods every day. You can also go directly to the [kendrikí laikí agorá] **κεντρική λαϊκή αγορά** *central market*, which is open five or six days a week in many cities. You will also find a [psaragorá] **ψαραγορά** *fish market* in many places, especially those close to the sea.

Greece produces several types of fruit, including [stafília] **σταφύλια** *grapes*, [karpoózia] **καρπούζια** *watermelons*, [portokália] **πορτοκάλια** *oranges* and [míla] **μήλα** *apples*. It also produces many different vegetables, such as [patátes] **πατάτες** *potatoes*, [domátes] **ντομάτες** *tomatoes* and [karóta] **καρότα** *carrots*. Some fish local to Greece are [barboónia] **μπαρμπούνια** *red mullet*, [tsipoóres] **τσιπούρες** *bream*, [lavrákia] **λαυράκια** *bass* and [péstrofes] **πέστροφες** *trout*. Don't miss the opportunity to ask for local products wherever you are – many of them have a seal awarded by the National Food Association which testifies to their good quality. Look for products with the words **ΠΟΠ (Προϊόντα με Ονομασία Προέλευσης)** *Produce with Designation of Origin* or **ΠΓΕ (Προϊόντα με Γεωγραφική Ένδειξη)** *Produce with Geographical Indication*.

134

The words for the different types of fruit, vegetables and fish in the text are in the plural. Can you work out what the singular forms are?

#  Vocabulary builder

**ΦΡΟΥΤΑ, ΛΑΧΑΝΙΚΑ ΚΑΙ ΜΥΡΩΔΙΚΑ** *FRUIT, VEGETABLES AND HERBS*

 **1 10.01 Look at the words and complete the missing English expressions. Then listen and try to imitate the pronunciation of the speakers.**

| [froóta] | **Φρούτα** | **Fruit** |
|---|---|---|
| [o ananás] | ο ανανάς | _____ |
| [i banána] | η μπανάνα | *banana* |
| [i fráoola] | η φράουλα | *strawberry* |
| [to stafíli] | το σταφύλι | *grape* |
| [to pepóni] | το πεπόνι | *melon* |
| | | |
| **[lahaniká]** | **Λαχανικά** | **Vegetables** |
| [i patáta] | η πατάτα | _____ |
| [i domáta] | η ντομάτα | _____ |
| [to karóto] | το καρότο | _____ |
| [to kolokitháki] | το κολοκυθάκι | *courgette* |
| | | |
| **[miroTHiká]** | **Μυρωδικά** | **Herbs** |
| [o ánithos] | ο άνιθος | *dill* |
| [o maindanós] | ο μαϊντανός | *parsley* |
| [to aláti] | το αλάτι | _____ |
| [to pipéri] | το πιπέρι | _____ |

**2** **10.02** The following are useful questions and answers that will help you if you go grocery shopping in Greece. Read the phrases and complete the missing English expressions. Then listen and repeat after the speakers.

| [póso thélete]? | Πόσο θέλετε; | How much do you want? |
|---|---|---|
| [pósa thélete]? | Πόσα θέλετε; | How many _____? |
| [pósa kilá]? | Πόσα κιλά; | How _____ kilos? |
| [póso káni]? | Πόσο κάνει; | How _____ is it? |
| [póso kánoon]? | Πόσο κάνουν; | How much _____? |
| [éna kiló]. | Ένα κιλό. | One kilo. |
| [THío kilá parakaló]. | Δύο κιλά παρακαλώ. | Two kilos please. |
| [misó kiló féta THoTHónis]. | Μισό κιλό φέτα Δωδώνης. | Half a _____ of Dodonis feta. |
| [triakósia ghramária parakaló]. | Τριακόσια γραμμάρια παρακαλώ. | Three hundred _____ please. |
| [kánoon tría evró akrivós]. | Κάνουν τρία ευρώ ακριβώς. | They are three euros exactly. |
| [káni THío evró ke íkosi leptá]. | Κάνει δύο ευρώ και είκοσι λεπτά. | It's two _____ and 20 cents. |

 **3** **10.03** Read the following Greek words and for each one choose the correct English equivalent from the box. Then listen and compare your answers. Listen again and repeat after the speakers.

> supermarket    hypermarket
> fruit and vegetable shop
> greengrocer    grocery store
> mini market
> weekly fruit and vegetable market

**a** [pandopolío] παντοπωλείο
**b** [manáviko] μανάβικο
**c** [oporopantopolío] οπωροπαντοπωλείο
**d** [laikí agorá] λαϊκή αγορά
**e** [super market] σούπερ
**f** [iperaghorá] υπεραγορά
**g** [bakáliko] μπακάλικο

# Conversation 1 **Έρχεσαι μαζί μου;** *Are you coming with me?*

**NEW WORDS AND EXPRESSIONS 1**

**10.04** **Listen to the words and expressions that are used in the next conversation. Note their meanings.**

| | | |
|---|---|---|
| [koorazméni] | κουρασμένη | *tired* |
| [yiatí rotás]? | γιατί ρωτάς; | *Why do you ask?* |
| [prépi na páo] | πρέπει να πάω | *I have to go* |
| [agorá] | αγορά | *market* |
| [laikí agorá] | λαϊκή αγορά | *fruit and vegetable market* |
| [yia lígo] | για λίγο | *for a little while* |
| [érhese]? | Έρχεσαι; | *Are you coming?* |
| [iTHéa] | ιδέα | *idea* |
| [me ta póTHia] | με τα πόδια | *on foot* (lit. *with the feet*) |
| [meriká] | μερικά | *some* |

**10.05** *Elpitha has to go to the local fruit and vegetable market. She asks Mary to join her.*

**1   Listen to the conversation a couple of times. Will Mary go with Elpitha?**

| | | |
|---|---|---|
| **Elpitha** | Mary, [íse koorazméni]? | Mary, are you tired? |
| **Mary** | [óhi], [yiatí rotás]? | No, why do you ask? |
| **Elpitha** | [prépi na páo] [stin laikí agorá] [yia lígo]. [érhese mazí moo]? | I have to go to the fruit and vegetable market for a little while. Are you coming with me? |
| **Mary** | [oréa iTHéa]. [poo íne]? | Good idea. Where is it? |
| **Elpitha** | [íne kondá]. [boroóme na páme] [me ta póTHia]. [thélo na agoráso] [meriká froóta] [ke lahaniká] | It's close by. We can go on foot. I want to buy some fruit and vegetables. |
| **Ελπίδα** | Mary, είσαι κουρασμένη; | |
| **Mary** | Όχι, γιατί ρωτάς; | |

| | |
|---|---|
| **Ελπίδα** | Πρέπει να πάω στην λαϊκή αγορά για λίγο. Έρχεσαι μαζί μου; |
| **Mary** | Ωραία ιδέα. Πού είναι; |
| **Ελπίδα** | Είναι κοντά. Μπορούμε να πάμε με τα πόδια. Θέλω να αγοράσω μερικά φρούτα και λαχανικά. |
| **Mary** | Έλα. Πάμε. |

2 **Now read the conversation and answer the questions.**
   a Is the fruit and vegetable market far away?
   b How will they get there?

 3 **Listen again and pay special attention to the words which run together. Practise speaking the part of Elpitha.**

# Language discovery 1

1 **The conversation has three expressions that contain the particle να. Look at their English translations and find the corresponding Greek phrase in each case. Can you see when this particle is used?**
   a I want to buy
   b We can go
   c I have to go

2 **It is useful to be able to say where people, objects or places are. Look at the following pairs of adverbs. Can you match them with their Greek counterparts?**
   a near/far          1 εδώ/εκεί
   b above/below       2 κοντά/μακριά
   c here/there        3 πάνω/κάτω

3 **Elpitha asks Mary if she is tired. If you look up the word for** *tired* **in a dictionary, you will find the following three forms. Decide which of the three is masculine, which is feminine and which is neuter.**
   a κουρασμέν-ος
   b κουρασμέν-η
   c κουρασμέν-ο

## 1 CONNECTING TWO VERBS

The word [na] **va** is a particle in Greek and is used to connect two verbs, hence it is also sometimes called a 'connector'. Connectors are sometimes omitted in English; for instance in the sentences *I like buying fruit* and *I must go there* the two verbs *like + buy* and *must + go* can coexist in the same sentence quite happily. In Greek, on the other hand, it is necessary to use [na] **va** to connect the two verbs:

| | | |
|---|---|---|
| [marési na agorázo froóta]. | **M'αρέσει να αγοράζω φρούτα.** | *I like buying fruit.* |
| [prépi na páo ekí]. | **Πρέπει να πάω εκεί.** | *I must go there.* |

There is no exception to this rule. An additional thing to bear in mind is that after [na] **va**, a different form of the verb is often used. You don't need to know more about this for the time being – just learn each verb on a case-by-case basis as you go along.

## 2 ADVERBS OF PLACE

In past units you learned some adverbs of time. If you got the answers to exercise 2 correct, you will have matched the following:

a *near/far*: **κοντά/μακριά**
b *above/below*: **πάνω/κάτω**
c *here/there*: **εδώ/εκεί**

Here are some more pairs of adverbs you will find useful when you want to indicate where something or someone is located. Try to learn them in pairs if you can.

| | |
|---|---|
| **μπροστά από/πίσω από** | *in front of/behind* |
| **μέσα σε/έξω από** | *inside/outside* |
| **δίπλα σε/γύρω από** | *next to/around* |

> **LANGUAGE TIP**
> Note that these words are all adverbs in Greek but in English *in front of*, *behind* and *next to* are all prepositions. *Inside*, *outside* and *around* can be either adverbs or prepositions.

## 3 ADJECTIVES DESCRIBING MOODS

You may have worked out by now that learning Greek adjectives can be challenging, as compared to only one form in English, Greek has different forms for singular and plural, as well as for the three genders.

**Look at the pictures showing the different moods listed. Can you give the correct gender and the English translation in each case?**

**a** [eftihizméni] ευτυχισμένη
**b** [thimoménos] θυμωμένος
**c** [lipiméni] λυπημένη
**d** [ékplikti] έκπληκτη
**e** [pinazménos] πεινασμένος
**f** [THipsazménos] διψασμένος
**g** [taragméni] ταραγμένη
**h** [koorazméni] κουρασμένη

The two adjectives [pinazménos] **πεινασμένος** *hungry* and [THipsazménos] **διψασμένος** *thirsty* are not used very frequently. Instead the verbs [pináo] **πεινάω** *be hungry* and [THipsáo] **διψάω** *be thirsty* are normally used instead. You should remember that you met the questions [pináte]? **πεινάτε;** *are you hungry?* and [THipsáte]? **διψάτε;** *are you thirsty?* in Unit 6.

# Conversation 2 **Στη λαϊκή αγορά** *At the fruit and vegetable market*

**NEW WORDS AND EXPRESSIONS 2**

**10.06 Listen to the words and expressions that are used in the next conversation. Note their meanings.**

| [kózmos] | κόσμος | people (here: crowded place) |
| [poloós] | πολλούς | many |
| [anthrópoos] | ανθρώπους | people |
| [pánda] | πάντα | always |
| [ipárhoon] | υπάρχουν | there are |
| [míla] | μήλα | apples |
| [portokália] | πορτοκάλια | oranges |
| [banánes] | μπανάνες | bananas |
| [na pároome] | να πάρουμε | to get/to buy (lit. to take) |
| [karpoózia] | καρπούζια | watermelons |
| [epohí] | εποχή | season |
| [fisiká] | φυσικά | naturally |
| [pio] | πιο | more, further |
| [fréska] | φρέσκα | fresh |
| [maroóli] | μαρούλι | lettuce |
| [agoória] | αγγούρια | cucumbers |

 **10.07** *Elpitha and Mary are walking in a noisy, crowded market among stalls with fresh fruit and vegetables.*

## 1 Listen to the conversation a couple of times. Is the market always busy?

| **Mary** | [po-po kózmos]! [polis kózmos]! | *Wow! It's crowded! Very crowded!* |
| **Elpitha** | [ne], [pánda éhi poloós anthrópoos eTHó]. [na]! [eTHó ipárhoon] [oréa míla] [portokália ke banánes]. [ti sarési na pároome]? | *Yes, there are always a lot of people. Here! There are some nice apples, oranges and bananas. What would you like us to get?* |
| **Mary** | [na pároome míla]. [ipárhoon karpoózia] [aftí tin epohí]? | *Let's get some apples. Are there any watermelons at this time of the year?* |
| **Elpitha** | [ne, fisiká]. [lígo pio káto]. [eTHó éhi] [kalá ke fréska] [lahaniká]. [thélo nagoráso] [éna maroóli], [THío agoória] [kéna kilo domátes]. | *Yes, of course. A little bit further down. Here are some nice fresh vegetables. I want to buy one lettuce, two cucumbers and one kilo of tomatoes.* |

| Mary | Πω-πω κόσμος! Πολύς κόσμος! |
| **Ελπίδα** | Ναι, πάντα έχει πολλούς ανθρώπους εδώ. Νά! Εδώ υπάρχουν ωραία μήλα, πορτοκάλια και μπανάνες. Τι σ'αρέσει να πάρουμε; |
| **Mary** | Να πάρουμε μήλα. Υπάρχουν καρπούζια αυτή την εποχή; |
| **Ελπίδα** | Ναι, φυσικά. Λίγο πιο κάτω. Εδώ έχει καλά και φρέσκα λαχανικά. Θέλω ν'αγοράσω ένα μαρούλι, δύο αγγούρια κι ένα κιλό ντομάτες. |

2 **Now read the conversation and answer the questions.**
   a  What would Mary like to get?
   b  What vegetables does Elpitha want?

3 **Listen again and pay special attention to the words which run together. Practise speaking the part of Elpitha.**

## 💡 Language discovery 2

1 **The conversation has three expressions that use the particle [na] να. Look at their English translations and find the corresponding Greek phrase in each case.**
   a  I'd like to get
   b  What would you like us to get?
   c  Let's get some apples.

2 **The conversation has also a fourth να but this time the α has a stress mark – νά. What does νά mean?**

3 **There are three instances of an adjective describing a noun in this conversation. Look at their English translations and find the corresponding Greek phrase in each case. Can you work out the rule of thumb with regard to the endings of the adjectives?**
   a  nice apples
   b  fresh vegetables
   c  many people

### 1 OMITTING ONE OF TWO VERBS

As you have seen in this unit, the particle [na] **να** is necessary when two verbs are connected in one sentence. Here are some important verbal constructions that use this particle:

| [prépi na] | **πρέπει να** | *must/have to/is necessary to* |
| [boró na] | **μπορώ να** | *can/be able to* |
| [borí na] | **μπορεί να** | *may/is possible to* |
| [thélo na] | **θέλω να** | *want to/would like to* |
| [marési na] | **μ'αρέσει να** | *like to* |

In this second conversation, you may have noticed a sentence with the particle [na] **να** where the first verb was omitted: [na pároome míla]. **Να πάρουμε μήλα.** This is an idiomatic use and you will encounter it especially in everyday language. In English, it is always necessary to use both verbs. Look at the following examples and their translations:

| **Να πάρουμε μήλα.** | *Let's get some apples.* |
| **Να πάρουμε μήλα;** | *Shall we get some apples?* |
| **Να ακούσουμε μουσική.** | *Let's listen to some music.* |
| **Να ακούσουμε μουσική;** | *Shall we listen to some music?* |

## 2 WORDS WITH OR WITHOUT A STRESS MARK

As exercise 2 will have shown you, there are a few words in Greek where the stress mark will signal a difference in either pronunciation or meaning or both! Here are a few examples, beginning with the one you have already seen:

**να/νά**: the first is the particle *to* and the second the word *here* or *there* when you show someone something.

**η/ή**: the first is the article *the* and the second the word *or*. The second word is pronounced differently – with a longer sound – than the first.

**που/πού**: the first is the relative pronoun *where*, *who* or *which* and the second the question word *where?*

**μια/μία**: both words mean *a*, *an* or *one*, although they are pronounced differently.

## 3 THE NUMBERS 1,000–10,000

**10.08 Now practise the numbers 1,000 to 10,000. If you prefer, you can say the numbers first and then listen and compare your pronunciation.**

| | | |
|---|---|---|
| [hílji], [hílies], [hília] | **χίλιοι** (m), **χίλιες** (f), **χίλια** (n) | *1,000* |
| [THío hiliáTHes] | **δύο χιλιάδες** | *2,000* |
| [tris hiliáTHes] | **τρεις χιλιάδες** | *3,000* |
| [téseris hiliáTHes] | **τέσσερις χιλιάδες** | *4,000* |
| [pénde hiliáTHes] | **πέντε χιλιάδες** | *5,000* |
| [éksi hiliáTHes] | **έξι χιλιάδες** | *6,000* |
| [eptá hiliáTHes] | **επτά χιλιάδες** | *7,000* |
| [októ hiliáTHes] | **οκτώ χιλιάδες** | *8,000* |
| [eniá hiliáTHes] | **εννιά χιλιάδες** | *9,000* |
| [THéka hiliáTHes] | **δέκα χιλιάδες** | *10,000* |

---

**GREEK MONEY**

The currency used in Greece is the euro. The word for *euro* is [evró] **ευρώ** (note the stress on the second syllable) and it does not change in the plural. Some examples:

| [éna evró] | **ένα ευρώ** | *one euro* |
|---|---|---|
| [THéka evró] | **δέκα ευρώ** | *ten euros* |
| [hília evró] | **χίλια ευρώ** | *1,000 euros* |
| [pénde hiliádes evró] | **πέντε χιλιάδες ευρώ** | *5,000 euros* |

### 4 YES AND NO

The words [ne] **ναι** *yes* and [óhi] **όχι** *no* will come in useful in most situations. You might also encounter some other ways of answering affirmatively: [fisiká] **φυσικά** *naturally*, [vévea] **βέβαια** *of course/sure*, [amé] **αμέ** *yeah*.

Bear in mind that non-verbal ways of saying *yes* and *no* are probably different from what you are familiar with. Greeks express *yes* by tilting their head downwards and keeping it down. A non-verbal *no* is expressed by tilting the head backwards and looking up, with eyebrows raised. To answer *no*, it is sometimes enough just to raise the eyebrows.

 Practice

1 **There are some fruits, herbs and vegetables mixed up in the box. Can you separate them into three groups?**

| ΦΡΟΥΤΑ | ΛΑΧΑΝΙΚΑ | ΜΥΡΩΔΙΚΑ |
|--------|----------|----------|
|        |          |          |
|        |          |          |
|        |          |          |

**2  Remember that the various forms for the definite article (the word** *the*) **can be challenging in Greek. Go back to the previous exercise and add both the singular and the plural form of the definite article to each word. The first ones have been done for you.**

[i banána] – [i banánes]

[to kolokitháki] – [ta kolokithákia]

**3  Can you now write out all the words in the previous exercise in Greek script? Give it a try and see how familiar you have now become with the Greek alphabet. The first ones have been done for you.**

η μπανάνα – οι μπανάνες

το κολοκυθάκι – τα κολοκυθάκια

**4  Look at the picture. Can you name the fruit and vegetables? The new vocabulary you need has been provided. Give the appropriate singular or plural form as needed. The first ones have been done for you.**

| [to skórTHo] | το σκόρδο | *garlic* |
| [to ahláTHi] | το αχλάδι | *pear* |

**a** [ta karóta]          **1** [to portokáli]

**b** _____     **2** _____

**c** _____     **3** _____

**d** _____     **4** _____

**5** The shopkeeper has told you how much you need to pay for the things you have just bought. Write the transliteration and/or Greek script for each amount.

    **a** 50€ _____

    **b** 17€ _____

    **c** 100€ _____

    **d** 12€ _____

    **e** 34€ _____

    **f** 70€ _____

**6** Match each figure with the correct words.

    **a** 1650           **1** οχτώ χιλιάδες τριακόσια

    **b** 2500           **2** πέντε χιλιάδες εφτακόσια πενήντα

    **c** 4100           **3** δύο χιλιάδες πεντακόσια

    **d** 5750           **4** έξι χιλιάδες εννιακόσια

    **e** 6900           **5** χίλια εξακόσια πενήντα

    **f** 8300           **6** τέσσερις χιλιάδες εκατό

**7** Use the phrases in the box to help you translate the following sentences.

> [prépi na]   [thélo na]   [boró na]
> [marési na]   [borí na]

    **a** I like going for walks with you.

    **b** I want to go to the fruit and vegetable market.

    **c** I must see you.

    **d** I can become angry.

    **e** Perhaps her name is Helen.

**8** Look at the people in the picture and work out what mood they are in. Then choose the correct word from the right-hand column. Work with the transliteration or, for more of a challenge, the Greek script.

 a
 b
 c
 d
 e
 f

| | | |
|---|---|---|
| a \_\_\_\_ | **1** | [lipiméni] λυπημένη |
| b \_\_\_\_ | **2** | [thimoménos] θυμωμένος |
| c \_\_\_\_ | **3** | [eftihizméni] ευτυχισμένη |
| d \_\_\_\_ | **4** | [pinazménos] πεινασμένος |
| e \_\_\_\_ | **5** | [THipsazménos] διψασμένος |
| f \_\_\_\_ | **6** | [koorazméni] κουρασμένη |

**9** 10.09 **Listen again to Conversation 2 and complete each sentence by choosing one word from the box. Note that one answer is used twice!**

> [kiló]  [fisiká]  [epohí]
> [agoória]  [lahaniká]
> [káto]  [portokália]  [ipárhoon]

| | |
|---|---|
| **Mary** | [po-po kózmos]! [polís kózmos]! |
| **Elpitha** | [ne], [pánda éhi poloós anthrópoos eTHó]. [na]! [eTHó] **a** _____ [oréa míla] **b** _____ [ke banánes]. [ti sarési na pároome]? |
| **Mary** | [na pároome míla]. **c** _____ [karpoózia] [aftí tin] **d** _____? |
| **Elpitha** | [ne] **e** _____ [lígo pio] **f** _____ [eTHó éhi] [kalá ke fréska ] **g** _____ [thélo nagoráso] [éna maroóli], [THío] **h** _____ [kéna] **i** _____ [domátes]. |

## Test yourself

**1** Name four different fruits that you like.

**2** Name four of your favourite vegetables or herbs.

**3** Tell a friend about your moods. Name at least four.

**4** How do you say the following numbers in Greek?

a  450

b  670

c  1,200

d  3,900

e  5,000

f  7,400

g  9,500

h  10,000

**5** Name three different places where you might buy food.

**6** Ask for half a kilo of apples and one kilo of oranges.

**7** Can you ask for the price of something? State both possible ways.

## SELF CHECK

**I CAN. . .**

- . . . ask for things in different amounts and quantities.
- . . . ask how much something costs.
- . . . say the names of different fruit, vegetables and herbs.
- . . . describe different moods I am in.
- . . . count from 1,000 to 10,000.

**1** **Some people tell you at which time they do certain activities. Match each clock face with the correct phrase.** *(12 points)*

**a** [THoolévo apó tis októ méhri tis téseris].
**b** [i maría íne sto spíti apó tis eniámisí méhri tis éksi].
**c** [THen tró-o poté apó tis THoTHekámisi méhri tis eniá].
**d** [íme sti THooliá apó tis eftá méhri tis téseris].
**e** [THen marési na THoolévo apó tis eniá méhri tis pénde].
**f** [o yiórgos vlépi tileórasi apó tis THekámisi méhri tis eptámisi].

**2** **Now translate each phrase from exercise 1 into English.**
*(12 points)*

a _____
b _____
c _____
d _____
e _____
f _____

## 3 Match the phrases with the illustrations. *(12 points)*

**a** [i maría íne stin koozína ke mayirévi].
**b** [o yiánis íne ékso apó to spíti].
**c** [i mitéra moo vlépi polí tileórasi].
**d** [o patéras moo pánda THiavázi efimeríTHa].
**e** [o kóstas akoó-i moosikí óli tin iméra].
**f** [i eléni íne sto grafío apó tis eniá méhri tis mía].

## 4 Now translate each phrase from Activity 3 into English. *(12 points)*

**a** _____
**b** _____
**c** _____
**d** _____
**e** _____
**f** _____

## 5 Can you match each action phrase to the correct illustration?
*(10 points)*

| | | | | |
|---|---|---|---|---|
| **a** | [káno dooz] | **f** | [páo sti THooliá] |
| **b** | [tró-o proinó] | **g** | [févgo apó ti THooliá] |
| **c** | [páo yia ípno] | **h** | [sikónome apó to kreváti] |
| **d** | [ksipnáo stis eptá] | **i** | [etimázome yia THooliá] |
| **e** | [THiavázo sto kreváti] | **j** | [etimázome yia ípno] |

**6 Now write the ten phrases in exercise 5 in Greek script.** *(10 points)*

a _____    f _____
b _____    g _____
c _____    h _____
d _____    i _____
e _____    j _____

**7 Look at the pictures and describe the daily routine in Greek.**
*(24 points)*

| a | _____ | g | _____ |
| b | _____ | h | _____ |
| c | _____ | i | _____ |
| d | _____ | j | _____ |
| e | _____ | k | _____ |
| f | _____ | l | _____ |

8 **Match each phrase to the correct illustration. There are two extra illustrations.** *(8 points)*

**a** Η Μαρία είναι πολύ θυμωμένη σήμερα.
**b** Ο Άγγελος είναι πολύ κουρασμένος τώρα.
**c** Η Ελένη διψάει πολύ. Ένα ποτήρι νερό ...
**d** Ο Κώστας πεινάει τώρα. Θέλει να πάρει κάτι ...

**TOTAL: 100 POINTS**

Congratulations! You have now completed the last exercise in this book. We hope that your journey through *Get started in Greek* was an entertaining one and that you learned many things about this language and rich culture along the way. We also hope that you are going to continue this journey, either by revising some past units or moving on to *Teach yourself Greek, complete course*. No matter what you do, we'd like to wish you **Καλό ταξίδι!**

8 Match each phrase to the correct illustration. There are two extra illustrations to each.

TOTAL: 100 POINTS

# Grammar summary

This grammar summary is intended mainly to act as a reference guide to the language used in the course. It is by no means a complete grammar, although some elements in this section do not appear in the course and are included for learners who wish to progress a little further.

You can skim through this section before you start Unit 1 and you can always refer back whenever you meet a new grammatical point in a unit and compare it with the notes here. Grammatical explanations in the units are somewhat short and to the point, with some examples for practical application. Here the approach is different and more organized and systematic in terms of grouping grammatical points together.

The most important grammatical groups outlined in this section are: **Articles**, **Nouns**, **Adjectives**, **Adverbs**, **Pronouns**, **Prepositions** and **Verbs**. In most instances you will find tables to which the different groups belong, along with a few examples and direct references back to units.

## 1 Articles

The words *a*, *an* and *the* are called **articles** in English. *A* and *an* are called **indefinite articles** and *the* is called the **definite article**. All articles come before a noun. Greek articles have a lot more than three forms! This is because the nouns they define are divided into three genders: masculine (m), feminine (f) and neuter (n). The Greek words for *a*, *an* and *the* are therefore different for each gender. In addition, each noun group has further forms in the singular and plural, so the articles have to agree with these, too.

Greek also has different endings for nouns and their articles (and adjectives – see below) when nouns are used in different ways within a sentence – for example, if they are the subject or the object of the sentence. These different forms of nouns are called **cases**. There are three main cases: nominative (nom), used when the word is the subject of the sentence; genitive (gen), used to show possession, i.e., that something belongs to someone; and accusative (acc), used when the word is the object of the sentence. English grammar has lost virtually all examples of case. The English word *who* is one of the few that can illustrate the idea of case. It is *who* in the nominative case, *whose* in the genitive case and *whom* in the accusative case. The following tables show the different forms of Greek articles.

**INDEFINITE ARTICLE** *A/AN*

|  | Masculine | Feminine | Neuter |
|---|---|---|---|
| nom | **ένας** [énas] | **μία** [mía] | **ένα** [éna] |
| gen | **ενός** [enós] | **μίας** [mías] | **ενός** [enós] |
| acc | **έναν** [énan] | **μία** [mía] | **ένα** [éna] |

**DEFINITE ARTICLE** *THE*

|  | Singular | | | Plural | | |
|---|---|---|---|---|---|---|
|  | Masculine | Feminine | Neuter | Masculine | Feminine | Neuter |
| nom | **ο** [o] | **η** [i] | **το** [to] | **οι** [i] | **οι** [i] | **τα** [ta] |
| gen | **του** [too] | **της** [tis] | **του** [too] | **των** [ton] | **των** [ton] | **των** [ton] |
| acc | **το(ν)** [to(n)] | **τη(ν)** [ti(n)] | **το** [to] | **τους** [toos] | **τις** [tis] | **τα** [ta] |

Articles are often used with the preposition **σε** [se] *at, to, in, on*, creating compound definite articles in the genitive and accusative cases only. The words in the singular are: **στου** [stoo], **στης** [stis], **στο(ν)** [sto(n)], **στη(ν)** [sti(n)], and in the plural: **στων** [ston], **στους** [stoos], **στις** [stis], **στα** [sta]. These compound words cannot stand as two separate words, e.g. **σε του** [se] [too].

# 2 Nouns

The names of people and things are called **nouns**. As already stated, Greek nouns are divided into three genders, and each noun has a singular and plural form, and changes according to the role it plays in the sentence (its case) – nominative, genitive, accusative. When you look up nouns in a dictionary you will find them in the nominative singular form. You can usually tell their gender by their endings. Most masculine nouns end in **-ας** [-as], **-ης** [-is] and **-ος** [-os], most feminine nouns in **-α** [-a] and **-η** [-i], and most neuter nouns in **-ι** [-i], **-ο** [-o] and **-μα** [-ma]. The course has introduced most nouns in the nominative case either in singular or plural. Some genitive and accusative forms have appeared in a few conversations without any special mention. As a rule of thumb, remember that nouns in the nominative case come before the verb and indicate the subject of the sentence, nouns in the accusative case come after the verb and indicate the object. The genitive case is used to show possession. The different forms are set out as follows:

## MASCULINE NOUNS

| | Singular | Plural |
|---|---|---|
| nom | **ο φίλος** [o fílos] | **οι φίλοι** [i fíli] |
| gen | **του φίλου** [too fíloo] | **των φίλων** [ton fílon] |
| acc | **τον φίλο** [ton fílo] | **τους φίλους** [toos fíloos] |

## FEMININE NOUNS

| | Singular | Plural |
|---|---|---|
| nom | **η κουζίνα** [i koozína] | **οι κουζίνες** [i koozínes] |
| gen | **της κουζίνας** [tis koozínas] | **των κουζινών** [ton koozinón] |
| acc | **την κουζίνα** [tin koozína] | **τις κουζίνες** [tis koozínes] |

## NEUTER NOUNS

| | Singular | Plural |
|---|---|---|
| nom | **το βιβλίο** [to vivlío] | **τα βιβλία** [ta vivlía] |
| gen | **του βιβλίου** [too vivlíoo] | **των βιβλίων** [ton vivlíon] |
| acc | **το βιβλίο** [to vivlío] | **τα βιβλία** [ta vivlía] |

# 3 Adjectives

**Adjectives** are words which describe people or things. They give more information about the noun they describe. Note: *a car* (noun), *a **big** car* (adjective-noun), *a **big red** car* (adjective-adjective-noun). The endings of adjectives change according to the noun they describe, i.e. masculine, feminine or neuter endings, singular or plural, nominative, genitive, accusative. Most adjectives have the same endings as the word **μεγάλος** [megálos] *big*:

## SINGULAR

| | Masculine | Feminine | Neuter |
|---|---|---|---|
| nom | **μεγάλος** [megálos] | **μεγάλη** [megáli] | **μεγάλο** [megálo] |
| gen | **μεγάλου** [megáloo] | **μεγάλης** [megális] | **μεγάλου** [megáloo] |
| acc | **μεγάλο** [megálo] | **μεγάλη** [megáli] | **μεγάλο** [megálo] |

## PLURAL

| | Masculine | Feminine | Neuter |
|---|---|---|---|
| nom | **μεγάλοι** [megáli] | **μεγάλες** [megáles] | **μεγάλα** [megála] |
| gen | **μεγάλων** [megálon] | **μεγάλων** [megálon] | **μεγάλων** [megálon] |
| acc | **μεγάλους** [megáloos] | **μεγάλες** [megáles] | **μεγάλα** [megála] |

# 4 Adverbs

**Adverbs** are words which usually describe the way things happen. Unlike adjectives, which give more information about the nouns they describe, adverbs give more information about the verbs they describe. Many Greek adverbs end in **-α** [-a] or **-ως** [-os], similar to the ending *-ly* of many English adverbs. Some examples include: **γρήγορα** [grígora] *quickly*, **καλά** [kalá] *well, nicely*, **βέβαια** [vévea] *of course, surely*.

Many Greek adverbs are formed from their corresponding adverbs. Notice the changes below: **γρήγορος** [grígoros] *fast, quick*, **γρήγορα** [grígora] *quickly*, **καλός** [kalós] *good, nice*, **καλά** [kalá] *nicely*, **βέβαιος** [véveos] *certain, sure*, **βέβαια** [vévea] *surely*. Unlike adjectives, adverbs have only one form. There is a small exception to this remark regarding a few adverbs which have two almost similar forms which are interchangeable in use. Some examples are **βέβαια** [vévea] and **βεβαίως** [vevéos] *of course, surely* and **σπάνια** [spánia] and **σπανίως** [spaníos] *rarely*.

# 5 Pronouns

Words such as *I, you, he* or *my, your, his* or *myself, yourself, himself* or *me, you, him*, etc. are pronouns. Pronouns are grouped in several sub-categories: personal, reflexive, demonstrative, possessive, relative, interrogative and indefinite pronouns.

**PERSONAL PRONOUNS**

| | Nominative | | Genitive | | Accusative | |
|---|---|---|---|---|---|---|
| | strong | weak | strong | weak | strong | weak |
| *I* | **εγώ** [egó] | – | **εμένα** [eména] | **μου** [moo] | **εμένα** [eména] | **με** [me] |
| *you* (sing/infml) | **εσύ** [esí] | – | **εσένα** [eséna] | **σου** [soo] | **εσένα** [eséna] | **σε** [se] |
| *he* | **αυτός** [aftós] | **τος** [tos] | **αυτού** [aftoó] | **του** [too] | **αυτόν** [aftón] | **τον** [ton] |
| *she* | **αυτή** [aftí] | **τη** [ti] | **αυτής** [aftís] | **της** [tis] | **αυτή(ν)** [aftí(n)] | **τη(ν)** [ti(n)] |
| *it* | **αυτό** [aftó] | **το** [to] | **αυτού** [aftoó] | **του** [too] | **αυτό** [aftó] | **το** [to] |
| *we* | **εμείς** [emís] | – | **εμάς** [emás] | **μας** [mas] | **εμάς** [emás] | **μας** [mas] |

| you (pl/ fml) | εσείς [esís] | – | εσάς [esás] | σας [sas] | εσάς [esás] | σας [sas] |
| they | αυτοί [aftí] | τοι [ti] | αυτών [aftón] | τους [toos] | αυτούς [aftoós] | τους [toos] |
|  | αυτές [aftés] | τες [tes] | αυτές [aftés] | τις/τες [tis/tes] |  |  |
|  | αυτά [aftá] | τα [ta] | αυτά [aftá] | τα [ta] |  |  |

Personal pronouns have both a strong and a weak form in the genitive and accusative cases.

Most Greek verbs like **έχω** [ého] *I have* take the nominative form of the personal pronoun, which is not absolutely necessary as it is in English, because the ending of the verb itself shows who is the subject. Some verbs like **μου αρέσει** [moo arési] *I like* or **με λένε** [me léne] *I am called* take the genitive or accusative form of the personal pronoun respectively. All strong forms are used for the purpose of emphasis in Greek. It is even possible to use both the strong and weak forms for extra emphasis. For example, **εμένα μου αρέσει το ράδιο** [eména moo arési to ráTHio] *I like the radio* or **εμένα με λένε Δημήτρη** [eména me léne THimítri] *I am called Dimitri*.

### REFLEXIVE PRONOUNS

Words like *myself, yourself,* etc. are reflexive pronouns. They are not as common in Greek as in English and they usually appear only in the accusative form with prepositions, e.g. **με τον εαυτό μου** [me ton eaftó moo] *with myself,* **για τον εαυτό της** [yia ton eaftó tis] *for herself,* **στον (σε | τον) εαυτό τους** [ston eaftó toos] *to themselves.*

### DEMONSTRATIVE PRONOUNS

|  | **Masculine** | **Feminine** | **Neuter** |
|---|---|---|---|
| this | αυτός [aftós] | αυτή [aftí] | αυτό [aftó] |
| these | αυτοί [aftí] | αυτές [aftés] | αυτά [aftá] |
| that | εκείνος [ekínos] | εκείνη [ekíni] | εκείνο [ekíno] |
| those | εκείνοι [ekíni] | εκείνες [ekínes] | εκείνα [ekína] |
| such a | τέτοιος [tétios] | τέτοια [tétia] | τέτοιο [tétio] |
| such (pl) | τέτοιοι [tétyi] | τέτοιες [téties] | τέτοια [tétia] |
| so much | τόσος [tósos] | τόση [tósi] | τόσο [tóso] |
| so many | τόσοι [tósi] | τόσες [tóses] | τόσα [tósa] |

Note that the different forms in the singular and plural for **αυτός**, **εκείνος** and **τόσος** are identical to the adjective **μεγάλος, -η, -ο** as shown in the previous paragraph in this section.

Note too that the demonstrative pronouns **αυτός** and **εκείνος** need the corresponding article for the noun in use, e.g. **αυτός ο άντρας** [aftós o ándras] *this man*, **εκείνη η γυναίκα** [ekíni i yinéka] *that woman*, **αυτά τα παιδιά** [aftá ta peTHiá] *these children*.

## POSSESSIVE PRONOUNS

| | | |
|---|---|---|
| *my* | **μου** | [moo] |
| *your* (sing/infml) | **σου** | [soo] |
| *his* | **του** | [too] |
| *her* | **της** | [tis] |
| *its* | **του** | [too] |
| *our* | **μας** | [mas] |
| *your* (pl/fml) | **σας** | [sas] |
| *their* | **τους** | [toos] |

Possessive pronouns have only one form in Greek. They always come after the noun they modify, whereas in English they come before the noun. In Greek, the noun is accompanied by its corresponding article, e.g. **το σπίτι μου** [to spíti moo] *my house*, **τα σπίτια μας** [ta spítia mas] *our houses*, **ο φίλος της** [o fílos tis] *her friend*, **οι φίλοι τους** [i fíli toos] *their friends*.

These words are called possessive pronouns in Greek grammar and possessive adjectives in English grammar!

## RELATIVE PRONOUNS

| | | |
|---|---|---|
| *who* | **που** | [poo] |
| *which* | **που** | [poo] |
| *that* | **που** | [poo] |
| *whatever* | **ό,τι** | [óti] |

## INTERROGATIVE PRONOUNS

| | | |
|---|---|---|
| *what?* | **τι;** | [ti]? |
| *where?* | **πού;** | [poo]? |

| | | |
|---|---|---|
| *how?* | **πώς;** | [pos]? |
| *why?* | **γιατί;** | [yiatí]? |
| *when?* | **πότε;** | [póte]? |

| | Masculine | Feminine | Neuter |
|---|---|---|---|
| *who? which?* | **ποιος;** [pios]? | **ποια;** [pia]? | **ποιο;** [pio]? |
| *how much?* | **πόσος;** [pósos]? | **πόση;** [pósi]? | **πόσο;** [póso]? |
| *which ones?* | **ποιοι;** [pyi]? | **ποιες;** [pies]? | **ποια;** [pia]? |
| *how many?* | **πόσοι;** [pósi]? | **πόσες;** [póses]? | **πόσα;** [pósa]? |

Question words like *what? who? how? where?* are interrogative pronouns.
Some have only one form, some more than one for m/f/n use.

## INDEFINITE PRONOUNS

| | | |
|---|---|---|
| *all, everything* | **όλα** | [óla] plural |
| *something, anything?* | **κάτι** | [káti] |
| *nothing, anything?* | **τίποτα** | [típota] |
| *every, each* | **κάθε** | [káthe] |

| | Masculine | Feminine | Neuter |
|---|---|---|---|
| *everyone* (m/f/n) | **καθένας** [kathénas] | **καθεμία** [kathemía] | **καθένα** [kathéna] |
| *everybody* (m/f/n) (pl) | **όλοι** [óli] | **όλες** [óles] | **όλα** [óla] |
| *some* (pl) | **μερικοί** [merikí] | **μερικές** [merikés] | **μερικά** [meriká] |
| *someone, something* (m/f/n) | **κάποιος** [kápios] | **κάποια** [kápia] | **κάποιο** [kápio] |
| *one, one* (person) (m/f/n) | **κανείς** [kanís] | **καμία** [kamía] | **κανένα** [kanéna] |
| *no one, nothing* (m/f/n) | **κανένας** [kanénas] | **καμία** [kamía] | **κανένα** [kanéna] |

Words like *each one, everyone, someone, no one,* etc. are indefinite
pronouns. Some have only one form, some more than one for m/f/n use.

# 6 Prepositions

**Prepositions** in English are such words as *between, from, in, by, for, with,*
etc. All corresponding Greek prepositions have only one form. Greek
prepositions will sometimes be followed by a noun in the genitive or
more often in the accusative case. Some frequent prepositions are:

## GENITIVE

| εναντίον | [enandíon] | *against* |
| μεταξύ | [metaxí] | *between* |
| υπέρ | [ipér] | *in favour, for* |

## ACCUSATIVE

| από | [apó] | *from* |
| για | [yia] | *for, to, over* |
| με | [me] | *with, by* |
| χωρίς | [horís] | *without* |
| μετά | [metá] | *after* |
| μέχρι | [méhri] | *until* |
| πριν | [prin] | *before* |
| προς | [pros] | *towards* |
| σε | [se] | *to, in, on, at* (place) |
| στις | [stis] | *at* (time) |

There are also some two-word prepositions. All of them are followed by nouns in the accusative.

## ACCUSATIVE

| πάνω από | [páno apó] | *over, above* |
| κάτω από | [káto apó] | *underneath, below* |
| μπροστά από | [brostá apó] | *in front of* |
| πίσω από | [píso apó] | *behind* |
| κοντά σε | [kondá se] | *close to* |
| δίπλα σε | [THípla se] | *next to* |
| γύρω από | [yíro apó] | *around from* |
| μέσα σε | [mésa se] | *inside* |
| έξω από | [ékso apó] | *outside, out of* |

# 7 Verbs

Words that indicate action, being, or feeling are called verbs. **Κάνω** [káno] *I do*, **μιλάω** [miláo] *I speak* or **μένω** [méno] *I live* are three examples from the several verbs this course includes.

Remember that a dictionary will list these three verbs, and all others, using the *I* form of the verb. This is the main form used for reference to Greek verbs (as the infinitive form in English – *to do, to speak, to live*, etc. – does not exist in Greek) as well as for the *I* form in the present tense.

Verb tenses refer to different points in time, such as the present, the future, and the past. This course relies mostly on present tense, touches on the future and past tenses, and introduces some forms after the word **να** [na] and imperatives.

Also, remember that personal pronouns, words like *I, he, they*, etc. in English, are not necessary in Greek because of the change in the verb ending. So, **κάνω** can be seen as **κάν-** (the verb stem which remains unchanged) and **-ω** (the verb ending which tells you whether *I, he* or *they*, etc. is performing the action). There are two verb endings in Greek for the *I* form: **-ω** [-o] and **μαι** [-me], e.g. **περιμένω** [periméno] *I wait* and **κάθομαι** [káthome] *I sit*.

The course introduces you to the main verb groups (or conjugations – there are two main conjugations) in both the active voice (verbs ending in **-ω**) and the passive voice (verbs ending in -**ομαι/-αμαι**).

The present tense for the main verb groups found in the course are set out as follows. Once you memorize the different endings, you will be confident enough to use them in context. Remember that the majority of Greek verbs fall into the first conjugation.

## ACTIVE VOICE

### 1st conjugation

| | | |
|---|---|---|
| **έχω** | [ého] | *I have* |
| **έχεις** | [éhis] | *you have* (sing/infml) |
| **έχει** | [éhi] | *he/she/it has* |
| **έχουμε** | [éhoome] | *we have* (pl/fml) |
| **έχετε** | [éhete] | *you have* |
| **έχουν(ε)** | [éhoon(e)] | *they have* |

| θέλω | [thélo] | *I want* |
| θέλεις | [thélis] | *you want* (infml/sing) |
| θέλει | [théli] | *he/she/it wants* |
| θέλουμε | [théloome] | *we want* |
| θέλετε | [thélete] | *you want* (fml/pl) |
| θέλουν(ε) | [théloon(e)] | *they want* |

## 2nd conjugation

Both groups in the second conjugation include verbs always stressed on the last syllable in their main form.

GROUP A

| πεινάω/πεινώ | [pináo/pinó] | *I am hungry* |
| πεινάς | [pinás] | *you are hungry* (infml/sing) |
| πεινά(ει) | [piná(-i)] | *he/she/it is hungry* |
| πεινάμε | [pináme] | *we are hungry* |
| πεινάτε | [pináte] | *you are hungry* (fml/pl) |
| πεινούν(ε) | [pinoón(e)] | *they are hungry* |

GROUP B

| μπορώ | [boró] | *I can* |
| μπορείς | [borís] | *you can* (infml/sing) |
| μπορεί | [borí] | *he/she/it can* |
| μπορούμε | [boroóme] | *we can* |
| μπορείτε | [boríte] | *you can* (fml/pl) |
| μπορούν(ε) | [boroón(e)] | *they can* |

| χαίρομαι | [hérome] | *I am glad* |
| χαίρεσαι | [hérese] | *you are glad* (infml/sing) |
| χαίρεται | [hérete] | *he/she/it is glad* |
| χαιρόμαστε | [herómaste] | *we are glad* |
| χαίρεστε | [héreste] | *you are glad* (fml/pl) |

| | | |
|---|---|---|
| **χαίρονται** | [héronde] | *they are glad* |
| **λυπάμαι** | [lipáme] | *I am sorry* |
| **λυπάσαι** | [lipáse] | *you are sorry* (infml/sing) |
| **λυπάται** | lipáte] | *he/she/it is sorry* |
| **λυπόμαστε** | [lipómaste] | *we are sorry* |
| **λυπάστε** | [lipáste] | *you are sorry* (fml/pl) |
| **λυπούνται** | [lipoónde] | *they are sorry* |

## PASSIVE VOICE

All verbs in the passive voice end in **-μαι** [-me].

## FUTURE TENSE

The future tense in Greek is formed with the particle **θα** [tha] (equivalent to *will* in English) and the verb. Some verbs do not change their form in the future tense, but most do. There follows a list of verbs belonging to both groups:

### Verbs without any different form in the future

| | | |
|---|---|---|
| **θα είμαι** | [tha íme] | *I will be* |
| **θα έχω** | [tha ého] | *I will have* |
| **θα ξέρω** | [tha kséro] | *I will know* |
| **θα πάω** | [tha páo] | *I will go* |

### Verbs with a different form in the future

Most verbs belong to this sub-group. Examples are:

| | | | |
|---|---|---|---|
| **δίνω** | **θα δώσω** | [tha THóso] | *I will give* |
| **θέλω** | **θα θελήσω** | [tha thelíso] | *I will want* |
| **μένω** | **θα μείνω** | [tha míno] | *I will stay* |
| **παίρνω** | **θα πάρω** | [tha páro] | *I will take* |
| **στέλνω** | **θα στείλω** | [tha stílo] | *I will send* |
| **φέρνω** | **θα φέρω** | [tha féro] | *I will bring* |
| **φεύγω** | **θα φύγω** | [tha fígo] | *I will leave* |

## Verbs with an irregular form in the future

Some verbs have a completely new form in the future. Examples are:

| βλέπω | θα δω | [tha THo] | *I will see* |
| έρχομαι | θα έρθω | [tha értho] | *I will come* |
| ζω | θα ζήσω | [tha zíso] | *I will live* |
| τρώω | θα φάω | [tha fáo] | *I will eat* |
| χαίρομαι | θα χαρώ | [tha haró] | *I will be glad* |

The different endings for *I, he/she/it, you*, etc. are the same as those in the present tense. Below are two verbs **έχω** and **στέλνω** with their full forms in the future:

| θα έχω | [tha ého] | *I will have* |
| θα έχεις | [tha éhis] | *you will have* (infml/sing) |
| θα έχει | [tha éhi] | *he/she/it will have* |
| θα έχουμε | [tha éhoome] | *we will have* |
| θα έχετε | [tha éhete] | *you will have* (fml/pl) |
| θα έχουν | [tha éhoon] | *they will have* |

| θα στείλω | [tha stílo] | *I will send* |
| θα στείλεις | [tha stílis] | *you will send* (infml/sing) |
| θα στείλει | [tha stíli] | *he/she/it will send* |
| θα στείλουμε | [tha stíloome] | *we will send* |
| θα στείλετε | [tha stílete] | *you will send* (fml/pl) |
| θα στείλουν | [tha stíloon] | *they will send* |

Here again is the full table for **είμαι** [íme], the verb *to be*:

| θα είμαι | [tha íme] | *I will be* |
| θα είσαι | [tha íse] | *you will be* (infml/sing) |
| θα είναι | [tha íne] | *he/she/it will be* |
| θα είμαστε | [tha ímaste] | *we will be* |
| θα είσαστε/είστε | [tha ísaste] | *you will be* (fml/pl) |
| θα είναι | [tha íne] | *they will be* |

## THE IMPERATIVE FORM

The imperative is a form of the verb you can use to request, tell or order someone to do something, e.g. *Come here!*, *Stop!*, *Don't speak!*, *Turn left!*, *Go now!*. This form is very frequent and important in everyday language. Remember that since Greek has two *you* forms (informal/singular and formal/plural), you need to learn two individual words for the imperatives.

| (sing/infml) | (pl/fml) | |
|---|---|---|
| **πήγαινε** [píyene]! | **πηγαίνετε** [piyénete]! | *Go!* |
| **στρίψε** [strípse]! | **στρίψτε** [strípste]! | *Turn!* |
| **βγες** [vyes]! | **βγείτε** [vyíte]! | *Get off! Get out!* |
| **συνέχισε** [sinéhise]! | **συνεχίστε** [sinehíste]! | *Continue!* |
| **σταμάτησε** [stamátise]! | **σταματήστε** [stamatíste]! | *Stop!* |
| **περπάτησε** [perpátise]! | **περπατήστε** [perpatíste]! | *Walk!* |
| **οδήγησε** [oTHíyise]! | **οδηγήστε** [oTHiyíste]! | *Drive!* |

## OTHER TENSES

This course intentionally has not introduced the learner to other verb tenses, particularly past tenses. Some verbs have appeared in different tenses but there are few instances of these and they have not been dealt with in the grammar sections. One example to illustrate this is: **καλώς σας βρήκα!** [kalós sas vríka]! *Nice to have met you!*

Here is the past form of the verb **είμαι** *to be*:

| | | |
|---|---|---|
| **ήμουν** | [ímoon] | *I was* |
| **ήσουν** | [ísoon] | *you were* (infml/sing) |
| **ήταν** | [ítan] | *he/she/it was* |
| **ήμασταν** | [ímastan] | *we were* |
| **ήσασταν** | [ísastan] | *you were* (fml/pl) |
| **ήταν** | [ítan] | *they were* |

Here is the past tense of **έχω** *I have*:

| | | |
|---|---|---|
| **είχα** | [íha] | *I had* |
| **είχες** | [íhes] | *you had* (infml/sing) |
| **είχε** | [íhe] | *he/she/it had* |
| **είχαμε** | [íhame] | *we had* |
| **είχατε** | [íhate] | *you had* (pl/fml) |
| **είχαν** | [íhan] | *they had* |

# English–Greek glossary

(Note: m = masculine, f = feminine, n = neuter)

| | | |
|---|---|---|
| a.m. | [pi-mi] | π.μ. |
| a/an/one | [énas], [mía], [éna] | ένας, μία, ένα |
| about/approximately | [perípoo] | περίπου |
| across/opposite | [apénandi] | απέναντι |
| adventure story/thriller | [peripétia] | περιπέτεια (f) |
| afterwards, later | [metá] | μετά |
| again | [páli] | πάλι |
| agree | [simfonó] | συμφωνώ |
| aeroplane | [aeropláno] | αεροπλάνο (n) |
| airport | [aeroTHrómio] | αεροδρόμιο (n) |
| almost | [sheTHón] | σχεδόν |
| along/together | [mazí] | μαζί |
| always | [pánda] | πάντα |
| America | [amerikí] | Αμερική (f) |
| and | [ke] | και |
| angry | [thimoménos, -i, -o] | θυμωμένος, -η -ο |
| another, more | [álos, -i, -o] | άλλος, -η, -ο |
| apartment building | [polikatikía] | πολυκατοικία (f) |
| apartment/flat | [THiamérizma] | διαμέρισμα (n) |
| appetizer, starter | [orektikó] | ορεκτικό (n) |
| April | [aprílios] | Απρίλιος (m) |
| architect | [arhitéktonas] | αρχιτέκτονας (m/f) |
| area | [hóros] | χώρος (m) |
| armchair | [poliTHróna] | πολυθρόνα (f) |
| around, about | [yíro], [perípoo] | γύρω, περίπου |
| arrive | [ftháno] | φθάνω |
| as | [ópos] | όπως |
| Athens | [athína] | Αθήνα (f) |
| August | [ávgoostos] | Αύγουστος (m) |
| Australia | [afstralía] | Αυστραλία (f) |
| autumn/fall | [fthinóporo] | φθινόπωρο (n) |
| availability | [THiathesimótita] | διαθεσιμότητα (f) |

| baby | [moró] | μωρό (n) |
| baby boy | [bébis] | μπέμπης (m) |
| baby girl | [béba] | μπέμπα (f) |
| balcony/porch | [balkóni] | μπαλκόνι (n) |
| banana | [banána] | μπανάνα (f) |
| bank | [trápeza] | τράπεζα (f) |
| basement | [ipóyion] | υπόγειον (n) |
| basketball | [básket] | μπάσκετ (n) |
| bass (fish) | [lavráki] | λαβράκι (n) |
| bathroom, bathtub | [bánio] | μπάνιο (n) |
| bathroom, toilet | [tooaléta] | τουαλέτα (f) |
| be | [íme] | είμαι |
| be able | [boró] | μπορώ |
| be glad | [hérome] | χαίρομαι |
| be happy | [héro] | χαίρω |
| be interested | [enTHiaférome] | ενδιαφέρομαι |
| be pleased | [héro] | χαίρω |
| beach | [plaz] | πλαζ (f) |
| bean | [fasóli] | φασόλι (n) |
| beautiful, nice | [oréos, -a, -o] | ωραίος, -α, -ο |
| bed | [kreváti] | κρεβάτι (n) |
| bedroom | [krevatokámara], [ipnoTHomátio] | κρεβατοκάμαρα (f), υπνοδωμάτιο (n) |
| beef | [mosharísios, -a, -o] | μοσχαρίσιος, -α, -ο |
| beefsteak | [biftéki] | μπιφτέκι (n) |
| beer | [bíra] | μπύρα (f) |
| behind | [píso] | πίσω |
| beige | [bez] | μπεζ |
| bell | [kooTHoóni] | κουδούνι (n) |
| Berlin | [verolíno] | Βερολίνο (n) |
| between | [metaksí] | μεταξύ |
| beverage, drink | [potó] | ποτό (n) |
| big, large | [megálos, -i, -o] | μεγάλος, -η, -ο |
| bill | [logariazmós] | λογαριασμός (m) |
| black | [mávros, -i, -o] | μαύρος, -η, -ο |
| block | [tetrágono] | τετράγωνο (n) |
| blue | [ble] | μπλε |
| blues (music) | [blooz] | μπλουζ (n) |
| boat | [várka] | βάρκα (f) |

| | | |
|---|---|---|
| book | **[vivlío]** | βιβλίο (n) |
| bookshop | **[vivliopolío]** | βιβλιοπωλείο (n) |
| booklet | **[filáTHio]** | φυλλάδιο (n) |
| bottle | **[bookáli]** | μπουκάλι (n) |
| bottled (mineral) water | **[emfialoméno neró]** | εμφιαλωμένο νερό (n) |
| boy | **[agóri]** | αγόρι (n) |
| bravo | **[brávo]** | μπράβο |
| bread | **[psomí]** | ψωμί (n) |
| breakfast | **[proinó]** | πρωινό (n) |
| bridge | **[yéfira]** | γέφυρα (f) |
| brother | **[aTHelfós]** | αδελφός (m) |
| brown | **[kafé]** | καφέ |
| bus | **[leoforío]** | λεωφορείο (n) |
| bus station | **[stathmós leoforíon]** | σταθμός λεωφορείων (m) |
| bus stop | **[stási leoforíon]** | στάση λεωφορείων (f) |
| busy | **[apasholiménos, -i, -o]** | απασχολημένος, -η, -ο |
| but | **[alá], [ma]** | αλλά, μα |
| butcher's shop | **[kreopolíon]** | κρεοπωλείο |
| butter | **[voótiro]** | βούτυρο (n) |
| café | **[kafetéria]** | καφετέρια (f) |
| can | **[boró]** | μπορώ |
| can/tin | **[kootí]** | κουτί (n) |
| car | **[aftokínito]** | αυτοκίνητο (n) |
| car park | **[párkin]** | πάρκιν (n) |
| card | **[kárta]** | κάρτα (f) |
| carrot | **[karóto]** | καρότο (n) |
| cash desk | **[tamío]** | ταμείο (n) |
| celery | **[sélino]** | σέλινο (n) |
| central | **[kendrikós, -í, -ó]** | κεντρικός, -ή, -ό |
| centre | **[kéndro]** | κέντρο (n) |
| century | **[eónas]** | αιώνας (m) |
| cereal | **[dimitriaká]** | δημητριακά (n/pl) |
| chair | **[karékla]** | καρέκλα (f) |
| changing room | **[THokimastírio]** | δοκιμαστήριο (n) |
| cheap | **[fthinós, -í, -ó]** | φθηνός, -ή, -ό |
| checked | **[karó]** | καρώ (m/f/n) |

| | | |
|---|---|---|
| cheque | **[epitayí]** | επιταγή (f) |
| child | **[peTHí]** | παιδί (n) |
| church | **[eklisía]** | εκκλησία (f) |
| cigarette | **[tsigáro]** | τσιγάρο (n) |
| cinema | **[sinemá]** | σινεμά (n) |
| close to | **[kondá]** | κοντά |
| closed | **[klistós, -í, -ó]** | κλειστός, -ή, -ό |
| closet/wardrobe | **[doolápa]** | ντουλάπα (f) |
| coca cola | **[kóka kóla]** | κόκα κόλα (f) |
| coffee | **[kafés]** | καφές (m) |
| coffee house | **[kafenío]** | καφενείο (n) |
| coffee (medium sweet) | **[métrios]** | μέτριος (m) |
| coffee (sweet) | **[glikós]** | γλυκός (m) |
| coffee (without sugar) | **[skétos]** | σκέτος (m) |
| comedy | **[komoTHía]** | κωμωδία (f) |
| company | **[etería]** | εταιρεία (f) |
| computer | **[kompioóter]** | κομπιούτερ (n) |
| conservatory | **[tzamaría]** | τζαμαρία (f) |
| contrast, antithesis | **[antíthesi]** | αντίθεση (f) |
| cook | **[mayirévo]** | μαγειρεύω |
| cooked foods | **[mayireftá]** | μαγειρευτά (n/pl) |
| corner | **[gonía]** | γωνία (f) |
| counter | **[pángos]** | πάγκος (m) |
| country | **[hóra]** | χώρα (f) |
| courgette, zucchini | **[kolokitháki]** | κολοκυθάκι (n) |
| cousin | **[(e)ksaTHélfi],** | (ε)ξαδέλφη (f), |
| | **[(e)ksáTHelfos]** | (ε)ξάδελφος (m) |
| credit card | **[pistotikí kárta]** | πιστωτική κάρτα (f) |
| creme caramel | **[krem karamelé]** | κρεμ καραμελέ (n) |
| croissant | **[krooasán]** | κρουασάν (n) |
| cucumber | **[agoóri]** | αγγούρι (n) |
| cup | **[flitzáni]** | φλυτζάνι (n) |
| currency | **[nómizma]** | νόμισμα (n) |
| customs | **[telonío]** | τελωνείο (n) |
| cutlet | **[brizóla]** | μπριζόλα (f) |
| | | |
| dark | **[skoóros, -a, -o]** | σκούρος, -α, -ο |
| date | **[imerominía]** | ημερομηνία (f) |
| daughter | **[kóri]** | κόρη (f) |

| day | [(i)méra] | (η)μέρα (f) |
| December | [THekémvrios] | Δεκέμβριος (m) |
| deposit, down payment | [prokatavolí] | προκαταβολή (f) |
| dessert | [glikó] | γλυκό (n) |
| dialogue | [THiálogos] | διάλογος (m) |
| difficult | [THískolos, -i, -o] | δύσκολος, -η, -ο |
| dill | [ánithos] | άνιθος (m) |
| dining room | [trapezaría] | τραπεζαρία |
| dinner | [vraTHinó] | βραδινό (n) |
| disagree | [THiafonó] | διαφωνώ |
| discotheque | [THiskothíki] | δισκοθήκη (f) |
| dislike | [antipathó] | αντιπαθώ |
| doctor | [yiatrós] | γιατρός (m/f) |
| door | [pórta] | πόρτα (f) |
| dorado or gilthead | [tsipoóra] | τσιπούρα (f) |
| double room | [THíklino] | δίκλινο (n) |
| down | [káto] | κάτω |
| dress | [fórema] | φόρεμα (n) |
| drink | [píno] | πίνω |
| | | |
| early | [norís] | νωρίς |
| easy | [éfkolos, -i, -o] | εύκολος, -η, -ο |
| eat | [tró-o] | τρώω |
| eight | [októ]/[ohtó] | οκτώ/οχτώ |
| eight hundred | [oktakósia]/ | οκτακόσια/ |
| | [ohtakósia] | οχτακόσια |
| eighteen | [THekaoktó] | δεκαοκτώ |
| eighty | [ogTHónda] | ογδόντα |
| eleven | [éndeka] | έντεκα |
| England | [anglía] | Αγγλία (f) |
| English (language) | [angl-iká] | Αγγλικά (n/pl) |
| entrance | [ísoTHos] | είσοδος (f) |
| envelope | [fákelos] | φάκελος (m) |
| Euro | [evró] | ευρώ |
| evening | [vráTHi] | βράδυ (n) |
| every | [káthe] | κάθε |
| everything/all | [óla] | όλα |
| everywhere | [pandoó] | παντού |
| exactly | [akrivós] | ακριβώς |

| excuse me, | [signómi], | συγνώμη, με |
| pardon me | [me sinhoríte] | συγχωρείτε (pl/fml) |
| exit | [éksoTHos] | έξοδος (f) |
| | | |
| fall (verb) | [péfto] | πέφτω |
| family | [ikoyénia] | οικογένεια (f) |
| father | [patéras] | πατέρας (m) |
| February | [fevrooários] | Φεβρουάριος (m) |
| ferryboat | [féribot] | φέρυμποτ (n) |
| fifteen | [THekapénde] | δεκαπέντε |
| fifth | [pémptos, -i, -o] | πέμπτος, -η, -ο |
| fifty | [penínda] | πενήντα |
| film | [érgo] [film] | έργο (n), φιλμ (n) |
| finally | [teliká] | τελικά |
| finish | [telióno] | τελειώνω |
| first | [prótos, -i, -o] | πρώτος, -η, -ο |
| fish | [psári] | ψάρι (n) |
| fish restaurant | [psarotavérna] | ψαροταβέρνα (f) |
| five | [pénde] | πέντε |
| five hundred | [pendakósia] | πεντακόσια |
| flat, apartment | [THiamérizma] | διαμέρισμα (n) |
| flight | [ptísi] | πτήση (f) |
| floor | [órofos] | όροφος (m) |
| flying dolphin, hydrofoil | [iptámeno] | ιπτάμενο (n) |
| food | [trofí] | τροφή (f) |
| food cooked in oil | [laTHerá] | λαδερά (n/pl) |
| foot | [póTHi] | πόδι (n) |
| football | [poTHósfero] | ποδόσφαιρο (n) |
| for | [yia] | για |
| fork | [piróoni] | πιρούνι (n) |
| fortnight | [THekapenthímero] | δεκαπενθήμερο (n) |
| forty | [saránda] | σαράντα |
| four | [téseris, -is, -a] | τέσσερις, -ις, -α |
| four hundred | [tetrakósia] | τετρακόσια |
| fourteen | [THekatéseris, -is, -a] | δεκατέσσερις, -ις, -α |
| fourth | [tétartos, -i, -o] | τέταρτος, -η, -ο |
| France | [galía] | Γαλλία (f) |
| free | [eléftheros, -i, -o] | ελεύθερος, -η, -ο |
| French (language) | [galiká] | γαλλικά (n/pl) |

| | | |
|---|---|---|
| friend | **[fílos] [fíli]** | φίλος (m), φίλη (f) |
| from | **[apó]** | από |
| front | **[brostá]** | μπροστά |
| fruit | **[froóto]** | φρούτο (n) |
| fruit and vegetable market | **[laikí agorá]** | λαϊκή αγορά (f) |
| | | |
| garage | **[garáz]** | γκαράζ (n) |
| garlic | **[skórTHo]** | σκόρδο (n) |
| German (language) | **[yermaniká]** | Γερμανικά (n/pl) |
| Germany | **[yermanía]** | Γερμανία (f) |
| get up | **[sikónome]** | σηκώνομαι |
| girl | **[korítsi]** | κορίτσι (n) |
| glass | **[potíri]** | ποτήρι (n) |
| go | **[páo]** | πάω |
| go for a walk | **[páo vólta]** | πάω βόλτα |
| good evening | **[kalispéra]** | καλησπέρα |
| good morning | **[kaliméra]** | καλημέρα |
| goodnight | **[kaliníhta]** | καληνύχτα |
| grandchild | **[egóni]** | εγγόνι (n) |
| granddaughter | **[egoní]** | εγγονή (f) |
| grandfather | **[papoós]** | παππούς (m) |
| grandmother | **[yiayiá]** | γιαγιά (f) |
| grandson | **[egonós]** | εγγονός (m) |
| grape | **[stafíli]** | σταφύλι (n) |
| Greece | **[eláTHa]** | Ελλάδα (f) |
| Greek (language) | **[eliniká]** | Ελληνικά (n/pl) |
| green | **[prásinos, -i, -o]** | πράσινος, -η, -ο |
| grilled foods | **[psitá]** | ψητά (n/pl) |
| ground floor | **[isóyion]** | ισόγειον (n) |
| | | |
| hairdresser's | **[komotírio]** | κομμωτήριο |
| half | **[misós, -í, -ó]** | μισός, -ή, -ό |
| hallway | **[hol]** | χωλ (n) |
| hand | **[héri]** | χέρι (n) |
| hand basin | **[niptíras]** | νιπτήρας (m) |
| happy | **[eftihizménos, -i, -o]** | ευτυχισμένος, -η, -ο |
| have | **[ého]** | έχω |
| he | **[aftós]** | αυτός |

| heating | **[thérmansi]** | θέρμανση (f) |
| hello / goodbye | **[hérete]** | χαίρετε (pl/fml) |
| hello / goodbye | **[yiásas]** | γεια σας (pl/fml) |
| hello / see you | **[yiásoo]** | γεια σου (sing/infml) |
| her | **[tis]** | της |
| herb | **[aromatikó fitó]** | αρωματικό φυτό (n) |
| here | **[eTHó]** | εδώ |
| here you are! | **[oríste]** | ορίστε |
| hi | **[yia]** | γεια |
| his | **[too]** | του |
| hobby | **[hóbi]** | χόμπυ (n) |
| homemade | **[spitikós, -í, -ó]** | σπιτικός, -ή, -ό |
| hospital | **[nosokomío]** | νοσοκομείο (n) |
| hotel | **[ksenoTHohío]** | ξενοδοχείο (n) |
| house/home | **[spíti]** | σπίτι (n) |
| how/what | **[pos]** | πώς |
| hungry | **[pinazménos, -i, -o]** | πεινασμένος, -η, -ο |
| husband/wife, spouse | **[sízigos]** | σύζυγος (m/f) |
| | | |
| I | **[egó]** | εγώ |
| iced coffee/frappé | **[frapés]** | φραπές (m) |
| idea | **[iTHéa]** | ιδέα (f) |
| immediately | **[amésos]** | αμέσως |
| in | **[se]** | σε |
| information (piece of) | **[pliroforía]** | πληροφορία (f) |
| instant coffee | **[nes kafés]** | νες καφές (m) |
| interested (I'm) | **[enTHiaférome]** | ενδιαφέρομαι |
| interesting | **[enTHiaféron]** | ενδιαφέρον |
| introduce | **[sistíno]** | συστήνω |
| Ireland | **[irlanTHía]** | Ιρλανδία (f) |
| island music | **[nisiótika]** | νησιώτικα (n/pl) |
| it | **[aftó]** | αυτό |
| Italian (language) | **[italiká]** | Ιταλικά (n/pl) |
| Italy | **[italía]** | Ιταλία (f) |
| its | **[too]** | του |
| | | |
| January | **[ianooários]** | Ιανουάριος (m) |
| jazz music | **[tzaz]** | τζαζ (f) |
| job/work | **[THooliá]** | δουλειά (f) |

| | | |
|---|---|---|
| juice | [himós] | χυμός (m) |
| July | [ioólios] | Ιούλιος (m) |
| June | [ioónios] | Ιούνιος (m) |
| | | |
| keys | [kliTHiá] | κλειδιά |
| kilo | [kiló] | κιλό (n) |
| kiosk | [períptero] | περίπτερο (n) |
| kitchen | [koozína] | κουζίνα (f) |
| knife | [mahéri] | μαχαίρι (n) |
| know | [kséro] | ξέρω |
| | | |
| lamb | [arnáki] | αρνάκι (n) |
| late | [argá] | αργά |
| lawn/grass | [grasíTHi] | γρασίδι (n) |
| learn | [mathéno] | μαθαίνω |
| leave | [févgo] | φεύγω |
| left | [aristerá] | αριστερά |
| lemonade | [lemonáTHa] | λεμονάδα (f) |
| letter | [gráma] | γράμμα (n) |
| lettuce | [maroóli] | μαρούλι (n) |
| lift/elevator | [asansér] | ασανσέρ (n) |
| light (colour), open | [aniktós, -í, -ó] | ανοικτός, -ή, -ό |
| (I) like | [marési] | μ'αρέσει |
| likely, probably | [pithanós, -í, -ó] | πιθανός, -ή, -ό |
| little | [lígos, -i, -o] | λίγος, -η, -ο |
| live | [méno] | μένω |
| living room | [salóni] | σαλόνι (f) |
| London | [lonTHíno] | Λονδίνο (n) |
| love | [agápi] | αγάπη (f) |
| love story | [istoría agápis] | ιστορία αγάπης (f) |
| lucky | [tiherós, -í, -ó] | τυχερός, -ή, -ό |
| luggage | [aposkeví] | αποσκευή (f) |
| lunch | [mesimerianó] | μεσημεριανό (n) |
| lyre | [líra] | λύρα (f) |
| | | |
| Madrid | [maTHríti] | Μαδρίτη (f) |
| mainly | [kiríos] | κυρίως |
| man/husband | [ándras] | άνδρας (m) |
| map | [hártis] | χάρτης (m) |

| March | [mártios] | Μάρτιος (m) |
| market | [agorá] | αγορά (f) |
| marmalade/jam | [marmeláTHa] | μαρμελάδα (f) |
| May | [máios] | Μάιος (m) |
| may/is possible to | [borí na] | μπορεί να |
| me (after a preposition) | [(e)ména] | (ε)μένα |
| me (before a verb) | [moo] | μου |
| medium, middle | [meséos, -a, -o] | μεσαίος, -α, -ο |
| melon | [pepóni] | πεπόνι (n) |
| mezzanine (floor) | [imiórofos] | ημιόροφος (m) |
| midday/afternoon | [mesiméri] | μεσημέρι (n) |
| milk | [gála] | γάλα (n) |
| minute | [leptó] | λεπτό (n) |
| mirror | [kathréftis] | καθρέφτης (m) |
| Miss | [THespiníTHa] | δεσποινίδα |
| moment | [stigmí] | στιγμή (f) |
| month | [mínas] | μήνας (m) |
| more | [pio] | πιο |
| more | [perisóteros, -i, -o] | περισσότερος, -η, -ο |
| morning | [proí] | πρωί (n) |
| mother | [mitéra] | μητέρα (f) |
| motorcycle | [motosikléta] | μοτοσυκλέτα (f) |
| mountain | [voonó] | βουνό (n) |
| Mr/Sir | [kírios] | κύριος (m) |
| Mrs/Madam | [kiría] | κυρία (f) |
| much/very | [polís, polí, polí] | πολύς, πολλή, πολύ |
| museum | [moosío] | μουσείο (n) |
| mushroom | [manitári] | μανιτάρι (n) |
| music | [moosikí] | μουσική (f) |
| musician | [moosikós] | μουσικός (m/f) |
| must/have to | [prépi na] | πρέπει να |
| my | [moo] | μου |
| | | |
| name | [ónoma] | όνομα (n) |
| national | [ethnikós, -í, -ó] | εθνικός, -ή, -ό |
| naturally | [fisiká] | φυσικά |
| nought/zero | [miTHén] | μηδέν |
| near, close to | [kondá] | κοντά |

| need | [hriázome] | χρειάζομαι |
| neighbourhood | [yitoniá] | γειτονιά (f) |
| never | [poté] | ποτέ |
| New York | [néa iórki] | Νέα Υόρκη (f) |
| newspaper | [efimeríTHa] | εφημερίδα (f) |
| next to | [THípla] | δίπλα |
| nice, beautiful | [oréos, -a, -o], [ómorfos, -i, -o] | ωραίος, -α, -ο, όμορφος, -η, -ο |
| nine | [enéa]/[eniá] | εννέα/εννιά |
| nine hundred | [eniakósia] | ενιακόσια |
| nineteen | [THekaeniá] | δεκαεννιά |
| ninety | [enenínda] | ενενήντα |
| no | [óhi] | όχι |
| not | [THen] | δεν |
| nothing | [típota] | τίποτα |
| novel | [noovéla], [mithistórima] | νουβέλα (f), μυθιστόρημα (n) |
| November | [noémvrios] | Νοέμβριος (m) |
| now | [tóra] | τώρα |
| number, size (of clothes) | [noómero] | νούμερο (n) |
| nurse | [nosokóma], [nosokómos] | νοσοκόμα (f), νοσοκόμος (m) |

| October | [októvrios] | Οκτώβριος (m) |
| of course, naturally | [vévea] | βέβαια |
| often | [sihná] | συχνά |
| oh | [ah] | αχ |
| OK, all right | [kalá], [endáksi] | καλά, εντάξει |
| Olympic Air | [olimbiakí] | Ολυμπιακή (f) |
| one | [énas], [mía], [éna] | ένας, μία, ένα |
| one hundred | [ekató] | εκατό |
| one thousand | [hílies], [hílji], [hília] | χίλιες (f), χίλιοι (m), χίλια |
| one-family house | [monokatikía] | μονοκατοικία (f) |
| orange (colour) | [portokalí] | πορτοκαλί |
| orange (fruit) | [portokáli]] | πορτοκάλι (n) |
| orangeade | [portokaláTHa] | πορτοκαλάδα (f) |
| our | [mas] | μας |

| out, outside | [ékso] | έξω |
| oven | [foórnos] | φούρνος (m) |
| over | [péra] | πέρα |

| p.m. | [mi-mi] | μ.μ. |
| pair | [zevgári] | ζευγάρι (n) |
| Paris | [parísi] | Παρίσι (n) |
| parsley | [maindanós] | μαϊντανός (m) |
| passport | [THiavatírio] | διαβατήριο (n) |
| peach | [roTHákino] | ροδάκινο (n) |
| pear | [ahláTHi] | αχλάδι (n) |
| penthouse | [retiré] | ρετιρέ (n) |
| petrol/gas | [venzíni] | βενζίνη (f) |
| petrol/gas station | [pratírio venzínis] | πρατήριο βενζίνης (n) |
| pharmacy | [farmakío] | φαρμακείο (n) |
| phrase | [ékfrasi] | έκφραση |
| pianist | [i pianístria], | η πιανίστρια (f), |
|  | [o pianístas] | ο πιανίστας (m) |
| pineapple | [ananás] | ανανάς (m) |
| pink | [roz] | ροζ |
| plate | [piáto] | πιάτο (n) |
| play | [pézo] | παίζω |
| please/you're welcome | [parakaló] | παρακαλώ |
| police | [astinomía] | αστυνομία (f) |
| pop music | [laiká] | λαϊκά (n/pl) |
| pork | [hirinó] | χοιρινό (n) |
| portion | [meríTHa] | μερίδα (f) |
| post office | [tahiTHromío] | ταχυδρομείο (n) |
| potato | [patáta] | πατάτα (f) |
| pound (sterling) | [líra] | λίρα (f) |
| practical | [praktikós, -í, -ó] | πρακτικός, ή, -ό |
| prefer | [protimó] | προτιμώ |
| prepare | [etimázo] | ετοιμάζω |
| price | [timí] | τιμή (f) |
| private | [iTHiotikós], [-í], [-ó] | ιδιωτικός, -ή, -ό |
| problem | [próvlima] | πρόβλημα (n) |
| prospectus | [prospéktoos] | προσπέκτους (n) |
| purple | [mov] | μωβ |

| question | [erótisi] | ερώτηση (f) |
| radio | [raTHiófono] | ραδιόφωνο (n) |
| rain | [vrohí] | βροχή (f) |
| rarely | [spánia] | σπάνια |
| read | [THiavázo] | διαβάζω |
| realize, see | [vlépo] | βλέπω |
| reception | [ipoTHohí] | υποδοχή (f) |
| red | [kókinos, -i, -o] | κόκκινος, -η, -ο |
| red mullet | [barboóni] | μπαρμπούνι (n) |
| reservation | [krátisi] | κράτηση (f) |
| residence | [katikía] | κατοικία (f) |
| restaurant | [estiatório] | εστιατόριο (n) |
| return | [epistréfo] | επιστρέφω |
| return/round trip | [me epistrofí] | με επιστροφή (f) |
| right (direction) | [THeksiá] | δεξιά |
| right (justice) | [THíkio] | δίκιο (n) |
| river | [potamós] | ποταμός (m) |
| rock music | [rok] | ροκ (n) |
| Rome | [rómi] | Ρώμη (f) |
| room | [kámara]/[THomátio] | κάμαρα (f) / δωμάτιο (n) |
| round (in shape) | [strongilós, -í, -ó] | στρογγυλός, ή, ό |
| running | [troháTHin] | τροχάδην (n) |
| sad | [lipiménos, -i, -o] | λυπημένος, -η, -ο |
| salad | [saláta] | σαλάτα (f) |
| sale/discount | [ékptosi] | έκπτωση (f) |
| same | [íTHios, -a, -o] | ίδιος, -α, -ο |
| Saturday | [sávato] | Σάββατο (n) |
| saucer | [piatáki] | πιατάκι (n) |
| school | [sholío] | σχολείο (n) |
| science fiction | [epistimonikí fantasía] | επιστημονική φαντασία (f) |
| Scotland | [skotía] | Σκωτία (f) |
| sea | [thálasa] | θάλασσα (f) |
| season | [epohí] | εποχή (f) |
| second (adjective) | [THéfteros, -i, -o] | δεύτερος, η-, -ο |

| | | |
|---|---|---|
| second (with time) | [THefterólepto] | δευτερόλεπτο (n) |
| see | [vlépo] | βλέπω |
| see again | [ksanavlépo] | ξαναβλέπω |
| September | [septémvrios] | Σεπτέμβριος (m) |
| sesame bagel | [kooloóri] | κουλούρι (n) |
| seven | [eptá]/[eftá] | επτά/εφτά |
| seven hundred | [eptakósia]/ | επτακόσια/ |
| | [eftakósia] | εφτακόσια |
| seventeen | [THekaeftá] | δεκαεφτά |
| seventy | [evTHomínda] | εβδομήντα |
| shampoo | [sampooán] | σαμπουάν (n) |
| she | [aftí] | αυτή |
| ship | [plío] | πλοίο (n) |
| shirt | [pookámiso] | πουκάμισο (n) |
| shoe | [papoótsi] | παπούτσι (n) |
| shoe lace | [korTHóni] | κορδόνι (n) |
| shop window | [vitrína] | βιτρίνα (f) |
| shower | [dooz] | ντους (n) |
| side | [plevrá] | πλευρά (f) |
| single room | [monóklino] | μονόκλινο (n) |
| sister | [aTHelfí] | αδελφή (f) |
| sit | [káthome] | κάθομαι |
| sitting room | [kathistikó] | καθιστικό (n) |
| six | [éksi] | έξι |
| six hundred | [eksakósia] | εξακόσια |
| sixteen | [THekaéksi] | δεκαέξι |
| sixty | [eksínda] | εξήντα |
| size | [mégethos] | μέγεθος (n) |
| sky blue | [galázios, -a, -o] | γαλάζιος, -α, -ο |
| sleep | [kimáme] | κοιμάμαι |
| slip-ons (loafers) | [pandoflé] | παντοφλέ (n) |
| slipper | [pandófla] | παντόφλα (f) |
| small | [mikrós, -í, -ó] | μικρός, -ή, -ό |
| smoke | [kapnízo] | καπνίζω |
| smoking | [kápnizma] | κάπνισμα (n) |
| so | [étsi], [tósos, -i, -o] | έτσι, τόσος, -η, -ο |
| soap | [sapoóni] | σαπούνι (n) |
| soda water | [sóTHa] | σόδα (f) |
| sofa | [kanapés] | καναπές (m) |

| | | |
|---|---|---|
| soft | [malakós, -iá, -ó] | μαλακός, -ιά, -ό |
| soft pop | [elafrolaiká] | ελαφρολαϊκά (n/pl) |
| son | [yios] | γιος (m) |
| sorry | [signómi] | συγνώμη (m) |
| soup spoon | [kootáli] | κουτάλι (n) |
| space, area | [hóros] | χώρος (m) |
| Spain | [ispanía] | Ισπανία (f) |
| Spanish (language) | [ispaniká] | Ισπανικά (n/pl) |
| speak | [miláo] | μιλάω |
| sport | [spor] | σπορ (n) |
| spring | [ániksi] | άνοιξη (f) |
| stamp | [gramatósimo] | γραμματόσημο (n) |
| stay (verb) | [káthome] | κάθομαι |
| stay | [THiamoní], [paramoní] | διαμονή (f), παραμονή (f) |
| still/yet | [akóma] | ακόμα |
| stool | [skambó] | σκαμπό (n) |
| story/history | [istoría] | ιστορία (f) |
| straight | [efthía] | ευθεία |
| straight ahead | [efthía brostá], [ísia] | ευθεία μπροστά, ίσια |
| strawberry | [fráoola] | φράουλα (f) |
| striped | [riyé] | ριγέ (m/f/n) |
| studio/bedsit | [garsoniéra] | γκαρσονιέρα (f) |
| study (verb) | [THiavázo] | διαβάζω |
| stuffed peppers and tomatoes | [yemistá] | γεμιστά (n/pl) |
| suitcase | [valítsa] | βαλίτσα (f) |
| summer | [kalokéri] | καλοκαίρι (n) |
| Sunday | [kiriakí] | Κυριακή (f) |
| supermarket | [soópermarket] | σούπερμαρκετ (n) |
| sure! | [amé]! | αμέ! |
| surprised | [ékpliktos, -i, -o] | έκπληκτος, -η, -ο |
| sweet | [glikós, -iá, ó] | γλυκός, -ιά, -ό |
| swimming | [bánio] | μπάνιο (n) |
| Sydney | [síTHnei] | Σίδνεϋ (n) |
| | | |
| table | [trapézi] | τραπέζι (n) |
| table tennis | [ping pong] | πίνγκ πονγκ (n) |
| take | [pérno] | παίρνω |

| taxi | [taksí] | ταξί (n) |
| tea | [tsái] | τσάι (n) |
| tea spoon | [kootaláki] | κουταλάκι (n) |
| teacher | [THaskála], [THáskalos] | δασκάλα (f), δάσκαλος (m) |
| telephone booth | [tilefonikós thálamos] | τηλεφωνικός θάλαμος (m) |
| television | [tileórasi] | τηλεόραση (f) |
| ten | [THéka] | δέκα |
| tennis | [ténis] | τένις (n) |
| thanks (lit. I thank you) | [efharistó] | ευχαριστώ |
| thanks (lit. we thank you) | [efharistoóme] | ευχαριστούμε |
| that / who (in statements) | [poo] | που |
| the | [o], [i], [to] | ο, η, το |
| theatre | [théatro] | θέατρο (n) |
| their | [toos] | τους |
| them | [aftoós], [aftés] | αυτούς (m), αυτές (f) |
| then, afterwards | [metá] | μετά |
| then/after that/later | [épita] | έπειτα |
| there | [ekí] | εκεί |
| Thessaloniki | [thesaloníki] | Θεσσαλονίκη (f) |
| they (only females) | [aftés] | αυτές |
| they (only females | [aftí] | αυτοί |
| they (only things) | [aftá] | αυτά |
| think | [nomízo] | νομίζω |
| third | [trítos, -i, -o] | τρίτος, -η, -ο |
| thirsty | [THipsazménos, -i, -o] | διψασμένος, -η, -ο |
| thirteen | [THekatrís, -ís, -ía] | δεκατρείς, -είς, -ία |
| thirty | [triánda] | τριάντα |
| though, although | [ómos] | όμως |
| three | [tris, tris, tría] | τρεις, τρεις, τρία |
| three hundred | [trakósia] | τριακόσια |
| thriller/horror (film) | [thríler] | θρίλερ (n) |
| ticket | [isitírio] | εισιτήριο (n) |
| time | [óra], [hrónos] | ώρα (f), χρόνος (m) |
| timetable | [pínakas THromoloyíon] | πίνακας δρομολογίων (m) |
| tired | [koorazménos, -i, -o] | κουρασμένος, -η, -ο |

| | | |
|---|---|---|
| tiring | [koorastikós, -í, -ó] | κουραστικός, -ή, -ό |
| to (used with verbs) | [na] | να |
| to/ in/at the | [ston], [stin], [sto] | στον, στην, στο |
| to, until | [méhri] | μέχρι |
| today | [símera] | σήμερα (n) |
| toilet | [tooaléta] | τουαλέτα (f) |
| tomato | [domáta] | ντομάτα (f) |
| toothbrush | [oTHondóvoortsa] | οδοντόβουρτσα (f) |
| toothpaste | [oTHondópasta] | οδοντόπαστα (f) |
| towel | [petséta] | πετσέτα (f) |
| town/city | [póli] | πόλη (f) |
| train | [tréno] | τρένο (n) |
| train station | [stathmós trénon] | σταθμός τρένων (m) |
| travel agency | [taksiTHiotikó grafío] | ταξιδιωτικό γραφείο (n) |
| trip | [taksíTHi] | ταξίδι (n) |
| triple room | [tríklino] | τρίκλινο (n) |
| trout | [péstrofa] | πέστροφα (f) |
| truth | [alíthia] | αλήθεια (f) |
| twelve | [THóTHeka] | δώδεκα |
| twenty | [íkosi] | είκοσι |
| two | [THío] | δύο |
| two hundred | [THiakósia] | διακόσια |
| | | |
| underground | [metró] | μετρό (n) |
| understand | [katalavéno] | καταλαβαίνω |
| unfortunately | [THistihós] | δυστυχώς |
| until | [méhri], [óspoo] | μέχρι, ώσπου |
| up | [páno] | πάνω |
| upset | [taragménos, -i, -o] | ταραγμένος, -η, -ο |
| usually | [sínithos] | συνήθως |
| | | |
| vegetable | [lahanikó] | λαχανικό (n) |
| view | [théa] | θέα (f) |
| volley ball | [vólei] | βόλεϋ (n) |
| | | |
| WC | [vesé] | WC (no Greek script) (n) |
| wait | [periméno] | περιμένω |
| waiter | [servitóros] | σερβιτόρος |

| | | |
|---|---|---|
| waitress | [servitóra] | σερβιτόρα |
| wake up | [ksipnáo] | ξυπνάω |
| Wales | [oo-alía] | Ουαλία (f) |
| walk | [perpató] | περπατώ |
| walk, stroll, car ride | [vólta] | βόλτα (f) |
| want | [thélo] | θέλω |
| watch | [vlépo] | βλέπω |
| water | [neró] | νερό (n) |
| we | [emís] | εμείς |
| weather | [kerós] | καιρός (m) |
| week | [evTHomáTHa] | εβδομάδα (f) |
| weekend | [savatokíriako] | Σαββατοκύριακο (n) |
| well (e.g. I'm well) | [kalá] | καλά |
| well (e.g. Well, what?) | [lipón] | λοιπόν |
| what/how | [ti] | τι |
| when (in questions) | [póte] | πότε |
| when (within a sentence) | [ótan] | όταν |
| where | [poo] | πού |
| white | [áspros, -i, -o] | άσπρος, -η, -ο |
| white wine | [áspro krasí] | άσπρο κρασί (n) |
| why | [yiatí] | γιατί |
| window | [paráthiro] | παράθυρο (n) |
| wine | [krasí] | κρασί (n) |
| winter | [himónas] | χειμώνας (m) |
| woman/wife | [yinéka] | γυναίκα (f) |
| word | [léksi] | λέξη (f) |
| work (verb) | [THoolévo] | δουλεύω |
| work (noun) | [THooliá] | δουλειά (f) |
| world | [kózmos] | κόσμος (m) |
| write | [gráfo] | γράφω |
| writer | [sigraféas] | συγγραφέας (m/f) |
| | | |
| yard | [avlí] | αυλή (f) |
| year | [hrónos] | χρόνος (m) |
| yellow | [kítrinos, -i, -o] | κίτρινος, -η, -ο |
| yes | [ne] | ναι |
| Yes, sure! Of course! | [málista] | μάλιστα |
| you (pl/fml) | [esís] | εσείς |

| | | |
|---|---|---|
| *you* (pl/fml) (e.g. to you) | **[sas]** | σας |
| *you* (sing/infml) | **[esí]** | εσύ |
| *you're welcome* | **[parakaló]** | παρακαλώ |
| *your* (pl/fml) | **[sas]** | σας |
| *your* (sing/infml) | **[soo]** | σου |

# Answer key

**UNIT 1**

**Greetings, introductions and wishes**

**1** γεια, γεια σου, γεια σας
**2** Με λένε … / Είμαι ο/η …
**3** Από εδώ ο/η … / Από'δω ο/η …

**Vocabulary builder**

**Greetings:** goodbye, good night; **Wishes:** Welcome!, thanks

**Conversation 1**

**1** [ti kánis]? Τι κάνεις;
**2 a** Fine, just fine. **b** Fine. **c** He's waiting for two friends from London.

**Language discovery 1**

**1 a** είμαι, **b** είσαι, **c** περιμένω.
**2** Άγγελος is used when you speak about this person. Άγγελε is used when you speak directly to that person.

**Conversation 2**

**1** Καλώς ορίσατε στην Ελλάδα!
**2 a** (I) thank you and (we) thank you. **b** Από means *from* and Πώς *How?*

**Language discovery 2**

**a** ο John, **b** η Mary, **c** στην Ελλάδα

**Practice**

**1 a** [kaliméra], **b** [kalispéra], **c** [kaliníhta]
**2 a** 3, **b** 5, **c** 1, **d** 2, **e** 4
**3 a** 1, **b** 3, **c** 2, **d** 4
**4 a** 1, **c** 2, **e** 3, **b** 4, **d** 5
**5 a** [sto], **b** [to], **c** [tin], **d** [stin]
**6 a** [i], **b** [o], **c** [o], **d** [o], **e** [i], **f** [i]
**7 a** [sas], **b** [o], **c** [i], **d** [polí], **e** [stin], **f** [se], **g** [me]

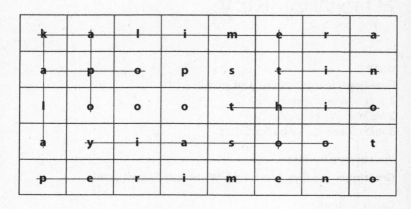

**9 a** [kalimera] καλημέρα, **b** [apo] από, **c** [stin] στην, **d** [thio] δύο, **e** [yiasoo] γεια σου, **f** [perimeno] περιμένω, **g** [kala] καλά, **h** [apo] από, **i** [etho] εδώ
**10 a** No, **b** No

**Test yourself**

**1 a** [yiásoo], **b** [ti kánis]?, **c** [ti kánis eTHó sto aeroTHrómio]?, **d** [efharistó], **e** [yiásas], **f** [kaliméra] – [kaliníhta], **g** [héro polí]
**2 a** [yia], **b** [yiásoo], **c** [yiásas], **d** [yia/yiásoo]
**3 a** [kalimera] καλημέρα good morning, **b** [apo] από from, **c** [stin] στην in (the), **d** [thio] δύο two, **e** [yiasoo] γεια σου hello/goodbye, **f** [perimeno] περιμένω I am waiting/I wait, **g** [kala] καλά good/fine, **h** [apo] από from, **i** [etho] εδώ here

**UNIT 2**

**Greece**
[athína] Αθήνα, [ólimbos] Όλυμπος, [kríti] Κρήτη

**Conversation 1**

**1** [eliniká] Ελληνικά, [angliká] Αγγλικά, [ghermaniká] Γερμανικά
**2 a** English and a little bit of Greek, **b** Greek, English and a little bit of German

**Language discovery 1**

**1 a** Εσύ, **b** Εγώ
**2 a** [eliniká] Ελληνικά, **b** [angliká] Αγγλικά, **c** [ghermaniká] Γερμανικά. All three languages end in -κά.

**Conversation 2**

**1** John comes from Australia and Mary is from the US.
**2 a** Anna comes from the island of Poros. **b** She lives in Athens now.

**Language discovery 2**

**1** The three articles are: το for neuter, την for feminine and τον for masculine. All Greek nouns are one of three genders.
**2 a** [esí] εσύ, **b** [esís] εσείς, **c** [eghó] εγώ, **d** [eghó] εγώ

**Practice**

**1 a** [eláTHa] Ελλάδα/[eliniká] ελληνικά, **b** [ispanía] Ισπανία/[ispaniká] ισπανικά, **c** [italía] Ιταλία/[italiká] ιταλικά, **d** [galía] Γαλλία/[galiká] γαλλικά, **e** [anglía] Αγγλία/[angliká] αγγλικά.
**2 a** 4, **b** 2, **c** 3, **d** 1
**3 a** [íne apó tin thesaloníki]. Είναι από τη Θεσσαλονίκη. He/she is from Thessaloniki. **b** [alá tóra méno stin pátra]. Αλλά τώρα μένω στην Πάτρα. But now I live in Patras. **c** [miláo italiká ke líga ispaniká]. Μιλάω Ιταλικά και λίγα Ισπανικά. I speak Italian and a little Spanish. **d** [i athína íne stin eláTHa]. Η Αθήνα είναι στην Ελλάδα. Athens is in Greece. **e** [ke to parísi sti galía]. Και το Παρίσι στη Γαλλία. And Paris in France.
**4 a** Athens, **b** Thessaloniki, **c** Patras, **d** Heraklion, **e** Larisa, **f** Volos
**5 a** 2, **b** 3, **c** 2, **d** 2, **e** 1, **f** 2
**6 a** [italía] Ιταλία, **b** [anglía] Αγγλία, **c** [ispanía] Ισπανία, **d** [galía] Γαλλία, **e** [yermanía] Γερμανία
**7 a** [apó], **b** [óhi], **c** [egó], **d** [esí], **e** [óhi], **f** [alá]
**8** You hear a dialogue mentioning the [pális] Πάλλης Pallis company.

**Test yourself**

**1** [apó poo íse]? or [apó poo íste]?
**2** [poo ménis tóra]? or [poo ménete tóra]?
**3** [íme apó to Cardiff] [alá tóra méno sto Manchester].
**4** [angliká], [galiká], [ispaniká], [yermaniká], [eliniká], [italiká]
**5** [lonTHíno], [rómi], [athína]

**UNIT 3**

**Employment in Greece**
It means to work/be employed. The text included the following words: [erghasía] employment and [erghátis-erghátria] worker.

## Vocabulary builder

musician, waitress, actress

## Conversation 1

**1** She is a teacher.
**2 a** He works in London. **b** He's an architect. **c** She writes children's books.
**d** No. She's a teacher.

## Language discovery 1

**1 a** αρχιτέκτονας, **b** συγγραφέας, **c** δασκάλα
**2** δάσκαλος – δασκάλα
**3 a** μένω, **b** δουλεύω, **c** γράφω, **d** είμαι

## Conversation 2

**1** Yes, she does.
**2 a** She knows Athens better. **b** [ne] [óchi]

## Language discovery 2

**1 a** ... ξέρεις ...;, **b** Πού μένεις;, **c** Μένεις ...
**2** The two words have a different sound for this double letter.

## Practice

**1 b** [esí], **c** [aftí]/[aftés]/[aftá], **d** [egó], **e** [aftós], **f** [aftí], **g** [emís], **h** [aftí]/
[aftés]/[aftá]
**2 a** [THen miláme yermaniká]. **b** [THen kséro ton ángelo]. **c** [THen ksérete
tin ána]. **d** [THen periméni tris fíloos]. **e** [THen ménoon sta yiánena].
**f** [THen íme apó tin amerikí]. **g** [THen íne apó tin italía].
**3 a** [esís ménete stin yermanía]? **b** [aftí íne apó tin afstralía]? **c** [kséris líga
eliniká]? **d** [aftés periménoon THío fíloos]? **e** [esí milás angliká]? **f** [esís THen
miláte ispaniká]? **g** [esís íste apó tin anglía]?
**4 a** [yiatrós] γιατρός, **b** [THaskála] δασκάλα, **c** [nosokóma] νοσοκόμα, **d**
[sigraféas] συγγραφέας, **e** [servitóros] σερβιτόρος, **f** [arhitéktonas] αρχιτέκτονας
**5 a** false, **b** true, **c** false, **d** true, **e** false, **f** true
**6** The man is [servitóros] σερβιτόρος and the woman [THaskála] δασκάλα.
**7 a** 4, **b** 5, **c** 1, **d** 2, **e** 3
**8 a** 2, **b** 1, **c** 2, **d** 3, **e** 2
**9 a** [íme servitóra. THen íme pianístria]. Είμαι σερβιτόρα. Δεν είμαι
πιανίστρια. I'm a waitress. I'm not a pianist. **b** [THen íme sigraféas]. Δεν
είμαι συγγραφέας. I'm not a writer. **c** [íste yiatrós]? [óhi], [íme moosikós].
Είστε γιατρός; Όχι, είμαι μουσικός. Are you a doctor? No, I'm a musician.

**d** [méno kondá sti thesaloníki]. Μένω κοντά στη Θεσσαλονίκη. I live close to (near) Thessaloniki. **e** [THen ímaste apó tin anglía]. Δεν είμαστε από την Αγγλία. We are not from England.

**10 a** [kséris], **b** [óhi], **c** [móno], **d** [poo], **e** [kondá], **f** [ne]
**11 a** -ου, **b** -ει, **c** -γγ

**Test yourself**

**1** [ti THooliá kánis]? [ti THooliá kánete]?
**2** [íme THáskalos / THaskála].
**3** He/she is a writer.
**4** I live in Manchester. I live close to Manchester.
**5** [íse] is informal, [íste] is more formal. The question means: Are you from England?
**6** what?, how/what?, where?, who/which/what?

**REVISION TEST 1**

**1 a** [kaliméra], **b** [hérete], **c** [kalispéra], **d** [kaliníhta], **e** [kaliníhta]
**2 a** [yiásas], **b** [yiásoo], **c** [pos íse]? **d** [kalá efharistó], [esí]? **e** [óhi áshima]/ [kalá], [efharistó].
**3** Γεια σου Νίκο! Χάρηκα! Ευχαριστώ. Χαίρομαι που είμαι εδώ. Όχι, είμαι από το Λίβερπουλ.
**4 a** Τι κάνεις εδώ; **b** Πώς είσαι; **c** Πώς σε λένε; **d** Μιλάς Ελληνικά; **e** Πού μένεις;
**5 a** 4, **b** 5, **c** 1, **d** 2, **f** 3
**6 a** [amerikí], **b** [yermanía], **c** [galía], **d** [italía], **e** [eláTHa], **1** [angliká], **2** [yermaniká], **3** [galiká], **4** [italiká], **5** [eliniká]
**7 a** 2, **b** 1, **c** 2, **d** 3, **e** 3
**8 a** 3, **b** 1, **c** 2, **d** 2, **e** 1, **f** 1
**9 a** [sigraféas], **b** [servitóra], **c** [athína], **d** [kaliméra], **e** [yiatrós], **f** [amerikí], **g** [moosikós], **h** [patéras], **i** [THoolévo], **j** [kondá], **k** [pianístas], **l** [THáskalos]
**10 a** [yiásoo maría]! [héro polí]! / [apó tin amerikí]. [apó tin néa iórki]. [esí]? / [ki'egó méno stin athína tóra]. [íme sigraféas peTHikón vivlíon].

**UNIT 4**

**A Greek home**

**1** Μένω σε ένα σπίτι / διαμέρισμα.
**2** [xílo] ξύλο, [túvlo] τούβλο, [pétra] πέτρα, [métalo] μέταλλο

**Vocabulary builder**

**3 a** Εγώ μένω σε μια πολυκατοικία. **b** Εγώ μένω σε ένα διαμέρισμα. **c** Εγώ μένω σε μια μονοκατοικία. **d** Εγώ μένω σε ένα σπίτι.

**Conversation 1**

**1** Anna lives in a four-room apartment in a block of flats.
**2 a** κουζίνα, μπάνιο, χωλ, **b** megalomania, megaphone, megahertz and microcomputer, microbiology, microfilm

**Language discovery 1**

**1 a** ένα χωλ, **b** ένα μπάνιο, **c** μία κουζίνα, **d** μία πολυκατοικία
**2 a** ένα, **b** μία, **c** τέσσερα

**Conversation 2**

**1** There are five bedrooms. [ipnoTHomátia]
**2 a** It's a detached house. [monokatikía], **b** [salóni] [trapezaría] [bánio] [ipnoTHomátio]

**Language discovery 2**

**1 a** [meghálo spíti], **b** [álo spíti], **c** [mikró hol], **d** [megálo salóni]
**2 a** [μπάνια], **b** [κτίρια], **c** [ξύλα], **d** [μέταλλα]

**Practice**

**1 a** 5, **b** 4, **c** 1, **d** 2, **e** 6, **f** 3
**2 a** [kondá] κοντά near – [makriá] μακριά far, **b** [póli] πόλη city – [hóra] χώρα country, **c** [spíti] σπίτι house – [THiamérizma] διαμέρισμα apartment/flat, **d** [salóni] σαλόνι living room – [kathistikó] καθιστικό sitting room, **e** [koozína] κουζίνα kitchen – [trapezaría] τραπεζαρία dining room, **f** [mikró] μικρό small – [megálo] μεγάλο big
**3 a** 4, **b** 2, **c** 1, **d** 5, **e** 3
**4** c, e, b, d, f, a
**5 a** [salóni], **b** [trapezaría], **c** [koozína], **d** [bánio], **e** [ipnoTHomátio], **f** [hol]
**6 a** [éna]/[miTHén]/[miTHén], **b** [éna] [éna] [THío], **c** [éna]/[tría]/[tésera], **d** [éna]/[éksi]/[éksi], **e** [éna]/[éksi]/[eniá], **f** [éna]/[eptá]/[éna], **g** [éna], [eniá], [eniá]
**7 a** [spíti], **b** [garsoniéra], **c** [salóni], **d** [koozína], **e** [bánio], **f** [retiré] vertical: saloni
**8 a** [spíti] σπίτι, **b** [garsoniéra] γκαρσονιέρα, **c** [salóni] σαλόνι, **d** [koozína] κουζίνα, **e** [bánio] μπάνιο, **f** [retiré] ρετιρέ, **g** vertical: [salóni] σαλόνι
**9 a** [sálo], **b** [pósa], **c** [megálo], **d** [mazí], **e** [pénde], **f** [polí]
**10** electricity: ηλεκτρισμού, programmes: προγράμματα

**Test yourself**

**1** [bánio], [tooaléta], [vesé]
**2** [tzamaría], [trapezaría], [ipnoTHomátio], [koozína] **3** [retiré],
[THiamérizma], [garsoniéra], [katikía]
**4** [méno se mía monokatikía sto lonTHíno]
**5** [mikró], [makriá], [polikatikía]
**6** [kathistikó], [tooaléta], [katikía]

**UNIT 5**

**Greek names**
Αγάπη, Ελπίδα, Ζωή

**Vocabulary builder**

mother, grandfather, grandchild, sister

**Conversation 1**

**1** They have two children, a boy and a girl.
**2 a** Μισό λεπτό. **b** The son is five years old. **c** The daughter is three years old.

**Language discovery 1**

**1 a** Έχεις οικογένεια; **b** πέντε χρονών **c** Μισό λεπτό. **d** Έχετε παιδιά; The underlined English words are not translated in Greek.
**2 a** ένα/μια-μία, **b** δύο, **c** τριών, **d** πέντε. When saying your age, you need a new form of the following numbers: 1 ενός, 3 τριών, 4 τεσσάρων. The rest of the numbers do not require a different form.
**3 a** σπίτι - σπίτια, **b** αγόρι – αγόρια, **c** κορίτσι - κορίτσια, **d** παιδί – παιδιά

**Conversation 2**

**1** They have three children, two boys and one girl.
**2 a** [servitóros], **b** 12 [THóTHeka] and 7 [eftá], **c** 10 [THéka]

**Language discovery 2**

**1 a** ο άντρας μου, **b** τα ονόματά τους. An article is necessary and the possessive adjective comes after the Greek noun. Word for word: the husband my and the names their
**2 a** His name is Yiorgos. **b** Your name is Yiorgos. **c** I want to see you again.
**d** I want to see him again.
**3 a** εφτά, **b** δέκα, **c** δώδεκα

**Practice**

**1 a** 4, **b** 2, **c** 3, **d** 6, **e** 5, **f** 3
**2 a** 6, **b** 2, **c** 4, **d** 3, **e** 5, **f** 1
**3 a** 4, **b** 3, **c** 1, **d** 5, **e** 2
**4 a** 15, **b** 17, **c** 12, **d** 13, **e** 11, **f** 14
**5 a** 7849321, **b** 9904057
**6 a** [to THiamérizmá too], **b** [to spíti mas], **c** [o papoós toos], **d** [i mitéra tis],
**e** [to THomátió moo], **f** [o ándras soo] or [o ándras sas] or [o sízigos soo] or
[o sízigos sas]
**7**

| p | a | p | o | o | s | y |
|---|---|---|---|---|---|---|
| a | n | p | l | h | e | i |
| m | y | i | n | e | k | a |
| e | o | a | e | n | a | y |
| k | o | r | i | t | s | i |
| k | m | i | t | e | r | a |

**8** Across: παππούς, γυναίκα, ένα, κορίτσι, μιτέρα, Down: πάμε, μου, πια, έχω, και, γιαγιά
**9 a** [ándras], **b** [ton], **c** [peTHiá], **d** [korítsi], **e** [níkos], **f** [hronón],
**g** [THótHeka], **h** [THéka], **i** [eptá], **j** [yiatí]
**10 a** /i/: υποκατάστημα, **b** /y/: γυαλιά, **c** /v/: Σταύρου, **d** /u/: Σταύρου,
ηλίου, βουτήματα, τσουρέκια, μπουφέ, Σεπτεμβρίου,

**Test yourself**

**1** [patéras], [mitéra], [peTHí], [papoós], [yiayiá], [yios], [kóri], [egonós],
[egoní], [aTHelfós], [aTHelfí], [(e)ksáTHelfos], [(e)ksaTHélfi]
**2** 11 [éndeka], 12 [THótHeka], 14 [THekatésera], 17 [THekaeptá] or
[THekaeftá], 19 [THekaeniá] or [THekaenéa], 20 [íkosi]
**3** Any answer is possible here. Say it to a native speaker!
**4** [póso hronón íse/íste]?
**5** [pos to léne] [sta eliniká]?

**UNIT 6**
**Ordering drinks**

**1** καφές, καφενείο, καφετέρια
**2** σκέτο, μέτριο, γλυκό

**Vocabulary builder**

**1** b, d, c, a
**2** a Greek coffee without sugar, an iced coffee with sugar, an orangeade, a lemonade, a medium Greek coffee, an instant coffee without milk
**3** Hot beverages: Greek coffee, iced coffee, tea, hot chocolate, Refreshments: Orangeade, lemonade, (pineapple) juice, (small) water, (Alcoholic) drinks: Beer, glass of wine, bottle of retsina, small carafe of ouzo
**4 a** 3, **b** 1, **c** 2

**Conversation 1**

**1** [kalós se vríkame] Καλώς σε βρήκαμε.
**2 a** Αντώνης, Γιωργία, **b** κύριε, κυρία

**Language discovery 1**

**1 d** Καλώς ορίσατε! The answers a and c are appropriate when you informally welcome a friend or relative. The answers b and d are used either formally when addressing one or more people or informally when addressing friends or relatives.
**2** The phrase is used by Mary, Andonis and Yioryía. Mary addresses the children, Andonis addresses John and Mary, and Yioryía addresses John and Mary.

**Conversation 2**

**1** She is asking them if they want to eat or drink something, e.g. coffee or cola.
**2 a** Nice house, very nice and very big. **b** Mary would like an orangeade and John an iced coffee.

**Language discovery 2**

**1 a** έλα-ελάτε, **b** κάθισε-καθίστε, **c** πάρε-πάρτε
**2 a** πεινάς-πεινάτε, **b** διψάς-διψάτε, **c** θέλεις-θέλετε. The first form is used when addressing a friend or relative and the second form when addressing one person formally or more people formally or informally.
**3 a** έναν καφέ, **b** μία κόκα κόλα, **c** μία πορτοκαλάδα, **d** ένα(ν) φραπέ. The choice of the article does not depend on the sound of the word that follows. It depends on the gender (masculine, feminine, neuter) of the noun.

**Practice**

**1 a** 3, **b** 5, **c** 4, **d** 6, **e** 1, **f** 2
**2 a** 3, **b** 5, **c** 4, **d** 6, **e** 1, **f** 2
**3 a** 4, **b** 5, **c** 1, **d** 3, **e** 2

**4** c, e, a, d, f, b
**5** [kondá soo]? [yiatí]? / [anglikå]? [egó], [thélo na miláo] [elinikå]! / [yiatí óhi]? [kafé stin arhí]. [éna frapé] [yia ména].
**6 a** [ksanavlépo], **b** [psomí], **c** [lemonáTHa], **d** [tsái], **e** [himós], **f** [frapés], **g** [kóka kóla]
**7 a** [eláte], **b** [kanapé], **c** [karékla], **d** [pináte], **e** [éna], **f** [mía], **g** [éhis], **h** [yia], **i** [ména]
**8 a** [thélo éna mikró bukáli neró], **b** [tha íthela éna meghálo bukáli neró], **c** [the íthela éna metalikó neró], **d** [éhete neró vrísis]?
**9 a** [énan métrio], **b** [Θα πάρω], **c** [Θα πάρω], **d** [μία λεμονάδα], **e** [καφέ], **f** [Μου φέρνετε], **g** [σκέτο χωρίς γάλα]
**10 a** [έναν ελληνικό γλυκό], **b** [ένα(ν) φραπέ με γάλα χωρίς ζάχαρη], **c** [ένα μικρό μπουκάλι νερό], **d** [ένα καραφάκι ούζο], **e** [μία μπίρα], **f** [μία ζεστή σοκολάτα]

## Test yourself

**1** [kafés], [portokaláTHa], [tsái], [himós], [lemonáTHa], [frapés], [gála]
**2** [éla ke kátse kondá moo]
**3** [éhete] [portokaláTHa i himó]?
**4** [kathíste] or [párte mía karékla]

## REVISION TEST 2

**1 b** [hol], **c** [koozína], **d** [salóni], **e** [ipnoTHomátio], **f** [trapezaría], **g** [bánio]
**2 1** b, **2** d, **3** e, **4** a, **5** c
**3 a** [tría], [pénde], **b** [eptá], [THéka], **c** [éndeka], [THóTHeka], [THekatésera], **d** [THekaéksi], [THekaeniá], [íkosi]
**4 1** c, **2** d, **3** e, **4** a, **5** b
**5** All five statements are false.
**6 a** 3, **b** 5, **c** 7, **d** 1, **e** 6, **f** 2, **g** 4
**7 a** This is my grandmother Artemis and my grandfather Odysseus. **b** My wife's name is Elpitha. **c** We have two children. A boy and a girl. **d** Our son's name is Angelos and our daughter's name is Niovi. **e** We live in a big apartment building.
**8 a** Δουλεύει ο άντρας σου τώρα; **b** Πόσα παιδιά έχετε; **c** Έχεις μεγάλη οικογένεια; **d** Πώς λένε τη γυναίκα σου; **e** Μιλάς καθόλου ελληνικά;
**9** Ευχαριστώ. Μεγάλο και ωραίο σπίτι! / Καλή ιδέα. Έναν καφέ για μένα. / Ναι. Ένα φραπέ μέτριο χωρίς γάλα. Και λίγο νερό παρακαλώ. / Ένα ποτήρι νερό παρακαλώ. / Δεν καταλαβαίνω. Πώς είναι αυτό στα Αγγλικά;

# UNIT 7
## Greek hospitality
ευχαριστώ, παρακαλώ, φιλοξενία, άδικο, διαμονή, παραμονή

## Vocabulary builder

**1** Το παράθυρο, η βιβλιοθήκη, η πολυθρόνα, η μπρίζα, το κάδρο, η πόρτα
**2 a** Η κουρτίνα, **b** η τηλεόραση, **c** το τηλέφωνο, **d** το τραπεζάκι, **e** η πόρτα, **f** ο καναπές
**3** ο πάγκος, ο νεροχύτης, ο καθρέφτης, ο νιπτήρας, η καρέκλα, η ντουλάπα, η μπανιέρα, η πολυθρόνα, το τραπέζι, το κρεβάτι, το τραπεζάκι, το κάδρο
**4** refrigerator, machine, stove, microwave oven, coffee

## Conversation 1

**1** She takes her to her bedroom.
**2 a** She saw an armchair and a big bed. **b** A big table can fit into the kitchen.

## Language discovery 1

**1 a** [polés], **b** [meghálo], **c** [oréa], **d** [meghálo], **e** [meghálo]
**2 a** Μπράβο, **b** μεγάλο, **c** υπνοδωμάτιο, **d** κουζίνα, **e** πολύ, **f** τραπέζι

## Conversation 2

**1** WC or guest bathroom
**2 a** She likes the round mirror a lot. **b** The bathroom is black and white.

## Language discovery 2

**1 a** [megháli], **b** [strongilós], **c** [mikró], **d** [praktikó]
**2 a** [Έχεις δίκιο], **b** [Ναι, βέβαια], **c** [Συμφωνώ], **d** [Μου αρέσει πολύ]
**3 a** [Μου αρέσει πολύ], **b** [Μου αρέσουν τα χρώματα]

## Practice

**1 a** [ble] + [áspro], **b** [prásino] + [áspro] + [kókino], **c** [mávro] + [kókino] + [kítrino], **d** [kókino] + [áspro], **e** [ble] + [áspro] + [kókino], **f** [kókino] + [kítrino]
**2 a** [moo arésoon i kathréftes], **b** [moo arésoon i kanapéTHes], **c** [moo arésoon i karékles], **d** [moo arésoon i polithrónes], **e** [moo arésoon ta bánia], **f** [moo arésoon ta krevátia]
**3 a** 5, **b** 4, **c** 1, **d** 3, **e** 2
**4 a** [mikró], **b** [oréo], **c** [THíkeo], **d** [lígo], **e** [áshimo], **f** [polí], **g** [áTHiko], **h** [megálo], **i** [tetrágono]

**5** e, b, d, a, f, c

**6 a** [praktikó], **b** [vénea], **c** [lootró], **d** [arésoon], **e** [kathréftis], **f** [áspro], **g** [alá], **h** [THíkio]

**7 a** false, **b** true, **c** true, **d** false, **e** true

**8 Mary:** I like Greece because it's small.
**Elpitha:** I don't agree. It's not very small.
**Mary:** I disagree but … I like the weather in Greece.
**Elpitha:** Here I agree with you. You are right.
**Mary:** Of course, because I don't prefer the rain in London.
**Elpitha:** You are not wrong.

**9** It is not Nikos' house.

## Test yourself

**1** [áspro], [mávro], [mov], [ble], [prásino], [kítrino], [portokalí], [kókino]

**2** [antipathó], [THiafonó], [ého áTHiko]

**3** [moo arési] or [moo arésoon], [simfonó], [ého THíkio]

**4** [antipathó], [THen marési]

**5** [karékla], [trapézi], [kanapés], [polithróna], [kreváti]

**6** [strongilós], [mikrós], [áspros]

**7** [tetrágonos], [megálos], [mávros]

**8** [fúrnos], [kafetiéra], [vrastíras], plindírio rúhon]

## UNIT 8

### Breakfast, lunch and dinner

κουλούρι, τυρόπιτα, τοστ, σπανακόπιτα

### Vocabulary builder

**1** I don't like …, hobby, day, I don't have …, sport

**2** Man: T, F, T, F, T, T Woman: F, F, F, F, T, T

**3** The phrases correspond to the cartoons: e, a, k, j, n, d, m, c, h, b, g, i, f, l

### Conversation 1

**1** She usually gets up at 7 o'clock.

**2 a** Έπειτα πάω για ψώνια. **b** She's not too happy about it. The word δυστυχώς helps us understand that.

### Language discovery 1

**1 a** τελικά, **b** έπειτα, **c** συνήθως, **d** νωρίς, **e** ακριβώς

**2 a** Τι ώρα είναι; **b** Είναι μία ακριβώς. **c** Συνήθως σηκώνομαι στις επτά.

**Conversation 2**

**1** Mary usually gets up at 7:30.
**2 a** She works from 10 a.m. to 4 p.m. **b** Around 7 p.m. at home or 8 p.m. when going out.

**Language discovery 2**

**1 a** Γύρω στις επτά στο σπίτι. **b** από τις δέκα μέχρι τις τέσσερις, **c** Ξυπνάω στις επτάμιση
**2 a** Επιστρέφω σπίτι, **b** Δουλεύω συνήθως, **c** Πάω στη δουλειά, **d** Παίρνω το τρένο, **e** Κάνω ένα ντους, **f** Τρώω πρωινό

**Practice**

**1** b, i, g, e, a, j, h, k, c, f, l, d
**2 a** I arrive at work at 8 o'clock. **b** I get up early. **c** I return home late. **d** I go to bed late. **e** I go to work. **f** I have dinner at 9 o'clock. **g** I don't have (lit. eat) breakfast, only coffee. **h** I have lunch at work. **i** I take a shower. **j** I have (lit. drink) a lot of coffee at work. **k** I finish work at 6 o'clock. **l** I watch some TV at 10 o'clock.
**3** There are no correct or incorrect answers in this exercise. Just remember that using a mix of different media will enhance your learning and speed up your tempo. Revision will always help you ensure that you have truly mastered a particular grammar or vocabulary point and it is recommended as your best double-check whenever you are learning alone.
**4 a** 3, **b** 5, **c** 1, **d** 6, **e** 2, **f** 4
**5 a** 8:05, **b** 8:30, **c** 10:30, **d** 1:45, **e** 11:45, **f** 7:05
**6 a** 2, **b** 2, **c** 4, **d** 3
**7 a** [óli], **b** [ksipnáo], **c** [tró-o], **d** [pérno], **e** [epistréfo], **f** [apó], **g** [méhri], **h** [tróte], **i** [yíro], **j** [ékso]
**8** Speaker 1: Το Σουβλάκι της Λωξάντρας, Speaker 2: Εδωδιμοπωλείο, Speaker 3: Ξενοδοχείο Ταξιάρχες

**Test yourself**

**1 a** [ekató tésera], **b** [ekató ogTHónda tésera], **c** [THiakósia triánda éna], **d** [tetrakósia penínda éksi], **e** [oktakósia íkosi eptá], **f** [eniakósia penínda éna] **g** [hília]
**2 a** [eftá ke íkosi], **b** [októmisi], **c** [eniá], **d** [éndeka ke tétarto], **e** [miámisi], **f** [téseris ke THéka], **g** [éksi pará tétarto] **3 a** [síkónome], **b** [ftáno], **c** [telióno], **d** [epistréfo], **e** [pérno]

**4 a** [pánda sikónome stis eksímisi]. **b** [poté THen ftáno sti THooliá norís].
**c** [merikés forés telióno ti THooliá moo argá]. **d** [spánia tró-o ékso].
**e** [sheTHón pánda pérno to tréno].
**5** [tileórasi] [básket] [poTHósfero] [ghimnastikí]

## UNIT 9
### Hobbies and Greek music

television: τηλεόραση, gym: γυμναστική, computer: κομπιούτερ, travelling: ταξίδι

### Vocabulary builder

**1** rock, blues, jazz, comedies, drama, novels, love stories, volleyball, basketball
**2** drama, crime story, love story, science fiction
**3** music, cinema, sports, you (sing/pl), a lot, have

### Conversation 1

**1** He likes to listen to music.
**2 a** John likes pop and rock music. **b** Angelos likes to watch TV or listen to the radio.

### Language discovery 1

**a** μ'αρέσει / μου αρέσει, **b** σ'αρέσει / σου αρέσει, **c** ν'ακούω / να ακούω

### Conversation 2

**1** Mary likes to do sports a lot.
**2 a** running, basketball and tennis, **b** Mary likes to go for a walk or stay home and read.

### Language discovery 2

**1** Words of Greek origin: το θέατρο, το βιβλίο, ο μύθος, η ιστορία, ενδιαφέρον, Words of English origin: το θρίλλερ, το σπορ, το μπάσκετ, το τέννις, το χόμπι / το χόμπυ
**2 a** βιβλίο/βιβλία, **b** μυθιστόρημα/μυθιστορήματα, **c** σπορ/σπορ, **d** χόμπι/χόμπι, **e** βόλτα/βόλτες: Loan words normally have only one form.

### Practice

**1** [THimítris] 1, 3, 6, 7, [níkos] 2, 3, 4, [maría] 1, 2, 5, 6
**2 a** 3, **b** 4, **c** 6, **d** 1, **e** 7, **f** 2, **g** 5
**3 a** 1, 2, 4, 5, **b** 1, 2, 4, 5, **c** 1, 2, 4, 5, **d** 3 **e** 1, 2, 4, 5

**4 a** [vlépi], **b** [akoón], **c** [moo arésoon] or [mas arésoon], **d** [THiavázoome],
**e** [sihénome], **f** [protimás] or [protimáte]
**5 a** Nick never watches TV. **b** Mary and James always listen to the radio.
**c** I like pop and rock music. **d** We read many books in Greece. **e** I despise
cigarettes. **f** Do you prefer the radio or the TV?
**6** [ángelos] 1, 2, 4, 6, [THéspina] 2, 3, 5, 6, [ariána] 1, 3, 4, 5
**7 a** [marésoon], **b** [enTHiaféron], **c** [troháTHin], **d** [forés], **e** [piyéno],
**f** [THiavázo], **g** [siníthos], **h** [istorías]

## Test yourself

**1** [laiká], [elafrolaiká], [rebétika]
**2** [noovéles], [mithistorímata], [astinomiká], [istoríes agápis], [peripéties]
**3** [komoTHíes], [THramatiká], [thríler], [astinomiká]
**4** [ti kánis ton eléfthero hróno soo]? and [pos pernás tis eléftheres óres
soo]?
**5** for example: [vlépo tileórasi], [káno vóltes], [páo théatro], etc.
**6** τροχάδην running, βόλτες walks/rides, ενδιαφέρον interesting, συνήθως
usually, κυρίως mainly
**7** [pánda], [sheTHón pánda], [sihénome] or [antipathó], [dramatiká]

## UNIT 10

### At the fruit and vegetable market

σταφύλι, καρπούζι, πορτοκάλι, μήλο, πατάτα, ντομάτα, καρότο,
μπαρμπούνι, τσιπούρα, λαυράκι, πέστροφα

### Vocabulary builder

**1** pineapple, potato, tomato, carrot, salt, pepper
**2** do you want, many, much, are they, kilo, grams, euro
**3 a** fruit and vegetable shop, **b** greengrocer, **c** grocery store, **d** weekly fruit
and vegetable market, **e** supermarket, **f** hypermarket, **g** mini market

### Conversation 1

**1** Mary will go with Elpitha.
**2 a** No, it's close by. **b** They will go on foot.

### Language discovery 1

**1 a** Θέλω να αγοράσω, **b** Μπορούμε να πάμε, **c** Πρέπει να πάω. This
particle is necessary when connecting two verbs.
**2 a** 2, **b** 3, **c** 1
**3 a** masculine, **b** feminine, **c** neuter

## Conversation 2

**1** Yes, it's always busy.
**2 a** She would like to get some apples and perhaps a watermelon. **b** One lettuce, two cucumbers and one kilo of tomatoes.

## Language discovery 2

**1 a** Θέλω ν'αγοράσω, **b** Τι σ'αρέσει να πάρουμε; **c** Να πάρουμε μήλα.
**2** It means *Here you are! Here! There!* especially when you point out something.
**3 a** ωραία μήλα, **b** φρέσκα λαχανικά, **c** πολλούς ανθρώπους. As a rule of thumb, the ending of the adjective normally matches the ending of the noun it modifies.

## Practice

**1**

| Fruit | Vegetables | Herbs |
|---|---|---|
| banána | kolokitháki | ánithos |
| fráula | agoóri | maindanós |
| roTHákino | domáta | |
| stafíli | karóto | |
| mílo | | |
| karpoózi | | |

**2**

| | | |
|---|---|---|
| i banana – i banánes | to kolokitháki – ta kolokithákia | o ánithos – i ánithi |
| i fráula – i fráules | to agoóri – ta agoória | o maindanós – i maindaní |
| to roTHákino – ta roTHákina | i domáta – i domátes | |
| to stafíli – ta stafília | to karóto – ta karóta | |
| to mílo – ta míla | | |
| to karpoózi – ta karpoózia | | |

**3**

| | | |
|---|---|---|
| Η μπανάνα -οι μπανάνες | Το κολοκυθάκι – τα κολοκυθάκια | Ο άνιθος – οι άνιθοι |
| Η φράουλα – οι φράουλες | Το αγγούρι – τα αγγούρια | Ο μαϊντανός – οι μαϊντανοί |
| Το ροδάκινο – τα ροδάκινα | Η ντομάτα – οι ντομάτες | |
| Το σταφύλι – τα σταφύλια | Το καρότο – τα καρότα | |
| Το μήλο – τα μήλα | | |
| Το καρπούζι – τα καρπούζια | | |

**4 b** [i patátes], **c** [i domátes], **d** [to skórTHo], **2** [to ahláTHi], **3** [ta stafília], **4** [i fráooles]
**5 a** [penínda evró] πενήντα ευρώ, **b** [THekaeftá evró] δεκαεφτά ευρώ, **c** [ekató evró] εκατό ευρώ, **d** [THóTHeka evró] δώδεκα ευρώ, **e** [triánda

tésera evró] τριάντα τέσσερα ευρώ, **f** [evTHomínda evró] εβδομήντα ευρώ

**6 a** 5, **b** 3, **c** 6, **d** 2, **e** 4, **f** 1

**7 a** [marési na piyéno vóltes mazí soo]. **b** [thélo na páo sti laikí agorá]. **c** [prépi na se THo]. **d** [boró na íme thimoménos]. **e** [borí na tin léne eléni].

**8** 1 c, **2** b, **3** a, **4** d, **5** e, **6** f

**9 a** [ipárhoon], **b** [portokália], **c** [epohí], **d** [fisiká], **e** [káto], **f** [lahaniká], **g** [agoória], **h** [kiló]

**Test yourself**

**1** [ananás], [hoormás], [yiarmás], [banána], [fráoola], [agriófrapa] or [gréipfroot], [stafíli], [pepóni], [roTHákino], [portokáli], [karpoózi]

**2** [ánithos], [maintanós], [arakás] or [bizéli], [patáta], [domáta], [melitzána], [karóto], [sélino], [kolokitháki], [maroóli], [agoóri]

**3** [eftihizménos], [pinazménos], [thimoménos], [THipsazménos], [lipiménos], [taragménos], [ékpliktos], [koorazménos]; (the masculine ending [-os] changes to [-i] for the feminine form)

**4 a** [tetrakósia penínda], **b** [eksakósia evTHomínda], **c** [hília THiakósia], **d** [tris hiliáTHes eniakósia], **e** [pénde hiliáTHes], **f** [eptá hiliáTHes tetrakósia], **g** [eniá hiliáTHes pendakósia], **h** [THéka hiliáTHes]

**5** [bakáliko, manáviko, pandopolío]

**6** [misó kilo míla parakaló] and [éna kiló portokália parakaló]

**7** [póso káni]? and [póso kánun]?

## REVISION TEST 3

**1 a** 5, **b** 2, **c** 4, **d** 1, **e** 6, **f** 3

**2 a** I work from 8:00 to 4:00. **b** Mary is at home from 9:30 to 6:00. **c** I never eat from 12:30 to 9:00. **d** I am at work from 7:00 to 4:00. **e** I don't like to work from 9:00 to 5:00. **f** George watches TV from 10:30 to 7:30.

**3 a** 4, **b** 2, **c** 1, **d** 3, **e** 6, **f** 5

**4 a** Mary is in the kitchen and is cooking. **b** John is outside the house. **c** My mother watches TV a lot. **d** My father always reads the newspaper. **e** Kostas listens to music all day. **f** Helen is in the office from 9:00 to 1:00.

**5 a** 8, **b** 2, **c** 1, **d** 9, **e** 3, **f** 4, **g** 10, **h** 6, **i** 7, **j** 5

**6 a** Κάνω ντους. I take a shower. **b** Τρώω πρωινό. I have breakfast. **c** Πάω για ύπνο. I go to bed (lit. sleep). **d** Ξυπνάω στις 7:00. I wake up at 7:00. **e** Διαβάζω στο κρεβάτι. I read in bed. **f** Πάω στη δουλειά. I go to work. **g** Φεύγω από τη δουλειά. I leave work. **h** Σηκώνομαι από το κρεβάτι. I get out of bed. **i** Ετοιμάζομαι για δουλειά. I get ready for work. **j** Ετοιμάζομαι για ύπνο. I get ready for sleep.

**7 a** [ksipnáo stis eptá]. **b** [sikónome apó to kreváti]. **c** [páo sto bánio]. **d** [káno dooz]. **e** [tró-o proinó]. **f** [akoó-o ráTHio]. **g** [páo sti THooliá]. **h** [epistréfo spíti]. **i** [káno vraTHinó]. **j** [pérno tiléfono éna fílo]. **k** [vlépo tileórasi]. **l** [páo yia ípno].
**8 a**-5, **b**-4, **c**-2, **d**-1

For learning on the go download our *Get Started in Greek* companion app:

# Greek: Teach Yourself

- **Choose how you learn** – our apps follow the same unit structure as our courses, so you can get extra practice wherever and whenever you want.
- **Make learning fun** – our apps are packed with interactive activities that give you immediate feedback.
- **Take your learning further** – compare your spoken answers and pronunciation to recordings of native speakers with our unique record and compare feature.
- **Listen as you learn** – our apps include full audio to accompany dialogues and listening exercises.
- **Control your learning** – track your progress and your scores to quickly identify what you need to review.

# "Global scale" of the Common European Framework of Reference for Languages: learning, teaching, assessment (CEFR)

| | | |
|---|---|---|
| **Advanced** | CEFR LEVEL C2 | Can understand with ease virtually everything heard or read. Can summarise information from different spoken and written sources, reconstructing arguments and accounts in a coherent presentation. Can express him/herself spontaneously, very fluently and precisely, differentiating finer shades of meaning even in more complex situations. |
| | CEFR LEVEL C1 | Can understand a wide range of demanding, longer texts, and recognise implicit meaning. Can express him/herself fluently and spontaneously without much obvious searching for expressions. Can use language flexibly and effectively for social, academic and professional purposes. Can produce clear, well-structured, detailed text on complex subjects, showing controlled use of organisational patterns, connectors and cohesive devices. |
| **Intermediate** | CEFR LEVEL B2 (A Level) | Can understand the main ideas of complex text on both concrete and abstract topics, including technical discussions in his/her field of specialisation. Can interact with a degree of fluency and spontaneity that makes regular interaction with native speakers quite possible without strain for either party. Can produce clear, detailed text on a wide range of subjects and explain a viewpoint on a topical issue giving the advantages and disadvantages of various options. |
| | CEFR LEVEL B1 (Higher GCSE) | Can understand the main points of clear standard input on familiar matters regularly encountered in work, school, leisure, etc. Can deal with most situations likely to arise whilst travelling in an area where the language is spoken. Can produce simple connected text on topics which are familiar or of personal interest. Can describe experiences and events, dreams, hopes and ambitions and briefly give reasons and explanations for opinions and plans. |
| **Beginner** | CEFR LEVEL A2: (Foundation GCSE) | Can understand sentences and frequently used expressions related to areas of most immediate relevance (e.g. very basic personal and family information, shopping, local geography, employment). Can communicate in simple and routine tasks requiring a simple and direct exchange of information on familiar and routine matters. Can describe in simple terms aspects of his/her background, immediate environment and matters in areas of immediate need. |
| | CEFR LEVEL A1 | Can understand and use familiar everyday expressions and very basic phrases aimed at the satisfaction of needs of a concrete type. Can introduce him/herself and others and can ask and answer questions about personal details such as where he/she lives, people he/she knows and things he/she has. Can interact in a simple way provided the other person talks slowly and clearly and is prepared to help. |